FAMILIES AND FARM
IN NINETEENTH-CENTU

FAMILIES
AND
FARMHOUSES
IN NINETEENTH-CENTURY
AMERICA

*Vernacular Design and
Social Change*

Sally McMurry

New York   Oxford

OXFORD UNIVERSITY PRESS

1988

Oxford University Press

Oxford   New York   Toronto
Delhi   Bombay   Calcutta   Madras   Karachi
Petaling Jaya   Singapore   Hong Kong   Tokyo
Nairobi   Dar es Salaam   Cape Town
Melbourne   Auckland

and associated companies in
Berlin   Ibadan

Copyright © 1988 by Oxford University Press, Inc.

Published by Oxford University Press, Inc.,
200 Madison Avenue, New York, New York 10016

Oxford is a registered trademark of Oxford University Press

Library of Congress Cataloging-in-Publication Data
McMurry, Sally Ann, 1954–
1. Farmhouses—United States.
   Families and farmhouses in nineteenth-century America
   Based on author's thesis—Cornell University.
   Bibliography: p.   Includes index.
2. Vernacular architecture—United States.
3. Architecture, Modern—19th century—United States.
4. Architecture and society—United States.
I. Title.
NA8208.5.M36   1988   728'.67'0973   87-24787
ISBN 0-19-504475-4

1 3 5 7 9 8 6 4 2

Printed in the United States of America
on acid-free paper

For my parents

PREFACE

The stylistic and technical terms used to describe architecture can contribute to dense, highly detailed description. As a student intern learning how to use those labels, I was fascinated to realize that with the proper vocabulary, I could write a great deal even about a relatively unpretentious building. Yet even after a building had been described down to the last stringcourse, it seemed to me as though something was missing. How did that building fit into its social context, and how were its inhabitants using the space enclosed by its walls? Questions about the social context of design are more difficult to answer, but they must be asked in order to see how and why building forms change. Many architectural histories deal with the social context of design indirectly, for example by analyzing how a pattern-book author thought families would use his designs. These works are major contributions to cultural history, but they still rely on an assumed link between designer and audience. This study uses a more direct means of linking design and social context: the owner-designed house plan. It analyzes several hundred house plans published in American agricultural periodicals, designed by "progressive" farmers—innovators, capitalists, experimenters. Their unsophisticated drawings appeared alongside attractive farmhouse designs by architects, but it is precisely their origin outside the architectural profession which makes the amateur house plans interesting. As house planners, progressive farm men and women gave form to their values. Working independently, and usually without professional aid, they drew from a variety of sources to fashion plans which met their specific requirements.

This study approaches the architecture of the progressive farmer's home as an index of social and cultural history, proceeding from the premise that house forms both influence and reflect the fundamental patterns of culture, including family life, child-rearing practices, and the role of the individual. How were industrialization, urbanization, and agricultural change expressed in the architecture of the progressive farmhouse? Conversely, how can the progressive farmhouse be used to help determine the nature of these social changes? For historians, the problem in researching the social history of domestic architecture stems from the paradox that the very familiarity of the home lends it a measure of obscurity: people do not often analyze their everyday surroundings or examine the assumptions which go into shaping them. To recover the everyday meaning of these domestic structures, I have combined conventional historical analysis of written documents with the analysis of plans, illustrations, and of the houses themselves, treating them all as equally important sources.

With these premises in mind, I compiled a set of questions which probed what J. Meredith Neil has called the "perceptual world" of domestic environments.[1] The first set of questions sought fundamental facts about the activities which took place in each room, at different times of the day and year; the identity of the participants; the areas of the house which were most heavily used; and the ways in which space was used for fixed functions such as meals. Other questions probed the social implications of these arrangements. How did progressive farm family members interact socially at home? Can nineteenth-century concepts of "public" and "private" space be inferred from the depiction or description of people living in these houses? Were there social "zones" defined by status or function? Some questions concerned broad issues of nomenclature and general arrangement. Were there differences between the designers' designated uses for spaces and their actual uses? Why? How and why did names for rooms change? What was the relationship among rooms? Finally, I asked how the house itself fit into its surroundings. How were the social and physical boundaries of the house delineated, for example, in the accessibility and prominence of entrances? What was the relationship between the house and its natural setting? I also sought to discover how and why any of these attributes had changed over the course of the century.

A second set of questions asked about the moral qualities of domestic design. What normative or emotional values did progressive families assign to different places or objects in the house? What was the relationship between assigned value and actual use? How was the domestic environment manipulated for the ends of social reform?

In the last generation, interest in material culture has grown as scholars have sought to discover how ordinary people lived in the past. Historians in this expanding field contend that the remains of everyday life survive as often in the form of objects as they do in documents, and recent thought has focused upon the philosophical and methodological issues raised in interpreting artifacts as primary sources in historical inquiry. Students of material culture ask (in addition to the fundamental questions about identification, description, and authentication): What was the relationship between the artifact and its maker? What was the artifact's original meaning, and how do we, generations removed, come to know what it meant originally? What were the private and public meanings of a given object? What social strategies and systems did an object express?[2]

Together, these questions were used to analyze a specific group of vernacular buildings, and to help explain why their forms changed significantly over the course of the nineteenth century.

NOTES

1. J. Meredith Neil, "What About Architecture?" *Journal of Popular Culture* (Fall 1971): 280–89.

2. Kenneth Ames, Tuesday colloquium, National Museum of American History, Fall 1981. Cary Carson, "Doing History with Material Culture," in Ian M. G. Quimby, ed., *Material Culture and the Study of American Life* (New York: Norton, 1978), 41–65, put forth the notion of the artifact as a "source of ideas." *Journal of American Culture* (Winter 1980); *AQ* (Bibliography 1983); E. McClung Fleming, "Early American Decorative Arts as Social Documents," *Mississippi Valley Historical Review* 45 (September 1958): 276–285; Thomas Schlereth, ed., *Material Culture Studies in America* (Nashville: AASLH, 1982); Edward T. Hall, *The Hidden Dimension* (Garden City, N.Y.: Anchor Books, 1969); Amos Rapoport, *House Form and Culture* (Englewood Cliffs, N.J.: Prentice-Hall, 1969); Jack Goody, ed., *The Developmental Cycle in Domestic Groups* (London: Cambridge University Press, 1958); J. Littlejohn, "Temne Space," *Anthropological Quarterly* 36 (January 1963): 1–17; Mary Douglas, "Symbolic Orders in the Use of Domestic Space," in Peter Ucko, ed., *Man, Settlement, and Urbanism* (London: Duckworth, 1972), 513–523; Dorothy Smith, "Household Space and Family Organization," *Pacific Sociological Review* 14 (January 1971): 53–79.

ACKNOWLEDGMENTS

I have received invaluable and much appreciated assistance in the course of writing this book. As it began as a dissertation at Cornell University, I would first like to thank members of the Cornell faculty who contributed to the project at its beginning: Fred Somkin, the dissertation director, offered full encouragement to explore other disciplines, to utilize Cornell's varied resources, and to emulate models of historical rigor; Joan Jacobs Brumberg has given me much appreciated support, from her detailed, insightful commentary on drafts to her daily encouragement and enthusiasm; Professor Emeritus Paul Wallace Gates offered valuable commentary; and Mary Beth Norton taught me what it means to revise. Thanks also to Rodris Roth of the National Museum of American History, Smithsonian Institution, who showed enthusiastic interest in my research, helped me gain access to libraries and collections, and introduced me to ideas of material culture studies.

Several people read drafts or parts of the manuscript at various stages. I am especially grateful to my husband, Barry Kernfeld, for his help. I thank Mark Reinberger, Norma Prendergast, David C. Smith, Thomas Hubka, Paul Harvey, Peirce Lewis, Hal Barron, Dell Upton, and Bernard Herman. I would also like to thank two anonymous reviewers for Oxford University Press.

I owe thanks to all of the people, many of them volunteers at local historical societies, who helped to uncover biographical information on the farmer house planners who appear in this study: Mildred H. Airy, Macedon (New York) Town Historian; Raymond Beecher, Greene County (New York) Historical Society; George Berkhofer, South Charleston, Ohio; Mrs. Lena Bushnell, Newark Valley, New York; Mrs. C. A. Church, Schenectady County (New York) Historical Society; Hugh E. Claremont, Redding, Connecticut; Mrs. Leroy Coryell, Romulus, New York; Mrs. Robert Dauchy, Clayville, New York; Jerald DeGroff, Genesee Township (Allegany County, New York) Historian; Gene DeGruson, Pittsburg (Kansas) State University; Claire Dempsey, Massachusetts Historical Commission; Mary S. Dibble, Patterson Library and Art Gallery, Westfield, New York;

Mrs. Merle Dommell, Grand Island (New York) Historical Society; Mr. and Mrs. Robert Geddes, Beverly, Ohio; Virginia Gibbs, Yates County (New York) Genealogical and Historical Society; Jean Gordon, Champaign County (Illinois) Historical Archives; Maxine Geerkes, Newark Valley, New York; Bill Greene, Jr., Allegany County (New York) Museum; Mrs. Dale Green, Chenango County (New York) Museum; Richard P. Hartung, Rock County (Wisconsin) Historical Society; John H. Herbruck, Beaver, Pennsylvania; Helen Hackett, Jacksonville, Illinois; Lillian Holley, Crown Point, Indiana; Mary Irvin, Lower Muskingum (Ohio) Historical Society; Mrs. Jean Jerred, Cambria, Wisconsin; Teresa Lasher, Niagara County (New York) Historian; William Lay, Jr., Tioga County (New York) Historical Society; Charles Lindquist, Lenawee County (Michigan) Historian; Bruce Lockhart, Fairfield, Connecticut; Cynthia Longwisch, Madison County (Illinois) Historical Society; Jeanne Martin, Ontario County (New York) Historical Society; Mrs. Robert McCready, Jaffrey, New Hampshire; Irma Mastrean, Princetown (New York) Historical Society; Marjorie Miller, Sheboygan, Wisconsin; Maurice Montgomery, Rock County (Wisconsin) Historical Society; C. L. Norlin, Jones County (Iowa) Historical Society; Gordon Olson, Grand Rapids (Michigan) Historian; Charles C. Pace, Jr., New Hartford (New York) Historical Society; Douglas Preston, Oneida County (New York) Historical Society; Katherine Rankin, Madison, Wisconsin; Herman Sass, Buffalo and Erie County (New York) Historical Society; Earle G. Shettleworth, Maine Historic Preservation Commission; Cara Sutherland, Chemung County (New York) Historical Society; Katherine Thompson, Rush (New York) Town Historian; Thomas Trombley, Historical Society of Saginaw County (Michigan); Esther Walton, Hastings, Michigan; Charles B. Wallace, Harrison County (Ohio) Historical Society; Lorraine Wagner, Somerset (New York) Historian; H. Wade White, Fairfield, Connecticut; Dohron Wilson, Mechanicsburg, Ohio; John Wilson, Wyoming County (New York) Historian; Mary Williams, Bureau County (Illinois) Historical Society; Allen Yale, Derby, Vermont.

Part of Chapter 3 appeared as "Progressive Farm Families and Their Houses, 1830–1855: A Study in Independent Design," *Agricultural History* 58 (July 1984): 330–347. Part of Chapter 5 appeared as "City Parlor, Country Sitting Room: Rural Vernacular Design and the American Parlor, 1840–1900," *Winterthur Portfolio* 20 (Winter 1985): 261–280.

The production of this book would not have been possible without the help of the numerous people who typed, gathered photos, proofread, and arranged for interlibrary loans. In particular, I thank Patricia Shier, Mona Perchonok, Carol Lee, Cornell University Libraries Interlibrary Services,

Penn State University Interlibrary Loan, Lori Ginzberg, David Faries, Doug Reddy, Laura Gottlieb, and the Penn State Photo Services Division.

Finally, many thanks to Joyce Berry, Nancy Lane, and Karen Lundeen at Oxford University Press, who ably guided the book through the entire production process.

CONTENTS

FAMILIES AND FARMHOUSES
IN NINETEENTH-CENTURY AMERICA

ONE

Introduction

NINETEENTH-CENTURY FARMHOUSES are evocative of the "Farmer's Age," reminders of a way of life that has long since disappeared. To many, they represent a more stable and placid world than the one we inhabit today. Yet in the middle decades of the nineteenth century, the northern rural landscape of the United States was highly dynamic. From the settled agricultural regions of New England westward to barely opened frontiers, new farmhouses and communities were appearing everywhere, and old ones were being transformed.[1]

This transformation was occurring within the vernacular landscape, and the farmhouses analyzed in this book are vernacular buildings. Most often "vernacular" is defined in negatives: it is not high style, not monumental, not professionally designed. But Dell Upton and John Michael Vlach point out that there is also a positive way to characterize vernacular architecture. It is distinguished by its common, "communally-sanctioned" qualities, its "intensity of social representation." The farmhouses discussed here fit into the category of vernacular because they were designed by the people who inhabited them, and because collectively they represent a specific sub-culture of northern rural society.[2]

This book is the story of how one particular class of northern farm families literally reshaped the domestic landscapes in which they lived and worked as America underwent the transformation from an agrarian society to an urban, industrial nation. I have chosen the term "progressive" to refer to them because it is a characterization they would—and in fact, did—readily apply to themselves.[3] Self-styled progressive farm men and women aimed to reform American agriculture and rural life through the introduction of capitalist method, technological innovation, scientific experimentation, and the reorganization of social and family life. Their domestic land-

3

scapes—the physical and perceptual homes that they shaped—bore the imprint of their reforming mentality.

Much attention has been paid to the social history of cities during the nineteenth century, yet the countryside was changing, too, and not always in response to change initiated elsewhere. In fact, progressive farm families helped to shape the elements of change, especially those agricultural shifts which accelerated urbanization and eventually led to the almost complete separation between food production and individual consumers today. Progressive farm families led the way in introducing these changes to the rural North. They were cultural mediators, poised between past and future, rural and urban, folk and popular cultures, and their historical significance extends further than their relatively small numbers suggest.

Historical change on a grand scale can be seen in microcosm in the farmhouse plans of amateur designers that appeared in northern agricultural periodicals over a period of some seventy years. The designers almost invariably explained their plans with brief letters. Farm handbooks are a second source of plans and commentaries. I have also traced several plans to the houses built from them and interpreted the material artifacts as they were realized from the plan.

Progressive farmhouse designers' plans appeared, beginning in the 1830s, in a newly emerging forum for rural and agricultural affairs, the agricultural journals. The plans considered here were published in eleven different journals: the *American Agriculturist* (New York), the *Prairie Farmer* (Chicago), the *Genesee Farmer* (Rochester), the *Ohio Farmer* (Cleveland), *Rural Affairs* (Albany), the *Cultivator* (Albany), the *Michigan Farmer* (Detroit), *Moore's Rural New Yorker* (Rochester), the *New England Farmer* (Boston), the *American Farmer* (Baltimore), and the *Ohio Cultivator* (Columbus). Once the journals were established, lower postal rates, technological innovation, new marketing tactics, and the emergence of advertising enabled the agricultural press to increase its circulation from 100,000 for several dozen periodicals in 1850 to 250,000 for more than fifty in 1860. Their emphases varied depending upon individual editors' interests, but their general goals were improved agricultural education; establishment of agricultural societies; promotion of soil science; publicity for new varieties of plants, stock breeds, fertilizers, and machinery; abolition of superstition; and improvement of rural culture. The farm journals are a rich source of information on daily farm work, leisure activities, child-rearing advice, women's duties, and social life.[4]

The journals appealed to progressive farmers, and welcomed commentary on all matters concerning agriculture. Often they issued appeals for readers' farmhouse plans. Sometimes contests were held, but more often an editor simply asked subscribers to forward house plans much as he might solicit information on crop experiments. Readers regularly responded, and between 1830 and 1900 several hundred owner-designed plans appeared in the journals.

Two kinds of supplementary material contribute to an understanding of these house plans. Biographical information was available for some of these amateur designers, the data pieced together from a variety of sources, such as atlases, local histories, federal census manuscripts, local directories, probate inventories, diaries, and local historical society files. Other sources included farm memoirs and autobiographies, architectural pattern books, domestic economy texts, and child-rearing handbooks.

These sources in turn form the basis for analyzing the evolution of the progressive farm home. The farmhouse of the 1830s and 1840s, a social and conceptual whole, gave way by the last decade of the century to a collection of specialized rooms that more carefully filtered people by age, class, and sex, as well as by activities, especially leisure and work.

The dates 1830 and 1900 frame a distinct period in independent rural house design. Beginning about 1830, detailed discussions of farm homes began to appear in the agricultural journals, coinciding with an increasing interest in "domesticity" throughout the wider culture. By 1900, the minority status of American farmers was already obvious. The contributions of independent planners in the agricultural papers had begun to decline both in numbers and in prestige. Challenging the independent tradition were the increasingly influential architectural profession, home economists offering expert advice, and the industrialization of construction.

The appearance of house plans in the agricultural press about 1832 reflected both the farmers' growing prosperity and their heightened interest in domestic matters. The form, meaning, and significance of a home were beginning to attract attention in all types of publications—agricultural journals, housekeeping guides, child-nurture literature, and domestic novels. Yet the idea of the progressive farm home differed markedly from the concept of urban, middle-class domesticity. At mid-century, farmhouse plans, some designed by women, featured efficiency for greater productivity, placed children's nurseries close to the kitchen, and designated rooms for farm "helps." This contrasted with the emerging ideal in urban literature of the home as an asylum, where the emphasis was on women furnishing but not planning their houses, where children's spaces were prominent, kitchens were isolated or hidden, and home and work were sharply differentiated. The rural planners' homes suggest that the mid-century ideal of domesticity was not monolithic, that instead it took different forms in different settings.

Between about 1855 and 1885, agricultural mechanization and the rise of the city brought marked changes to northern rural society. Progressive farmers both initiated and responded to these changes, and planned their homes accordingly. As farmers specialized (particularly in the dairy and fruit industries), men took over tasks formerly done by women. Mechanization, which occurred in the field but not in the home, further intensified the growing differentiation between men's and women's work. Women began to criticize this disparity, viewing their work as household drudgery. Mechanization also brought intensified class divisions; increased capital costs of farming prevented farmhands from rising. These new social divisions found expression in domestic space. The ideal of the farmhouse as a unified workplace began to erode, and there were noticeable shifts in the arrangement of rooms. The kitchen, now specialized and isolated, often faced toward the public roadway rather than toward the farm grounds. In keeping with urban values of leisure and child nurture, the nursery was moved away from the kitchen, while playrooms and other specialized children's spaces began to appear. Rooms for farmhands were isolated or eliminated. The house was becoming a collection of individual rooms, the gap between work and family growing more and more pronounced.

Yet the development of individual, specialized spaces did not proceed uniformly. The nature of the rural parlor was constantly debated. Columnists and planners in the farm journals urged readers to abandon this isolated, gloomy, seldom-used room for an open, informal, multipurpose family sitting room. The parlor, which farmer-designers associated with urban culture and especially with urban women, represented the undesirable qualities of formality, family disintegration, economic waste, and idleness. The sitting room, on the other hand, was seen as symbolizing country virtues—honest informality, family solidarity, thrift, and industry. The sitting room ideal reflected distinctly rural patterns of social life, because sitting rooms admitted people of all ages and both sexes. In contrast, the urban parlor was primarily for women. But the sitting room came dangerously close to imitating the urban forms it was supposed to challenge. Nonetheless, progressive farmhouse designers enthusiastically experimented with alternatives to the parlor, and by the turn of the century, fully one-half of them had omitted the parlor altogether, replacing it with a sitting or living room. These experiments may have provided a fund of experience for other, nonrural designers to draw upon later in the century as Americans everywhere abandoned the parlor.

The introduction of separate bedrooms for children and adolescents, occurring from about 1880 to 1900, was the last major transformation in the development of the progressive farm's domestic landscape. This was a significant step in the segregation of family members and reflected the rising importance of children in American culture. Children had long been the subject of devoted attention, but the nature of that attention had changed. During the early nineteenth century, advice to mothers focused upon young children. Obedience, subordination, and moral character were the qualities to be developed, and the supervision implied in this ideal was architecturally expressed by adjoining family rooms and nurseries. By the latter part of the century, however, the emphasis was on limited autonomy, play, and individual character formation. Adolescence was now seen as a crucial stage of life. Ideally, a house would have a single room for each child, especially for each adolescent. By this time, single rooms were more feasible because families were smaller and living standards were higher. In the progressive farm home, activities which once took place in communal areas now moved to the individual child's room, further contributing to a sense of social atomization.

The reorganization of the farm home between 1830 and 1900 challenged the old rural ideal of family cooperation and solidarity, but may also be seen as a realistic adjustment to persistent problems and to new currents of thought. In the mid-century, while the farmhouse may have signified cooperation, it also implied excessive work, lack of privacy, and little opportunity for recreation. As farm mechanization and specialization increased, there was less need for women and children to do farm work. The new interest in leisure and children's play probably reflected this. The labor needed on farms also declined, and the proportion of the American population engaged in farming dropped steadily. As their children migrated to the city, progressive farm parents reluctantly faced the prospect that their sons and daughters would not farm. The prescriptive ideals of the sitting room and later of individual bedrooms evolved in part as attempts to keep farm children at home. These spaces, associated with ambivalence about the future, show that progressive farm families were successful in pursuing capitalistic agriculture, but paid a price in the transformation of the traditional family farm.

This study asks: What did progressive farmers' houses look like? Who were the people who designed them? It then describes what was going on behind these farmhouse façades, how domestic spaces were arranged and rearranged for work, play, socializing, and how, as they reshaped their lives, progressive farm families also reshaped their domestic landscapes.

NOTES

1. Bernard Herman, *Architecture and Rural Life in Central Delaware, 1700–1900* (Knoxville: University of Tennessee Press, 1987), demonstrates physical and cultural transformations beginning with rural buildings themselves. Steven Hahn and Jonathan Prude, *The Countryside in the Age of Capitalist Transformation: Essays in the Social History of Rural America* (Chapel Hill and London: University of North Carolina Press, 1985), is a set of collected essays. Robert St. George, "Set Thine House in Order: The Domestication of the Yeomanry in Seventeenth-Century New England," in *New England Begins* (Boston: Museum of Fine Arts, 1982), vol. 2, 159–352, establishes a background against which later developments can be measured.

2. Dell Upton and John Michael Vlach, *Common Places: Readings in American Vernacular Architecture* (Athens: University of Georgia Press, 1986), xvi, xvii. My understanding of "vernacular" has also been shaped by other viewpoints. See especially Camille Wells, *Perspectives in Vernacular Architecture II* (Columbia: University of Missouri Press, 1986), introduction. John Kouwenhoven raised the issue of vernacular over twenty years ago in his classic, *The Arts in Modern American Civilization,* 2nd ed. (New York: Norton, 1967). Henry Glassie, in *Folk Building in Middle Virginia* (Knoxville: University of Tennessee Press, 1975) and *Pattern in the Material Folk Culture of the Eastern United States* (Philadelphia: University of Pennsylvania Press, 1968) distinguishes between "folk" and "popular" building. Richard Bushman, "American High-Style and Vernacular Cultures," in Jack Greene and J. R. Pole, eds., *Colonial British America* (Baltimore: Johns Hopkins University Press, 1984), 345–384, offers suggestions for studying the interactions among cultures.

3. John Adams Nash, *The Progressive Farmer* (New York: A. O. Moore, 1857).

4. On the general context of the magazine and publishing industries, see John Tebbel, *History of Book Publishing in the United States,* 5 vols. (New York: R. R. Bowker, 1972–1981) and Frank Luther Mott, *History of American Magazines,* 5 vols. (Cambridge: Harvard University Press, 1938–68). Mott, 2:10, notes that the *Country Gentleman's* circulation in the 1850s competed well with such general periodicals as *Frank Leslie's Weekly* and *Harper's Weekly.* On agricultural journalism, the main authorities are Paul Gates, *The Farmer's Age: Agriculture 1815–1860* (New York: Holt, Rinehart, and Winston, 1960); Donald Marti, *To Improve the Soil and the Mind* (Ann Arbor: University Microfilms International, 1979); Percy Wells Bidwell and John Falconer, *History of Agriculture in the Northern United States, 1620–1860* (1925. Reprint, New York: Peter Smith, 1941), 166; Marti, "Agricultural Journalism and the Diffusion of Knowledge," *Ag. History* 54 (January 1980): 28–37; Albert L. Demaree, "The Farm Journals, their Editors, and their Public, 1830–1860," *Ag. History* 15 (October 1941): 182–188; George Lemmer, "Early Agricultural Editors and their Farm Philosophies," *Ag. History* 31 (October 1957): 3–23; Gilbert Tucker, *Historical Sketch of American Agricultural Periodicals* (Albany, privately printed, 1909); William E. Ogilvie, *Pioneer Agricultural Journalists* (Chicago: Arthur G. Leonard, 1927); Richard Farrell, "Advice to Farmers: the Content of Agricultural Newspapers, 1860–1910," *Ag. History* 51 (January 1977): 209–217; Albert Demaree, *The American Agricultural Press 1819–1860* (New York: Columbia University Press, 1940); Richard Bardolph, *Agricultural Literature and the Early Illinois Farmer* (Urbana: University of Illinois Press, 1948). For the idea of "gentleman farmer," see Rexford Sherman, "Daniel Webster, Gentleman Farmer," *Ag. History* 53 (April 1979): 475–488; Chester M. Destler, "The Gentleman Farmer and the New Agriculture: Jeremiah Wadsworth," *Ag. History* 46 (January 1972): 135–143. On Jesse Buel, editor of the *Cultivator,* see Harry J. Carman, "Jesse Buel, Albany County Agriculturist," *New York History* 14 (July 1933): 241–250. See also

Carman's full-length biography, *Jesse Buel* (New York: Columbia University Press, 1947). And for analyses of specific journals' emphases, see Kathleen Smith, "Moore's Rural New Yorker: A Farm Program for the 1850s," *Ag. History* 45 (January 1971): 39–46, and Frances Kaye, "The Ladies' Department of the Ohio Cultivator, 1845–55: A Feminist Forum," *Ag. History* 50 (April 1976): 414–424.

TWO

The Progressive Agriculturist's Vernacular

NINETEENTH-CENTURY FARMHOUSES, common features of the rural landscape in the northern states, first catch the observer's eye with their rich variety of styles and materials—from Gothic to Greek, cobblestone to clapboard. This chapter describes five progressive farmers' houses from the outside, the way an observer would initially see them. The houses strongly testify that the progressive farmer's vernacular took a variety of forms, produced within a culture eager to experiment. This description of exteriors will help us understand how and why progressive farm families manipulated their domestic interiors. The five examples discussed here are among the best documented of the houses that have been traced from several hundred owner-designed plans.

Vermont Farmer

Derby, Vermont, is a far northern small town only a few miles from the Canadian border. Settled originally in 1795, Derby enjoyed a brief period of prosperity as a center of a mixed farming and lumbering economy until about 1850. It was from a Derby farmer, William Verback, that one of the entries in the Albany *Cultivator's* first house-plan contest came. The house, of plank construction, dates from about 1825 and still stands, only slightly altered (Figures 2–1, 2–2). Plank construction was common in northern New England from the earliest days of settlement until about 1850; it consists of 2-inch-thick planks set into timber plates and sills. The planks, inexpensively produced at a sawmill, replaced some structural elements of the traditional timber frame. Plank construction allowed the owner to fol-

Fig. 2–1. William Verback house, Derby, Vermont (c. 1825), photographed in 1986.

Fig. 2–2. William Verback house, elevation (1839).

low the current fashion, especially regarding interior and exterior finishes. William Verback, for example, chose to cover his plank frame with brick, signaling to his neighbors his prosperity and community standing; his farm was worth $3,000 and he was a longtime deacon of the local Congregational church. As there were only two other brick houses in town at the time, Verback had joined the select few. In combining local building traditions with the unconventional, Verback's house shared a key quality with the community but also stood apart.[1]

New York Farmer

The town of Pike in Wyoming County, western New York, had, like the rural neighborhoods surrounding it, developed a mixed farming economy by the 1840s—the years when New York state was the most productive agricultural state in the nation. C. Butler Rider (1792–1869), according to a local history a "native of New Hampshire and a prosperous farmer and influential citizen of Pike," ran a 110-acre farm there. In 1850 he apparently concentrated on beef cattle, but also produced grain, wool, peas, potatoes, and hemp. Like many other farmers, Rider had several sidelines; he was known locally as a surveyor, sign painter, and artist, with his specialty "charcoal drawings." Perhaps it was this artistic bent that led Rider to design and build a new farmhouse around 1860 (Figures 2–3, 2–4).

Rider's design, like Verback's, mixed common practice with innovation. He used the balloon frame, fast becoming an important mode of construction in American domestic architecture. Rider succinctly described and illustrated the technique of balloon framing in *Moore's Rural New Yorker* (Figure 2–5), explaining that "a well-made 'balloon' frame is much cheaper and better for all houses of moderate height than a timber frame. It *adapts* itself better to circumstances. It is more *plastic,* so to speak." The balloon frame, first developed in Chicago in the 1830s and 1840s, replaced the cumbersome timber-framing system of massive beams held together with wooden pins. Instead, the balloon frame consisted of many light, uniformly sized and spaced studs nailed together. A few people could erect the frame using such simple tools as a hammer, saw, and nails. This innovation, which the agricultural press publicized extensively, may have made possible much of the progressive farmers' architectural experimentation, since it allowed for spatial variety and did not require sophisticated building skills.[2] By the last quarter of the century, most of the farmer-designers who mentioned their construction techniques employed balloon framing.

Rider wrote that he regarded the "Italian style" as "the one most perfectly adapted to the wants of the farming community." Why, he did not

Fig. 2–3. C. B. Rider, Italian rural farmhouse, Pike, New York (1860), photographed about 1910.

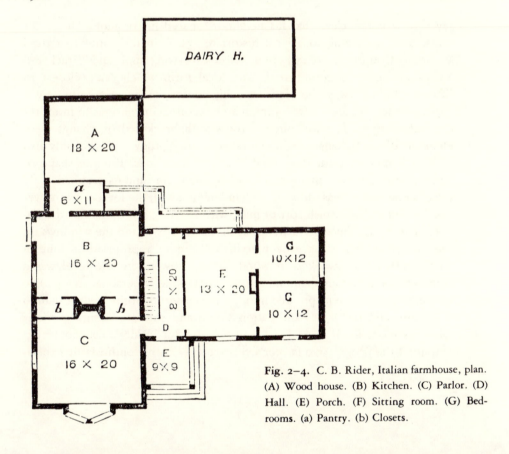

Fig. 2–4. C. B. Rider, Italian farmhouse, plan. (A) Wood house. (B) Kitchen. (C) Parlor. (D) Hall. (E) Porch. (F) Sitting room. (G) Bedrooms. (a) Pantry. (b) Closets.

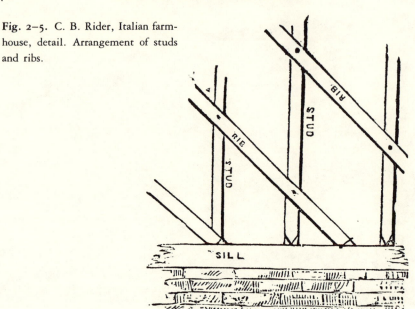

Fig. 2–5. C. B. Rider, Italian farmhouse, detail. Arrangement of studs and ribs.

say, and it is not clear that his neighbors shared his opinion. The Rider house was, according to a local historian, "rare" in the context of rural Wyoming County, an area where the Greek Revival temple and "Bracketed Victorian" forms predominated. The local form which came closest to Rider's "Italian" was the Italianate, hip-roofed cube surmounted by a cupola. Rider did use a few common architectural conventions to interpret the Italian style. The low-pitched roofs with bracketed overhangs were elements of the Italianate architectural vocabulary; they were probably also familiar sights on local Bracketed Victorian buildings. But the shape of Rider's house, with its main sections of equal volume and its proportionally large, squat tower, was idiosyncratic, in keeping with the local characterization of him as "a waspish sort of man, with a strong self-opinionated manner." The Renaissance-style arches at the tower's base and the windows on the third level would have been stylistically more appropriate if done in stucco rather than worked in wood. At the tower's middle level was a completely anomalous diamond-shaped boss, Rider's personal stamp. The balcony design, with its pointed hood, came closer to Gothic styling than to Italianate, and the board-and-batten siding and shuttered four-over-four windows more likely were local features by 1860. Rider's farmhouse exemplified the progressive farmer's vernacular—its overenthusiastic experimentation produced an amalgam of common technique, local practice, and provincial naïveté.

New York Country Merchant

The tiny crossroads town of Coventry, New York, perches atop a long ridge in the rolling dairy country of Chenango County; it is a collection of houses which straggle along two streets. Among the modest classical revival vernacular houses stands an octagon house (Figure 2–6), originally built by carpenter Lemuel Lewis for one Edgar Phillips, who sent the design to *Moore's Rural New Yorker* in 1860 (Figures 2–7, 2–8). Phillips, a prosperous dry-goods merchant, had grown up on a farm near Coventry and was closely involved with the farming community. Local histories show that the Phillips family were well established political, social, and religious figures in this town of 150 inhabitants. Phillips's house, like William Verback's and C. B. Rider's, combined unorthodox features with more common ones. It was originally built of 1½-inch vertical wooden planks with battened seams. Wooden brackets ornamented a projecting cornice, and conventional shutters covered each 2/2 window. Thus, in materials, details, and scale the

Fig. 2–6. Edgar Phillips, octagon farmhouse, Coventry, New York (1860), photographed in 1985.

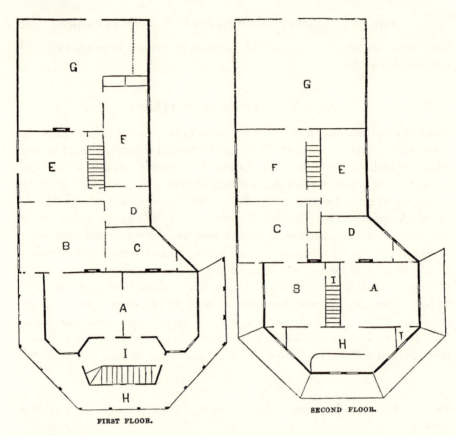

FIRST FLOOR.

SECOND FLOOR.

Fig. 2–7. Edgar Phillips house, plan. (Left) *First Floor:* (A) Parlors. (B) Dining room. (C) Bedroom. (D) Pantry. (E) Cook and Wash room. (F) Milk room. (G) Wood house. (H) False window. (I) Hall. (Right) *Second Floor:* (A, B) Parlor chambers. (C, D, E, F) Bedrooms. (G) Lumber room. (H) Hall. (I) Triangular closets.

Fig. 2–8. Edgar Phillips house, elevation.

building did not depart radically from convention. In fact, it defied Orson Squires Fowler, the octagon's prophet, who recommended "gravel walls" (concrete). Its shape, of course, made it quite distinct. Originally, a porch extended all the way around the building and must have further accentuated the octagon form. But the building is not visually coherent—odd recesses pierce two of the octagon's faces, detracting from the façade's visual impact, and a long, straight wing off the back seems to betray a lack of confidence in Fowler's prescription for a pure octagon.[3] The plan, too, is idiosyncratic; it does not even resemble any of the plans in Fowler's book. Whatever Phillips's motives were for erecting this strange conglomeration, it placed him in an ambiguous position in Coventry, with his house's shape emphatically proclaiming his individuality, yet the details expressing widely shared formulas.

Prairie Pioneer, Illinois

Cyrus Bryant (1798–1865) grew up on a farm in the hills of western Massachusetts. His family home was probably a traditional New England one-story, gambrel-roofed, center-chimney house. After finishing primary school, Bryant attended Hadley Academy, where his studies were punctuated by stints working on the family farm and teaching school. Bryant then moved into the world of commerce, working for nearly eight years as a clerk in Kinderhook, New York, and later in Columbia, South Carolina. At age 29 he resumed his education at Rensselaer Polytechnic Institute in Troy, New York, studying chemistry, botany, natural philosophy, mineralogy, geology, and astronomy. For a brief time after he received a degree in 1829, he toured as an itinerant lecturer, and in 1832 headed west, following the lead of friends and neighbors of his native Cummington. The same year he staked a claim in Princeton, Illinois, about 100 miles west of the little town of Chicago. There he ceased his peripatetic ways, remaining there until his death in 1865.

Bryant became a prominent citizen in Princeton. He organized the first library, served in county offices, and established an agricultural association. He was a prairie pioneer, but "loved the customs of his native Massachusetts" and yearly invited a few "congenial friends" to "talk and joke, eat apples, drink cider, and sing the old fugue songs."[4]

All of these experiences likely informed Bryant's thinking when he designed a house to succeed his pioneer dwelling. By 1843, in a letter to a relative back in Massachusetts, he wrote:

I intend to build a house next season if I shall be sufficiently pros-

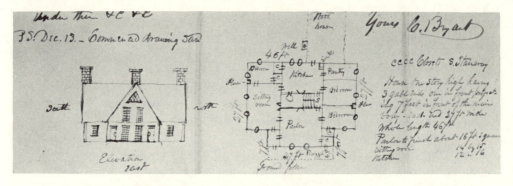

Fig. 2–9. Cyrus Bryant house, Princeton, Illinois (1844–45). Bryant's sketch of his plan as presented to Mr. John Everett, December 1843.

perous . . . I have 65,000 bricks and 250$ paid towards the carpenter's work. The mason work I can pay for in land. I have timber sufficient on my own land for hewing which I shall draw out this winter. I have also some lumber on hand, and some paid for which I shall probably be able to get home before spring. The sand must be hauled about 2 miles—And the lime I shall probably get at Dixon 35 miles—price $12\frac{1}{2}$ cts at the kiln-good-worth from $12\frac{1}{2}$ to 15 cts a bushel to haul it—lime can be had nearer but not so good.

At the close of the letter, Bryant sketched a rough draft of a plan for a cottage that he noted he would probably build (Figure 2–9).[5]

Bryant started construction in the spring of 1844, using bricks made in his own kiln, and moved his family into the house in 1845, the same year that the plan and elevation appeared in the *Prairie Farmer* (Figure 2–10). The house, still standing (Figure 2–11), was the first substantial post-pioneer era house in Princeton and shows that, except for substituting an elongated Gothic window for the planned triangular gable window, Bryant followed his plan closely.[6]

Bryant's house, like the others, added new elements to a conventional vernacular idiom. The most prominent features were its steep, bold gables, elements associated with the Gothic style and undoubtedly novel in an area only a decade removed from the pioneer stage. Thin, white octagonal porch supports were another Gothic accent. At the same time, the house retained elements that would have been familiar to his fellow pioneers, many of whom had migrated from New England and the mid-Atlantic states, where six-over-six sash windows and symmetry were well established architectural conventions. Bryant built with local materials, mostly from his own land, another practice which would have been familiar to people who remem-

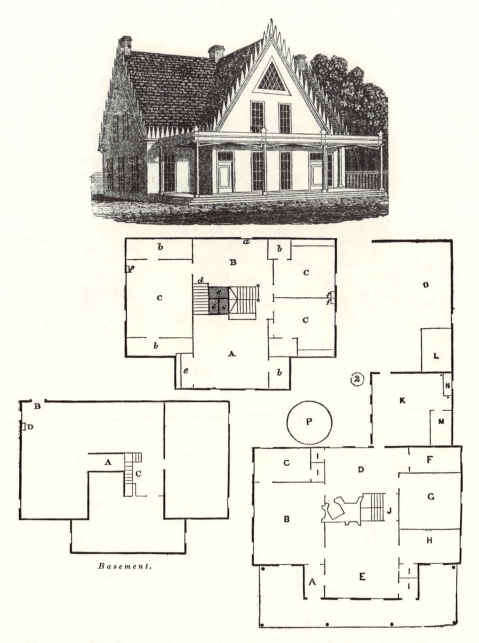

Fig. 2–10. Cyrus Bryant house, plan and elevation (1845). (Right) *Principal Floor:* (A) Front entry. (B) Dining or sitting room. (C, H, G) Bedrooms. (D) Kitchen. (E) Parlor. (F) Pantry. (I) Closets. (J) Passage. (K) Washroom. (L) Meal and flour room. (M) Milk room. (N) Sink. (O) Woodshed. (Q) Well. (P) Cistern. (Left) *Basement:* (A) Arch on which the chimney stands, supported by two piers, 16 in. thick. (B) An upright hatchway, or passage into the cellar. (C) Cellar stairs. (D) Flue. (Above) *Second Floor:* (A) Room for library, maps, pictures, and specimens in natural history. (B) Hall. (C) Bedrooms. (a) Dormant window [sic.] (b) Closets. (c) Shelves for books (not labeled, may be incorrectly labeled 'e' in 'A'). (d) Stairs to attic. (e) Chimneys. (f) Flues.

Fig. 2–11. Cyrus Bryant house, photographed in 1986.

bered Pennsylvania stone houses and New England timber-framed structures. Though Bryant gave his house a Gothic form, he chose to leave it
unembellished, omitting most Gothic trim. Its plain appearance thus reinforced the design's vernacular qualities.[7]

The three identical, prominent chimneys had both aesthetic and practical purposes. Only the central chimney opened into a large fireplace; the
other two were unnecessarily massive flues for stoves. Did Bryant design
them alike because of a desire for symmetry, for their visual effect in
association with the Gothic style, or out of a nostalgic attachment to the
massive chimneys of his native New England? Possibly he was influenced by
his more famous brother, William Cullen Bryant. An intriguing bit of correspondence indicates that Cyrus indeed maintained contact with the world of
architectural fashion through his brother. William Cullen knew Andrew
Jackson Downing, the famous pattern-book author and promoter of the
new, picturesque architectural taste. According to Downing's aesthetic,
chimneys signified family hearths, and muted colors a union with nature. In
1855, the poet Bryant advised his brother on what color to paint his house:

If I were you I would have but two colors. I would have the window blinds and the cornice of the same color. If I had the body of the house painted A according to the samples in Downing's book or B I would paint the cornice and blinds C. D it strikes me is not a bad color and if I adopted that I would have the cornice and window blinds F. I do not for my part think that a house with cornice and window blinds of the same color looks ill; though perhaps that would be more suitable for a house of which but one material is used. In a brick house it may be well to distinguish the wooden cornices doors, window frames and blinds by another color.

Cyrus may have acquired a taste for the picturesque through his brother; his home combined this with his own nostalgia for New England.[8]

The plan, like the exterior, mixed old familiar forms with variations on those forms. At first glance it does not resemble any common vernacular plan. The front gable extended about seven feet from the main mass, adding extra room and variety to the interior. Upstairs, a special room accommodated Bryant's scholarly interests. On the ground floor, highly detailed

Fig. 2–12. New England center-chimney plan. (A) One-story house, popularly known as a "Cape Cod." (B) Two-story house. Both types have similar floor plans. Reproduced from *Big House, Little House, Back House, Barn: The Connected Farm Buildings of New England* by Thomas C. Hubka, by permission of University Press of New England. Copyright 1984 by Trustees of Dartmouth College.

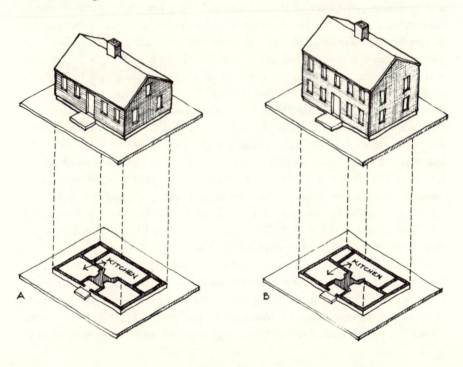

kitchen arrangements suggest that Bryant, or more likely his wife, took an interest in aids to women's work; a systematic approach to kitchen work spaces was unusual. But other elements of the plan derived from the traditional New England Cape Cod plan (Figure 2–12). The massive central fireplace anchored the plan elements; behind it, bedroom, kitchen, and pantry were arranged in typical sequence (south to north) across the rear. In the front half of the house, the traditional entranceway was widened and extended outward to create a parlor.[9]

Bryant's house reflected both the pioneer progressive farmer and the nostalgic traditionalist. It spoke both of its owner's prominence and his humble origins. The bold, jutting gables could not be missed, especially since the house was located on a "Round Point" isolated from the local woodlands, further enhancing the house's visual impact.[10] It was an appropriate setting for a leading citizen. Yet, by retaining familiar exterior and plan elements, Bryant also acknowledged a common background with his neighbors.

Ohio Farmer and Agricultural Educator

Joseph E. Wing (1861–1915) acquired a reputation in the community of Mechanicsburg, Ohio, as "Joe, the Alfalfa King," "on account of his ardent and intelligent advocacy of alfalfa culture." Wing preached progressive agriculture while a lecturer for state farmers' institutes, as a staff correspondent of the *Breeders' Gazette,* and as a government consultant. "Woodland," his 340-acre farm, was regarded as a model for sheep breeders, horticulturists, and indeed for farmers in general. At Woodland, Wing and his wife designed and built two houses, the first in 1892 and another, as their family grew, in 1904. They published the first plan in the *Country Gentleman.* In introducing the plan, Wing explained that he and his bride had first spent a year in a "rented house built cheaply and by contract" and determined to learn from the experience. "Not finding in the books of plans anything that just suited," Wing continued, "I worked out the plan adopted after much thought and consultation." The result was compact and carefully constructed, allowing for maximum use of a small area (Figures 2–13, 2–14, 2–15). The sitting room and dining room were joined by sliding doors; window seat and cupboards provided built-in storage space. The kitchen, equipped with stove, sink, and cupboards, was close to the pump and dairy. Water drawn from the pump ran through the dairy trough, automatically cooling milk stored there. Wing took special pains to construct a warm, tight house, improvising with materials he had on hand. He put lime mortar under the floorboards for insulation and soundproofing, and also filled the

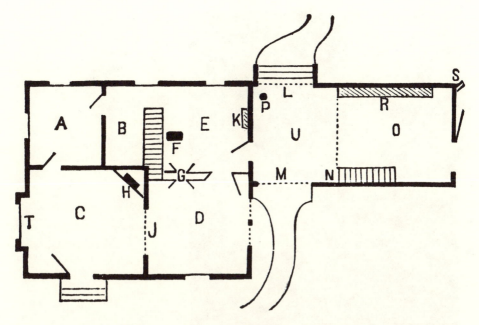

Fig. 2–13. Joe Wing house, Mechanicsburg, Ohio (1892), plan. (A) Bedroom. (B) Closet and Bath. (C) Living room. (D) Dining room. (E) Kitchen. (F) Stove. (G) Cupboards. (H) Hearth. (J, L, M) Sliding doors. (K) Sink. (N) Stove. (O) Woodshed. (P) Pump. (R) Cement trough for milk. (S) Drain. (T) Window seat. (U) Back porch.

Fig. 2–14. Joe Wing house, elevation.

23

Fig. 2–15. Joe Wing's wife and two of his sons photographed about 1901. They are seated in the living room next to the hearth (H) on the plan (Fig. 2–13).

Fig. 2–16. Joe Wing's house, photographed about 1920.

"spaces between siding and lath solidly with dry oak sawdust" for insulation. Sliding barn doors closed in the porch and shielded the kitchen entrance from the elements. For the exterior, Wing decided on stucco, using wire poultry netting to secure the plaster.[11]

From the outside, this modest building (Figure 2–16) is not so coherent as its plan, mostly because Wing's carpenter convinced him to put a hipped roof on one end. The result was a jumbled massing of exterior elements. The fenestration and simplicity of finish, though, clearly indicate room placement. In his choice of stucco Wing apparently was responding to a new fashion. According to a local historian, farmers in this prosperous area had long competed to "build larger and finer homes" than their neighbors. Then, "from around 1890 to 1920 a 'craze' hit this area, both out in the surrounding country-side and here in Mechanicsburg that to make your home look more aristocratic it should be stuccoed." Wing's house was small, but by stuccoing it he signaled his aspirations to high standing in the community. Yet the house, liver-red with bottle-green trim and ochre roof, must have blended unobtrusively into the landscape.[12] Joe Wing's place, like those of Verback, Phillips, and Bryant, stood apart from the neighboring houses without completely repudiating them.

These five buildings all indicate that their designers modified existing forms and adopted new styles, shapes, materials, and ideas. But their architectural experimentation had definite limits. The houses were usually quite plain; the planners shunned stylistic elegance, concentrating instead on interior arrangement, construction, and shape. They were thus variations in the common landscape, but not anomalies.

Progressive Farmer-Planners: A Group Profile

William Verback, C. B. Rider, Cyrus Bryant, Joe Wing, and Edgar Phillips were among more than 200 people who sent house plans to the agricultural journals between 1830 and 1900. Who were these progressive farmhouse designers and what was their position in their rural communities? Some historians have argued that "book farming" was unpopular, and that innovative farmers were a small, wealthy elite, far removed from the rank and file. Others believe that most farmers were quite receptive to innovation. An examination of these farmers' backgrounds, and especially of the houses they built, suggests that the notion of a sharp polarization between progressive agriculturists and the rest—hidebound, book-scorning traditionalists—cannot be sustained. True, these farmers were comfortably ensconced in the upper levels of rural society. But they were not isolated from their neighbors, nor were they always at odds with them. The progressive families had ambivalent relationships with their communities, at times co-operating, at times clashing with them. They acted as cultural mediators between past and future, country and city, folk and popular cultures. And nowhere is this more evident than in the physical forms of their houses.[13]

Most of these farmers simply signed their plans with initials or used pseudonyms. The "constant Reader" from Michigan, or "N.B.V." from Cayuga County remain anonymous. Of those planners who did give a name and location, many also have disappeared, too obscure to have even been remembered in a local history. Yet a surprising number are identified in local histories, directories, atlases, manuscript census returns, probate inventories, and even diaries. These data are not meant to make up the type of rigorous cliometric profile that historians are by now accustomed to seeing in social histories. County "vanity histories," for example, betray by their very sobriquets their limited reliability.[14] Nonetheless, these sources and the eloquent testimony of the houses themselves all contribute to a remarkably consistent image of the nineteenth-century progressive farm family and its place in the community.

Farmer-planners lived in twenty-two northern states and territories, from the east coast to the Great Plains. The largest concentration was in the mid-Atlantic region, especially New York state. This is not surprising, because the most prominent national agricultural periodicals—the *American Agriculturist* and the *Cultivator,* for example—were published in New York, the nation's leading agricultural state until the mid-1870s. But the geographic center of planning did shift westward over time. In the 1850s, two-thirds of the plans originated in the mid-Atlantic. In the next decade, the percentages were even, and by the 1880s, 23 of 28 came from Ohio and states to the west—a pattern that reflects the steady westward movement of the center of American population in the nineteenth century.[15]

The contributors of most plans lived close to towns or cities. H. B. Hart's farm in Monroe County, New York, was near Rochester, and James Ellis owned a large sheep farm about two miles from Syracuse. J. F. Chubb established his farm on the outskirts of the expanding Grand Rapids, Michigan. Other contributors lived in Adrian, Michigan (30 miles from Toledo, Ohio); Edwardsville, Illinois; Poland, Ohio (near Youngstown); Collinsville, Illinois (15 miles from St. Louis); and Farmington, Connecticut (near Hartford). Thus farmer-planners must have enjoyed frequent contacts with town society and business.[16]

Most of the planners were of Yankee or British stock. The non-natives had emigrated largely from the British Isles; only a few came from continental Europe. Most of the New Englanders were native-born, as were the

New Yorkers. Western contributors—those from Wisconsin, Michigan, Ohio, northern Illinois, and Iowa—hailed primarily from New England, New York, and Pennsylvania.[17]

Many of the planners had unusually strong roots in their communities. For example, of the five who lived in Connecticut, four were born in or near their communities and some, like Mrs. William H. Burr, came from long-established families. In New York state, where a greater proportion of newcomers might be expected, only a few had migrated from coastal states. Moreover, once settled, many stayed for a long time. Their names appeared regularly in federal census returns, local directories, and ultimately in country histories. Benjamin Steere, for example, is recorded in the federal census returns of Adrian, Michigan, for three decades beginning in 1850; James Smeallie farmed in Princetown, Schenectady County, New York, for a score of years; and Augustus Hurlburt lived in or near Utica, New York, his whole life.[18]

This stability may be exaggerated because longtime residents, of course, are more likely to appear in local records, while those who migrate frequently are more difficult to track down. Geographically stable families, however, still probably typified the group, and several characteristics of the house plan contributors suggest that they were less inclined to migrate than were their neighbors. They invested a great deal of thought and care in building their dwellings, obviously expecting that the houses would serve their families for many years. And their local success probably inclined them to stay where they were. Allan Bogue and others have noted that people who "persisted" in a given locality tended to be richer than those who left. As substantial farmers, businessmen, and professionals, these people had little reason to leave.[19]

Agriculture was the dominant profession among the planners whose occupations could be determined. Comparatively few, however, can simply be labeled "farmers"; most followed a combination of pursuits. Businessmen-farmers, successors of the gentlemen farmers of the eighteenth century and the distant ancestors of agribusiness practitioners, led their communities in applying business principles to agriculture. William Little of Ohio farmed 350 acres with hired labor and mechanical implements, producing dairy products, wheat, rye, corn, and oats, while running a "Dry goods, Groceries, and Variety Stores [sic]" in a nearby town. Perhaps he used his store as an outlet for his own farm goods. J. S. Peers farmed 50 acres in southern Illinois and was a partner in a local lumber business. The brothers Daniel and John Edwards of Little Genesee, New York, farmed 580 acres (they were also first in the area to purchase a mowing machine) and operated a sawmill and a cabinet shop. Harry B. Hart, who lived about

10 miles from Rochester, shrewdly balanced a diversified farming scheme, served as postmaster and merchant, and sold insurance. Peter Wykoff of Romulus, New York, made brooms. Others apparently preferred more intellectual complements with farming. Cyrus Bryant established a local reputation as a botanist and geologist; Waldo Brown of Ohio described himself as a farmer and agricultural reporter.[20]

Among the planners whose sole occupation was farming, innovators, organizers, and specialists predominated. From his father's 120-acre farm in Yates County, New York, Lorenzo D. Snook sent farm journals an endless stream of communications: "Improvements in Bee Hives," "Snook's Improved Corn Marker," "The Great Thistle Destroyer," "Renewing Strawberry Plantations." Nurseryman Benjamin Steere (Adrian, Michigan) organized the "first farmers' club west of the Allegheny Mountains," attended conventions of horticulturists and fruit growers, and held local Horticultural Society meetings in his home. Dairyman James Smeallie was probably one of the first farmers in Schenectady to take up his specialty on a substantial scale: in 1836 he milked twenty cows, earning an annual profit of $42.55 per cow from cheese and butter sales. Smeallie was also a leader of the local agricultural society. Davis Cossit, sheepman of Onondaga, New York, was interested in agricultural cooperation, serving as an officer in various farm organizations from 1853 to 1866.[21]

Some of the house designers did not rely on farms for income but still took an active interest in agriculture. Among them were clergymen, attorneys, physicians, politicians, carpenters, writers, a railroad agent, a druggist, a schoolmaster, an engineer, a carriage-maker, a machinist, and a factory hand. Thomas Thomas, an English civil engineer transplanted to Milwaukee, applied his expertise to agricultural projects and to house plans. The agricultural interests of the Rutland, Vermont, builder, railroad pioneer, editor, and politician John Cain stemmed from his awareness of agriculture's importance (especially sheep raising) in Vermont's economy. Carpenter-joiner Lewis Lorenzo Pierce of New Hampshire reported to the agricultural journals on the progress of local harvests and also described the results of his own experiments with mulches for fruit trees. In Wisconsin, B. X. Hoxie acquired an excellent reputation as a builder, and also established a cheese factory with a capacity for processing the milk of 600 cows.[22]

Only impressionistic conclusions can be made about wealth, but apparently most of the planners were well-to-do. Waldo Brown, of Butler County, Ohio, owned a farm worth $6,000 (well above the state average) in 1880. He reported that his farm machinery was worth $300, also an unusually high figure. George Cattell of Harrisville, Ohio, valued his farm at $8,000 in 1860, when the average rural male in his state owned only $1,500 worth of land and buildings. Benjamin Chase of Stillwater, New York, reported to the census taker in 1860 that his 150-acre farm had a cash value of $9,000 (the state average was $5,668) and that he owned $240 worth of agricultural implements (the average was $180). In 1850, Daniel Edwards owned one of only four farms that were over 500 acres in Allegany County, New York.[23]

Of the plans submitted between 1830 and 1900, at least twenty-one were by women. In 1895, when the *American Agriculturist* sponsored a house design contest, eleven of the thirty-one winners were women, including the first-prize winner. Reconstruction of women designers' biographies depends more upon inference, however, than the profiles of their male counterparts. Such signatures and pseudonyms as "Farmer's Wife" or "Maryland Matron" imply but do not confirm that their contributors were female. Even when women's names do appear in local histories or census returns, etc., the information typically describes their husbands, not the women.

Yet it is safe to conclude that women planners were farm wives, sometimes professionals and usually experienced in farming. They thought house design was a legitimate exercise of their duties. Mrs. Matilda Howard of Zanesville, Ohio, helped run a farm owned by her stockbreeder husband. Mrs. Howard apparently shared her husband's interest in progressive farming, for she contributed to the *Cultivator* her knowledge of dairying, indicating that she had taken "personal charge" of a small dairy in the early 1830s. Mrs. William H. Burr, from near Danbury, Connecticut, won a premium for her house plan in 1882. Mrs. James Ellis (Lucy Cudworth) was the wife of a prosperous sheep farmer from 1833 until 1854, when tragedy prompted the couple to leave farming.[24]

Several of the women house planners forged professional careers. Laura Lyman of Stamford, Connecticut, became a writer. Both she and her husband, Joseph Bardwell Lyman, wrote on agricultural topics for New York City newspapers, and they collaborated on the popular *Philosophy of Housekeeping*. Mrs. Lyman also contributed to *Hearth and Home*, publisher Orange Judd's sister journal to the *American Agriculturist*, in the 1870s. Leila Robinson Bedell, who sent her plan to *Moore's* in 1872, must have been influenced by her father, Solon Robinson, one of the nineteenth century's most articulate proponents of progressive agriculture. Her own career as a homeopathic physician, however, took her away from her Indiana farm to Chicago.[25]

The Design Process

What made these progressive agriculturists regard themselves as "progressive" was an outlook, a set of values that defined them. The culture of progressive farming emphasized book learning, innovation, and experimentation, and the planners' approach to design bore the imprint of this frame of mind. As Suel Foster of Muscatine, Iowa, explained in the *Prairie Farmer* (1855), the farmer ought to "seek for [his house] the most improved plan, as in the wagon, the plow, the reaper, etc."[26]

S. B. Shaw illustrated this approach when he sent a plan to the *Cultivator* in 1841. Shaw was an Episcopalian clergyman in western Massachusetts, home of the first Berkshire agricultural society. An accompanying letter explained his motivation for planning a house:

> Although a professional man, [I am] interested in the culture of the soil, and in all matters of general utility and improvement. I occupy a glebe of about thirty acres, upon which I have made some experiments in farming, and am convinced that scientific investigations may be made highly conducive to the advancement of good husbandry. I do not agree with some that the Rohan potato is to be discarded, or that snow is as good as eggs in flap-jacks; but I do agree with those who maintain that whatever discoveries may be made beneficial to the world . . . should be made public. In accordance with this principle, I send you the plan of a cheap house which I furnished one of my neighbors . . . The gentleman to whom I gave it has built twice from it, and has lately remarked that should he build twenty houses they should all be alike.[27]

Shaw thought of a good house plan as a "discovery," analogous to an ostensibly superior breed of potato. The Rohan potato was an experimental variety whose yields were tremendous, though many thought it was tough and unpalatable. Shaw's experimental nature played a prominent role in his search for a house design; he welcomed innovations as a solution to specific architectural problems.

The inclination to try different ways to solve a problem, to experiment with a variety of crops, fertilizers, or machines, could also manifest itself in a continual reevaluation of house designs. Obviously, a house could not be replanned at will, but within limits it could be altered. For some, then, designing never ceased. Numerous contributors made remarks similar to William Verback's note in 1839 that he had "sen[t] you the plan of my dwelling house with the improvements which several years' occupancy has suggested." Verback probably continually reassessed his design, noting deficiencies and attempting to correct them.[28]

Solon Robinson, a prominent agricultural reformer from Indiana, offered a variation on the idea of continual reevaluation and experimentation: he thought that farmers could economize by building in stages, "each part complete in itself." In 1847 he proposed a detailed program for a house which would be built (as the family's size and means increased) in carefully calculated increments from the original one-room cabin to a commodious farmhouse. By following this procedure, Robinson declared, the proprietor could be "building all the time and always having a perfect house."[29] Economy was foremost in his mind; he also systematized the way in which earlier generations of Americans had expanded their dwellings.

Many of these house plans were produced by joint effort, and perhaps by negotiation. The progressive farmer, who enthusiastically shared the results of his agricultural experiments with his colleagues, might encourage a similar exchange at home, especially between members of the household. Progressive farm women shared the values of progressive agriculture, applying these values to their usual role of housekeeping and incorporating their domestic experience into designing the house. Their place in determining the plan of progressive farmhouses and in differentiating independent vernacular planning from professional designs was a prominent one.

Some women contributed plans independently and under their own names while others influenced design from behind the scenes. Early on, the *Cultivator* sanctioned women's participation in design when it set the criteria for its 1839 contest: "To improve our farm dwelling-houses, to render them convenient, economize the cost, and lessen the burden of female labor." Solon Robinson, commenting on the contest, wrote "I hope that your readers, whose *wife* thinks he has a convenient house, will furnish you at least the plan." He added that in his estimation, "one story farmhouses . . . are much easier for the good woman." Robinson may have incorporated his own wife's suggestions in arriving at a house design; at the very least he must have been aware of her preferences. Solomon Jewett of Weybridge, Vermont (whose contribution to progressive agriculture was importing purebred sheep), won second prize in the contest. He too implied that women should have at least a consulting role: "the farmer's wife," he explained, "considers it very important, that the kitchen should be convenient to each apartment above and below." "H.A.P." of Buffalo, New York, wrote the *Cultivator* in 1846 to criticize a plan it had recently published:

> My better half, sitting at my elbow, says she would like to have some of your correspondents furnish a plan of a house or cottage, suitable for a large family, in which all the rooms should be on one floor . . . for, she says that running up and down stairs makes the women look old when they are young, and that a cellar kitchen is an abomination. And further,

she thinks that what little scolding and fretting is heard among them, is owing very much to the ill judged plans of their houses.[30]

By 1859, *Moore's Rural New Yorker* described a cooperative process of design: "Usually among our farming community the plan of a house is got up by the builder; or, rather, the proprietor decides upon the size and general shape, and then the carpenter subdivides it into apartments under the direction of the female head of the family."[31]

The culture of progressive agriculture, then, had a direct bearing upon the design process, since progressive farm families valued an experimental and cooperative approach to design. This approach in turn influenced the actual forms that the plans assumed.

Progressive farmhouse designs were inspired by three principal sources: common vernacular forms, original ideas, and pattern-book plans. Often all three would be combined to produce a syncretistic hybrid. Sometimes the result was obviously patched together, but in other instances the various styles were skillfully melded together.

Many of the independent planners began with familiar vernacular forms. Geographers and architectural historians have identified a number of basic vernacular forms which were ubiquitous in the North. Some classifying criteria are based upon plans, others upon sometimes deceptive exterior appearances. Because no comprehensive typology of plans exists, especially for houses in which balloon frame and innovations in stove design allowed for flexibility, types based on both plan and exterior appearance will be employed here. The plan of the "I" house, a two-story structure with its long side parallel to the road, consisted of two rooms separated by a hall-way. The "I" was common in the mid-Atlantic and upper South, but rare in New England. The common New England Cape Cod house was one-and-a-half stories, with a center chimney flanked by two large front rooms, and a large center room in back. A variation on the Cape Cod had a central stair in place of the chimney. The symmetrical Georgian plan, or "four over four," was two rooms deep with a center hall, and two stories high. As the Greek Revival gained popularity, "temple form" and "upright-and-wing" houses became common. The gable end of the temple form faced the road. Usually the upright-and-wing consisted of a two-story main block with one or two subordinate wings, and was most common in New England, New York, and Michigan. By the Civil War, new forms were gaining in popularity, such as the "bent" house, which consisted of a pair of intersecting wings of roughly equal volume. Cube-shaped volumes also became more popular.[32]

Independent farmer-planners like Cyrus Bryant often borrowed these and other vernacular forms as the basis of their plans. In an anonymous plan by "B." (1853) and a signed plan by L. L. Pierce (1857) (Figures 2–17, 2–18), several versions of the Classic Cottage are evident. Philip Ritz (1857) chose to build a one-and-a-half-story house based on the Cape Cod (Figure 2–19). "H.A.P." (1847) used the Georgian plan (Figure 2–20). The upright-and-wing form was also popular. In 1858 an anonymous "subscriber" sent an elaborate plan of this style to the *Genesee Farmer* (Figures 2–21, 2–22); a simpler variant of this form, signed "Farmer's Wife," was submitted to the *Cultivator* in 1849 (Figure 2–23). A. B. Tucker of Monticello, Iowa, designed a "Cornbelt Cube" (Figures 2–24, 2–25).

A second glance at these plans shows that their designers rarely left basic vernacular forms unaltered. "B.'s" plan substituted a sitting room and vestibule for the more conventional passageway. L. L. Pierce placed the kitchen in the front rather than in the rear, as was customary. "H.A.P.'s" design lacked the rigorous symmetry and formality of a conventional Georgian plan. In fact, he designed this one-story house with his wife in mind, arranging all of the family bedrooms within easy reach of the kitchen and "family room." No two upright-and-wing plans contained the same combination of rooms and shapes. The anonymous "subscriber" lavished attention on entrance, curved stairway, and nursery; the "Farmer's Wife," on the other hand, designed a compact plan and arranged all spaces to focus on the kitchen. A. B. Tucker's house combined two forms—the cube doubled as the "upright" in an upright-and-wing arrangement.

The tendency to tinker with traditional forms is exemplified by Lewis Falley Allen's designs. A land speculator and renowned stock breeder, Allen settled in Buffalo, New York, around 1830. His first farmhouse plan (Figure 2–26), published in the *Genesee Farmer* in 1832, was based upon a "Long Island Dutch" house he knew. A second plan (Figure 2–26) combined what Allen considered the best attributes of "Yankee" building (a two-story plan) with the benefits of the "Dutch" model (the subdivision of rooms and pattern of kitchen wing). Actually, both plans were versions of the symmetrical Georgian center-hall plan; Georgian houses of the "Dutch" regions are characterized by the narrowness of the back rooms in relation to the front rooms. Nevertheless, Allen's approach to design illustrated his interest in combining the forms of two disparate regions, exploiting the observations he had made on his travels. Apparently Allen did not feel bound to follow rigidly the vernacular forms of his native New England.[33]

Pattern-books were successors of an earlier genre of builders' guides for carpenters and craftsmen; they encompassed a wider range of topics and were geared to the general public. Whether or not they bought the books themselves, progressive farmers were exposed to numerous pattern-book designs in the agricultural press throughout the century.

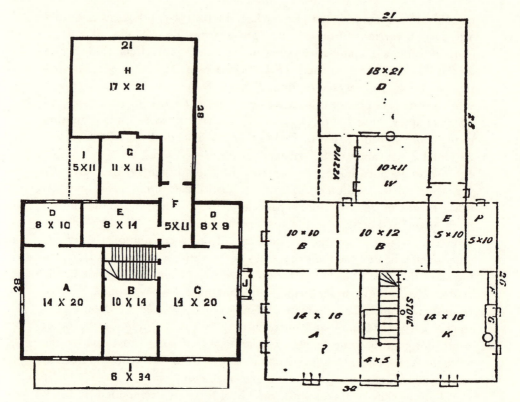

Fig. 2–17. Anonymous plan for a farmhouse (1853). (A) Parlor. (B) Sitting room. (C) Living and dining room. (D) Bedrooms. (E) Pantry. (F) Passage. (G) Washroom. (H) Wood house. (I) Verandas. (J) Portico. (Kitchen not indicated.)

Fig. 2–18. L. L. Pierce, plan for a farmhouse in Jaffrey, New Hampshire (1857). (A) Parlor. (B) Bedrooms. (D) Woodshed. (E) Passage. (F) Cupboard. (G) Sink with pump. (K) Kitchen. (P) Pantry. (W) Washroom.

Fig. 2–19. Phillip Ritz, plan for a farmhouse in Corvallis, Oregon (1857).

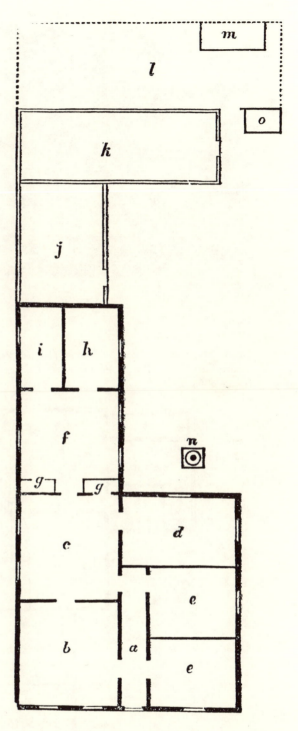

Fig. 2–20. Anonymous plan for a farm-house in Buffalo, New York (1847). (a) Hall. (b) Parlor. (c) Dining and Family room. (d) Family bedroom. (e) Bedrooms. (f) Kitchen. (g) Closets. (h) Bedroom. (i) Pantry. (j) Wood house. (k) Carriage house and Horse barn. (l) Barnyard. (m) Barn. (n) Well. (o) Hog pen.

35

Fig. 2–21. Anonymous design for a farmhouse in Mendon, New York (1858). Elevation.

Fig. 2–22. Farmhouse design, Mendon, plan. (A) Parlor. (B) Living room. (C) Nursery. (D) Winter kitchen. (E) Hall. (F) Bedrooms. (G) Clothes room. (H) Pantry. (I) Summer kitchen. (J) Wood house. (P) Piazzas.

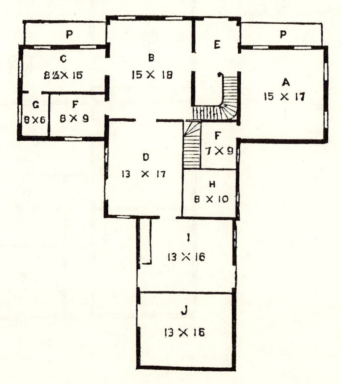

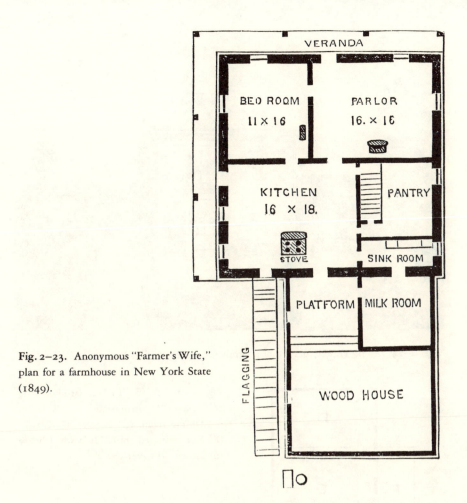

VERANDA

BED ROOM
11 × 16

PARLOR
16. × 16

KITCHEN
16 × 18.

PANTRY

STOVE

SINK ROOM

FLAGGING

PLATFORM | MILK ROOM

WOOD HOUSE

Fig. 2–23. Anonymous "Farmer's Wife," plan for a farmhouse in New York State (1849).

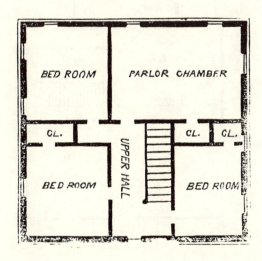

BED ROOM

PARLOR CHAMBER

CL.

CL.

CL.

BED ROOM

UPPER HALL

BED ROOM

37

Fig. 2–24. A. B. Tucker, design for a farmhouse in Monticello, Iowa (1885). Elevation.

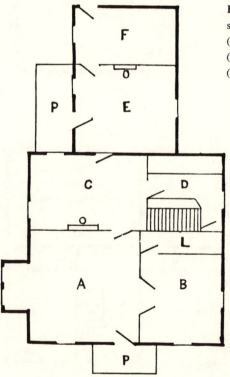

Fig. 2–25. A. B. Tucker, farmhouse design, plan. (A) Sitting room. (B) Bedroom. (C) Dining room. (D) Pantry. (E) Kitchen. (F) Not indicated, probably a wood house. (L) Closets. (P) Porches.

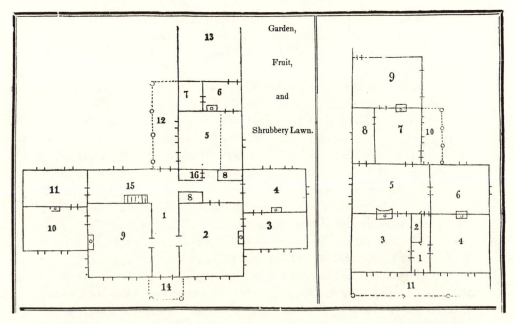

Fig. 2–26. Lewis F. Allen, farmhouse plans combining "Dutch" and "Yankee" plans (1832). (Left) *"Dutch" plan.* (1) Main hall. (2) Common parlor. (3) Family bedroom. (4) Nursery or Family room. (5) Kitchen. (6) Passage. (7) Ironing and Bathing Room. (8) Closets. (9) Parlor. (10, 11) Spare bedrooms. (12) Back porch. (13) Wood house. (14) Front porch. (15) Rear hall. (16) Cellar stairs. (Right) *"Combined" plan.* (1) Front entry. (2) Stairs. (3) Common sitting room. (4) Parlor. (5) Main kitchen. (6) Family bedroom. (7) Outer kitchen. (8) Milk room. (9) Wood house. (10) Rear porch. (11) Porch. (0) Fireplaces.

A. J. Downing (1814–1852), America's leading writer on country houses, set the standard for pattern-book writers. His first work, on landscape gardening, appeared in 1841. It was followed by *Cottage Residences* (1842), *The Architecture of Country Houses* (1850), *Hints to Persons Upon Building in the Country* (1851), and *Rural Essays* (1852). Downing was a nurseryman well-known in circles of progressive agriculture; consequently, his writings gained wide and favorable publicity in the agricultural press. He not only introduced a new source of house plans, but popularized a romantic philosophy of design which touched upon artistic, professional, and social life. Downing emphasized the importance of aesthetics (and therefore of architectural style) in forming moral character and cementing ties of sentiment. Downing believed that the rural resident, aided by a professional architect, ought to aim for aesthetic unity and individual expression in house design.[34] The plans he promoted reflected his interest in and knowledge of well-to-do suburban families in which the men worked outside the home; leisure and ceremonial spaces took up the largest areas and most prominent locations, and work areas (for "domestics") were screened away from living spaces.

Farmhouse architecture, he thought, especially needed reform. Of the independent amateur planners, he remarked that architecture was "not the mere province of the builder," much less of the farmer: the "ignorant ploughman" did not appreciate the "beauty of clouds or aerial perspectives in landscapes" in which he toiled. In *The Architecture of Country Houses* is a chapter entitled "What a Farm House Should Be." It opens with another jibe at the farmer-designer: "The designs continually published by agricultural journals, most of which emanate from the agricultural class, show the continual aiming after something better . . . But a large number of the better and more substantial farmhouses . . . are decidedly failures, considered in either a tasteful or architectural point of view."[35]

Downing addressed the agricultural community directly in "Hints on the Construction of Farm Houses," published in the June 1846 issue of the *Cultivator.* He began by proclaiming that the farmhouse was a worthy object of attention, invoking the agrarian ideal—after all, the sturdy yeoman farmer anchored the American republic. But he condemned farmers' pretensions in adding such unseemly details as Greek porticoes to their dwellings: "The beauty of propriety is a species of moral beauty even in houses and clothes." To fulfill the requirement for propriety, Downing argued, the farmhouse must express "manifest utility," because utility was the salient characteristic of farm life. Ornament should therefore "combine itself with the most important and useful features of the house."[36] He identified these as the verandah, an entranceway, gables (which indicated the utility of a sloping roof), and the chimney stacks, which signaled the family hearth within. He promoted the Gothic, Italianate, and "Swiss" styles as the most appropriate expressions of rural domestic qualities.

Downing mounted a forceful, coherent presentation of new ideas, and his books went through many editions. Farmer-designers were conspicuous among his targets, but they received his works with ambivalence. Lewis Falley Allen's selective adoption of Downing's ideas was typical of the reception that most progressive farmers gave to him.

Allen noticed Downing's work as soon as it appeared. In the *American Agriculturist* (January 1843) he condemned America's rural architecture as "uncouth" and recommended Downing's books to remedy architectural defects. His own house, he declared, would be "snug and convenient." In an agrarian variation of picturesque landscaping, Allen promised a "good kitchen garden," which would impart "a homelike appearance." Meanwhile,

Allen's brothers, Richard and Anthony, editors of the *American Agriculturist,* had favorably reviewed *Cottage Residences* and printed an engraving of design #2 from that work as its frontispiece.[37]

Later, in the same year, Lewis Allen gave notice that his farmhouse was now finished at a cost of about $1000. He explained why his design was superior to other plans:

> The grand difficulty with the plans of farm-houses that I find laid down in
> the books and papers is, that the constructors . . . sacrifice convenience to
> fancy. This is all wrong . . . Comfort and convenience are the main requi-
> sites, and these obtained, if the slightest good taste is used, the house will
> look well . . .[38]

If the woodcut (Figure 2–27) published in 1845 is accurate, Allen's house was indeed devoid of "fancy." It most resembles the plain, "uncouth" farmhouses which Downing tried to eradicate (Figure 2–28), though of course the latter engraving exaggerated for effect. In criticizing the designs which flaunted "fancy," Allen may have referred to one of Downing's books, since few other architectural books were available in 1845. It appears, therefore, that Allen was of two minds about Downing's architectural advice. He applauded the introduction of principles of "taste," even adopting Downing's language to some extent, but fretted about the devotion to "fancy," which he believed characterized the new styles. Perhaps Allen's ambivalence

Fig. 2–27. Lewis Allen, design for a farmhouse in Black Rock, New York (1845). Gable end.

Fig. 2–28. A. J. Downing, illustration of improved farmhouse style (1846). (Above) Before. (Below) After.

stemmed from his own social position. On the one hand, his rural background and devotion to farming made him aware of the practical demands of agricultural work; on the other, his spectacular success as a businessman may have influenced his interest in aesthetic considerations.

In 1848, Allen sent another plan and elevation, together with a long essay, "The Construction of Farm Cottages," to the journal. He evidently had further pondered Downing's philosophy, incorporating some of its tenets and rejecting others. The essay opened with his now customary tactic of criticizing the deficiencies of American houses. He also made note of a new kind of eyesore: "On the brow of yon eminence," he warned, "there may be seen a castle-like structure, 'embosomed high in tufted trees,' reminding the traveller . . . that he is surrounded by the feudal oppressors, who long made sorrowful the homes of the Old World." Allen bemoaned the "mania for building Gothic castles," associating the Gothic style with uncomfortable and inconvenient design. "The kitchen and living-room are in a basement, half under ground, throwing the fumes of the scullery . . . into the parlor above."[39] Whether or not Allen referred to designs inspired by Downing's works (several of the Gothic houses in *Cottage Residences* did have basement kitchens), he was clearly at odds with the evocations of Downing's favored styles.

In criticizing the Gothic house for its inconvenience, Allen did not disagree about the merits of a particular style. He analyzed the problem at a more fundamental level and concluded that

> most of the houses in this country have been planned by persons who have never studied the first principles of domestic architecture, such as builders, carpenters, etc., . . . or they have been designed by professional architects, . . . who have been reared in the rigid school of European precedent, if in any, imbued with prejudices at variance with the simplicity of our manners.

Apparently Allen sought a middle ground between folk building and "high-style," professionally designed monuments. He continued with his own interpretation of the "first principles of domestic architecture":

> The chief objects to be considered are, first, the number and character of the people it is intended to accomodate; 2d, the expense, or present means and prospective ability of the proprietor; 3d, regarding exposure to the sun, and in affording convenience to the outbuildings . . . 4th, consistency, or congruity, so far as it is considered as an object in landscape scenery, and its fitness . . . in promoting health and comfort . . . to the occupants within.[40]

Allen placed economy and convenience above beauty in his scheme of architectural priorities, where Downing had decried "mere utility" in favor of "beauty of form" and "expression." Yet Allen incorporated Downing's prescriptions for landscaping into his fourth point. Moreover, after a room-by-room description of his plan, Allen offered eighteen more points on color, style, landscaping, and ornament for "those who have not given much thought to the subject." Here Downing's influence was pervasive. For example, Allen suggested that a "high and massive chimney top in a cold climate like ours, gives a cottage an appearance of cheerfulness, because they are [sic] associated in the observer's mind with the glowing grates . . . within."[41]

Although Allen frequently referred to aesthetics in his eighteen points, the house shown in the 1848 essay (Figures 2–29, 2–30) again violated several of Downing's cardinal rules. First, if it could be said to have a style, it most resembled the hated Grecian, with its regular floor plan and Doric

Fig. 2–29. Lewis Allen, design for a farmhouse (1848). Plan. (Right) *Ground Floor:* (B) Bedroom. (C) Closets. (D) Dining room. (E) Entry. (H) Lobby. (K) Kitchen. (L) Library, Office, or Nursery. (P) Parlors. (S) Stairs. (V) Vault. (c) Chimney. (d) Trapdoor. (l) Lightning conductor. (Left) *Attic Floor:* (A, B) Bedrooms. (G) Garret. (S) Stairs. (c) Chimney. (f) Stove funnel.

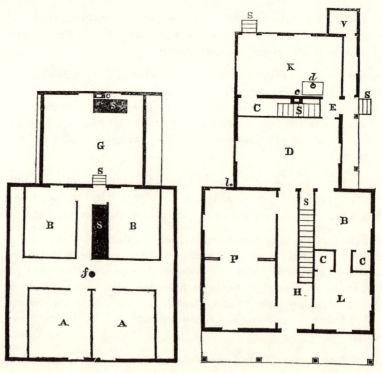

Fig. 2–30. Lewis Allen, 1848 design, elevation.

porch columns. Second, the white house stands boldly visible, not screened by foliage and muted in color as Downing would prescribe.

Allen's book *Rural Architecture* (1852) exhibited his most extensive intertwining of independent ideas with notions borrowed from Downing. He modeled the book itself after the pattern-books and paid homage to Downing's ideas; a farmhouse, Allen declared, should "express itself in everything." The elevations in the book definitely reflected prevailing styles, especially the Italianate. But Allen insisted that his plans addressed the "everyday wants of a strictly agricultural population," emphasizing family and work spaces instead of entertainment and leisure spaces.[42] Allen in fact did erect at least one farmhouse during his lifetime, probably more. One survives, on Grand Island, near Buffalo. He called it "River Lea," and it served as his summer residence. Its exterior (Figure 2–31) strongly resembles Design IV of Allen's book (Figure 2–32), especially the center gable and balcony, and graduated window proportions. It also has a center-hall plan, as does the model design. Allen had once more modified a standard vernacular plan, this time by clothing it with a mixture of stylistic touches.

Most farmer-planners used Downing's books, and pattern-books in general, as Allen did: they selectively embraced some stylistic reforms (for instance in the use of board-and-batten siding or Gothic detail), but continued their independent planning. As Victorian styles became more popular and as pattern-books proliferated, fewer of the independent planners followed vernacular plans, but they did not simply copy the new plans outright. Instead, they apparently consulted a variety of sources. One correspondent

Fig. 2-31. Lewis Allen residence, Grand Island, New York, designed about 1850, photographed about 1960.

Fig. 2-32. Lewis Allen, farmhouse design from *Rural Architecture* (1860). Elevation.

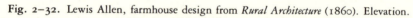

of the *Cultivator* wrote in December of 1859 to ask for advice. He had "searched through books on rural and domestic architecture," but had not yet found a plan which met his requirements: "The plan which best suits me, is one published in 'Rural Affairs,' p. 133, but the study or library is not in a sufficiently retired position. There is also a plan in Downing's Country Houses, p 304, which, if made smaller, would adapt itself very well to my wants, except that I cannot heat the library with a furnace." This particular correspondent probably ended up with a combination of plans. Another reader, Suel Foster, consulted "Gervase Wheeler's *Rural Houses*, . . . Downing's work, and Raunlette's [Ranlett's] *Architect*." He considered himself "amply paid for any cost or time in studying these works," but concluded that "ancient orders of architectural style" were "far less important than the internal arrangement."[43]

Pattern-books did not always promote conventional popular styles. Orson Squires Fowler believed he had discovered the most economical and efficient mode of house construction in the *Octagon and Gravel Wall Mode of Construction.* Numerous farmer-designers, like Edgar Phillips of Coventry, showed an interest in the octagon house, the architectural equivalent of the crazes which periodically swept the agricultural world for such oddities as the silkworm or the Rohan potato. Seventeen octagon plans appeared after 1850 in the farm press. Some contributors, like D. S. Curtis of Madison, Wisconsin, followed Fowler's prescriptions faithfully: "the Fowlers have very clearly and properly set forth the economy and convenience of this style of building," Curtis declared. Horticulturist H. T. Vose also adopted the octagon plan, but substituted guidelines published in the *Annual Register of Rural Affairs* for Fowler's recommendations. He explained that he had planned "in accordance with the rules given in the *Annual Register.*" Vose probably referred to an article entitled "Farm Houses—the Art of Planning Them." The fourth rule reads "More attention should be given to the arrangement and convenient disposition of such rooms as are in constant use, than those but occasionally occupied. Hence the kitchen and living room should receive more attention . . . than the parlor." In accordance with this rule, no doubt, Vose placed the parlor "up stairs."[44] Vose's plan was yet another example of freely combining different published sources in approaching an architectural problem.

The independence of the farmer-planners is apparent in the creative way in which they combined vernacular forms, pattern-book designs, and their own ideas, providing a significant source of innovation in American vernacular architecture. The major transition in American vernacular architecture, according to architectural historian Dell Upton, was from a regionally differentiated folk architecture in the early part of the century to a nationally distributed, popular architecture at the century's end. This transition did not occur through wholesale adoption of popular forms; instead, vernacular designers selectively adapted pattern-book styles to their own needs.[45]

The farmer-designers, then, should be considered part of a broader movement. They worked independently, but they used the agricultural press as a forum for the exchange of ideas on house design. They wrote to criticize other peoples' plans, to suggest improvements, to inform readers of the results when they built from a published plan, or to announce that their own plans had been copied by neighbors. A Pennsylvania farmer, for example, wrote to the *Genesee Farmer* that, in his opinion, Allen's plan had been the journal's most worthwhile offering since he had subscribed. He continued: "My house is now complete, and declared by all who see it, to be the best planned house in Union County. I expect to see before long two other houses erected in my neighborhood upon the same plan."[46] So, in a region with its own building traditions, miles away from western New York, a farmer chose to imitate a published plan rather than follow local, orally transmitted patterns. Agricultural journals had become an agent in the spread of ideas on house design and contributed to the broader transformation of American vernacular architecture.

Progressive farmer-designers' architectural behavior was symptomatic of their wider cultural position. Like their houses, progressive farm families stood out from their neighbors, but also shared important qualities with them. Progressive farmers were not representative of most rural people. But their position in the community allowed them the means and the outlook to function as cultural mediators in a variety of ways—between rural and urban cultures, and between "folk" and "popular" cultures, for example. This role was inherently invested with tension; ordinary farmers regarded their progressive counterparts with amusement, contempt, envy, and grudging respect. Their attitudes can be explained in part by the character of progressive agriculture, a blend of scientific inquiry and chicanery. The same farmer who found success by underdraining his lands with tile might also invest in such expensive follies as silkworms, or a potato plant that produced prodigious yields—of tough, inedible tubers. Yet, while the progressive farmer's experimentation succeeded or failed, the less adventurous and less well-to-do neighbors probably took note and watched to see what happened. In the competitive heat of capitalist agriculture, they sometimes found themselves imitating the progressives, whether they wanted to or not, if only to keep up with the rapid pace of agricultural change in the nineteenth century.

Progressive agriculturists also thought and wrote about issues of concern to the broader rural community—agricultural competition, rural-urban migration, education, transportation, women's issues. Their solutions to the challenges facing rural society may have been beyond the means of their neighbors, but the problems they addressed were common to all. And they were committed to rural life; most farmed at least part-time, and many stayed in the same place for years. They were tied to their communities, and their houses bear testimony to those ties. By contrast, their twentieth-century successors in rural reform, the country-life reformers, came mostly from cities and universities. Thus progressive farm families' homes, blends of tradition and innovation, local custom and independent ideas, reflected their occupants' position in the wider social context.[47]

The appearance of progressive farmers' owner-designed houses in the northern countryside testified both to the growing affluence of some farm families and to the search for new cultural forms that preoccupied so many Americans in the nineteenth century. Though the process by which progressive farmers incorporated new architectural ideals may have paralleled broader transformations taking place, the content of the plans reflected their own distinctive concerns. It is in the inner workings of the plans that we see the families' everyday lives evolve, as social change and architectural change intersected. In the years between 1830 and 1900, these independent planners were to draw on the variety of cultural resources available to them as they shaped and reshaped their homes to create a constantly changing rural scene.

NOTES

1. R. H. Howard and Henry E. Crocker, eds., *A History of New England* (Boston: Crocker & Co., 1881), II: 322–327; U.S. Census, Agriculture Schedule and Population Schedule, 1840, 1850, 1860; Abby Maria Hemenway, *Vermont Historical Gazetteer* (Burlington, Vt., 1877): 179; Jan Leo Lewandowski, "The Plank Framed House in Northeastern Vermont," *Vermont History* 53 (Spring 1985): 104–121; Dell Upton, "Traditional Timber Framing," in Brooke Hindle, ed., *Material Culture of the Wooden Age* (Tarrytown, N.Y.: Sleepy Hollow Press, 1981), 35–97. Fred Kniffen, "Folk Housing: Key to Diffusion," *Annals,* Association of American Geographers 55 (December 1965): 549–577; Fred Kniffin and Henry Glassie, "Building in Wood in the Eastern United States: A Time-Place Perspective," *Geographical Review* 56 (January 1966): 40–66. Since it is not clear what the original plan looked like, I have omitted it from discussion here. Thanks to Allen R. Yale, Derby, Vermont, for his generous help in locating and surveying the Verback house.

2. C. B. Rider, "Italian Farm House," *Moore's* 11 (January 1860): 5; C. Disturnell, *Gazetteer of the State of New York* (Albany, 1843), 323; *History of Wyoming County New York* (New York: F. W. Beers, 1880), 262; U.S. Census, Population Schedule, 1850, 1860, 1870, Agriculture Schedule, 1850; correspondence with John G. Wilson, Wyoming County Historian. On the balloon frame, see Paul Sprague, "The Origin of Balloon Framing," *JSAH* 40 (December 1981):

312–319; for coverage by agricultural periodicals, see for example George Woodward, "Balloon Frames," *AC* 3rd ser. 8 (January 1860): 20.

3. *Atlas of Chenango County New York* (Philadelphia: Pomeroy and Whitman, 1875), 23. U.S. Census, Population Schedule, 1850 and 1860; Janet MacFarlane, "Octagon Buildings in New York State," *New York History* 33 (April 1952): 216; Chenango County Cemetery Records Vol. 5: 18; James Hadden Smith, *History of Chenango and Madison Counties* (Syracuse, N.Y.: D. Mason, 1880), 186, 191; Oliver P. Judd, *History of the Town of Coventry* (Oxford, N.Y.: *Oxford Review,* 1912), 38–39, 66–67, 74–79. Thanks to the Chenango County Office of History for making this information available. Orson Squires Fowler wrote *A Home for All: the Gravel Wall and Octagon Mode of Building* (1848. Reprint, New York: Dover, 1973).

4. Information on Bryant courtesy of Mary W. Williams, Bureau County Historical Society Museum and Library. It comes from the Peoria *Journal-Transcript,* October 18, 1942; Bureau County *Republican,* August 6, 1936; Doris Parr Leonard, *A Pioneer Tour of Bureau County Illinois* (Princeton: Bureau County *Republican,* 1954), 9–10; and Henry C. Bradsby, ed., *History of Bureau County, Illinois* (Chicago: World Publishing Co., 1885), 297–298, 469–470; George B. Harrington, *Past and Present of Bureau County Illinois* (Chicago: Pioneer Publishing Co., 1906), 189–190; William Cullen Bryant II and Thomas G. Voss, eds., *Letters of William Cullen Bryant,* 3 vols. (New York: Fordham University Press, 1975), I: 295–298, 354–356, 362–363, 368–372, 376–379, 396–399, II: 112, III: 148, 324, 268; Charles H. Brown, *William Cullen Bryant* (New York: Charles Scribner's Sons, 1971), 188; Julia Hatfield, *The Bryant Homestead Book* (New York: G. P. Putnam & Son, 1870), 86; Helen Foster and William Streeter, *Only One Cummington* (Cummington, Mass.: Cummington Historical Commission, 1974); Gerard Chapman, "History in Houses: The William Cullen Bryant Homestead," *Antiques* 124 (October 1983): 782–788.

On migration of Yankee people and forms, see Thomas Schlereth, "The New England Presence in the Midwest Landscape," *Old Northwest* 9 (Summer 1983): 125–142; Peirce Lewis, "Common House, Cultural Spoor," *Landscape* 19 (January 1975): 1–22; Stanley D. Dodge, "Bureau and the Princeton Community," *Annals,* Association of American Geographers 22 (September 1932): 159–209.

5. Cyrus Bryant to John Everett, December 1, 1843. Many thanks to Mary W. Williams, Dr. K. Dexter Nelson, and Mr. Duncan Bryant, Princeton, Illinois, for sharing this letter with me. Local tradition says that Alvah Whitmarsh, an emigrant carpenter from Cummington, designed the house, but no documentation exists. Given Bryant's drawing, and that William Cullen Bryant's *Letters* (vol. II; p. 470–471) show that Whitmarsh probably built but did not design another Bryant house in Princeton, it is safe to assume that Cyrus was responsible for his own design.

6. "Residence of Cyrus Bryant Esq.," *PF* 5 (October 1845): 252–253.

7. Frederick Koeper, *Illinois Architecture from Territorial Times to the Present* (Chicago: University of Chicago Press, 1968); Douglas Meyer, "Folk Housing on the Illinois Frontier," *Pioneer America Society Transactions* 1 (January 1978): 30–42.

8. *DAB* 3: 200–202; Bryant II, ed., *Letters of William Cullen Bryant,* III, 368–369; Brown, *William Cullen Bryant.*

9. Bryant's addition of a large central gable may be seen as a more radical version of a similar tactic used by builders as they adapted the Gothic to traditional vernacular forms. As the Gothic became more popular, the central gable allowed builders to add Gothic trim without disrupting the basic plan. See Dell Upton, "Pattern-Books and Professionalism: Aspects of the Transformation of Domestic Architecture in America, 1800–1860," *WP* 19 (Summer/Autumn 1984): 141; Henry Glassie, *Folk Housing in Middle Virginia* (Knoxville: University of Tennessee Press, 1975), 158–159.

10. Leonard, *Pioneer Tour,* 9–10.

11. *History of Champaign County Ohio* (Chicago: W. H. Beers, 1881), 944–947; "Building a House," *CG* 57 (June 16, 1892): 464–465; Wing, "A Home for $4061 that Really Satisfied," *Country Life* 11 (March 1907): lxxxiii–xci.

12. "Building a House," 465. Thanks to Dohron Wilson, Mechanicsburg, Ohio, for information and research assistance.

13. See Chapter 3 for more discussion of book farming. There were more plans submitted than actually were published, especially for the contests.

14. James Malin, "The 'Vanity' Histories," *Kansas Historical Quarterly* 21 (Winter 1955): 598–643.

15. Paul Wallace Gates, "Agricultural Change in New York State, 1850–1890," *New York History* 50 (April 1969): 115–141; David Maldwyn Ellis, *A History of New York State* (Ithaca, N.Y.: Cornell University Press, 1967), 485.

16. *Monroe County Directory 1869–1870* (Syracuse, 1869), 265; *History of Monroe County New York* (Philadelphia: Everts, Ensign, & Everts, 1877), 258; U.S. Census, Population and Agriculture Schedules, 1850, 1860; Agriculture Schedule, 1870, 1880; New York State Census, 1855, 1865; *Atlas of Monroe County New York* (New York: F. W. Beers, 1872), 105, 112; communication with Katherine W. Thompson, Rush Town Historian. On Ellis, see below note 24; on Chubb: *History of Kent County, Michigan* (Chicago: Charles Chapman, 1881), 442, 777; *History and Directory of Kent County Michigan* (Grand Rapids, Mich.: Dillenback & Leavitt, 1870), 117; Grand Rapids *Directory 1859–60:* 48; Z. Lydens, ed., *The Story of Grand Rapids* (Grand Rapids, Mich.: Kregel Publishing, 1966), 264, 479; Albert Baxter, *History of Grand Rapids Michigan* (New York: Munsell, 1891), 20, 59, 72, 77, 143, 237, 391, 510; Dwight Goss, *History of Grand Rapids and Its Industries* (Chicago: C. F. Cooper, 1906), 165; U.S. Census, Population Schedule, 1840, 1850, Agriculture Schedule, 1850; Obituary, Grand Rapids *Eagle,* April 6, 1864. Thanks to Gordon Olson, Grand Rapids Public Library, for supplying some of this information.

17. Edward F. Alexander, "Wisconsin, New York's Daughter State," *Wisconsin Magazine of History* 30 (September 1946): 11–30, describes the origins of Wisconsin's population. See also Rexford Newcomb, *Architecture of the Old Northwest Territory* (Chicago: University of Chicago Press, 1950), 67; Hubert H. Wilhelm, "New England in Southeastern Ohio," *Pioneer America Society Transactions* 2 (1979): 13–29; William N. Parker, "From Northwest to Midwest," in David Klingaman and Richard Vedder, eds., *Essays in Nineteenth Century Economic History* (Athens, Oh.: Ohio University Press, 1975), 3–35.

18. *Fairfield County Commemorative Biographical Record* (Chicago: J. H. Beers, 1899), 776–777; U.S. Census, Population and Agriculture Schedule, 1880. Thanks to Hugh Claremont, Redding, Conn., for additional information. On Steere, information comes from the U.S. Census, Population and Agriculture Schedules, 1850, 1860, and 1870; R. L. Bonner, *Memoirs of Lenawee County* (Madison, Wis.: Western Historical Association, 1909), 674–675; *Combination Atlas Map of Lenawee County Michigan* (Chicago: Everts & Stewart, 1874), 69; *Michigan Pioneer Collections* 10 (1886): 80; Steere, "European Larch as an Ornamental," *CG* 38 (January 16, 1873): 38; Bentley Historical Collections, University of Michigan, William Doty diary. Thanks also to Charles Lindquist, Curator, Lenawee County Historical Museum, for information on Steere's landholdings. Smeallie appears in Princetown, Schenectady County, in 1836, 1840, and 1850. See also his letters to the Albany *Cultivator* 4 (July 1836): 85; *Schenectady Directory and City Register* (1841–1842): 8; U.S. Census, Population Schedule, 1840, 1850. Thanks also to Mrs. C. A. Church, Schenectady County Historical Society. On Hurlburt: Daniel Wager, *Oneida County* (Boston: Boston History Co., 1896), 310; Moses Bagg, *The*

Pioneers of Utica (Utica, N.Y.: Curtis & Childs, 1877), 549; U.S. Census, Population and Agriculture Schedules, 1850. Thanks to Charles C. Pace, Jr., of the New Hartford Historical Society and to Douglas Preston, Oneida Historical Society, for their painstaking and helpful research.

19. Allan Bogue, *From Prairie to Corn Belt: Farming in the Illinois and Iowa Prairies in the Nineteenth Century* (Chicago: University of Chicago Press, 1963), 24.

20. On Little, information is from U.S. Census, Population and Agriculture Schedules, 1850; *Ohio State Business Directory* (1853–54): 207. On Peers, information is from the *Illustrated Encyclopedia and Atlas Map of Madison County Illinois* (St. Louis: Brink, McCormick, 1873), 119; Collinsville directory for 1858; U.S. Census, Population and Agriculture Schedules, 1870; *History of Madison County* (Edwardsville, Illinois: Brink, 1882), 458–460. Thanks to Cynthia Longwisch of the Madison County Historical Society for supplying information from the 1912 Edwardsville *Intelligencer*. On the Edwards brothers, information appears in Mrs. G. D. Merrill, ed., *Centennial Memorial History of Allegany County* (Alfred, New York, 1896), 878; *History of Allegany County New York* (New York: F. W. Beers, 1879), 290–291; U.S. Census, Population and Agriculture Schedules, 1850, 1860, and 1870. Thanks also to Bill Greene, Jr., Historian, Allegany County Museum, for his generosity in sharing information on the Edwards brothers. On Hart, see above n. 16. Wykoff appears in the *Atlas of Seneca County* (Philadelphia: Pomeroy, Whitman, & Co., 1874), 30; in Hamilton Child's *Business Directory of Seneca County, New York* (Syracuse, 1894), 229; and in the U.S. Census, Population and Agriculture Schedules, 1860, 1870, and 1880. Thanks also to Mrs. Leroy Coryell, Romulus, New York, who informed me of the history of the Wykoff house.

It is difficult to know if these nineteenth-century businessmen/farmers followed the example of the many farmers who abandoned farming altogether in favor of other occupations. Yasuo Okada demonstrates in his analysis of one upstate New York farmer's diary how this farmer gradually moved away from agriculture. Percy Wells Bidwell has also pointed out that many New England farmers were forced to seek outside income because their farms no longer provided all of their wants. Because the biographical resources on the plan contributors are limited, there is no way to tell with any certainty if they were headed permanently away from agriculture. See Yasuo Okada, "Squires' Diary: New York Agriculture in Transition 1840–1860," *Keio Economic Studies* 7 (1970): 78–98; Percy Wells Bidwell, "The Agricultural Revolution in New England," *American Historical Review* 26 (July 1921): 683–703.

21. Biographical information on Snook from the U.S. Census, Agriculture Schedule, 1850 and 1880, Population Schedule, 1850, 1870, 1880; *CG* 32 (November 19, 1868): 340; *CG* 29 (May 9, 1867): 304; *CG* 24 (September 7, 1865): 155; *CG* 30 (July 18, 1867): 46. On Steere, see above note 18. On Smeallie, see above note 18. On Davis Cossit, see *Ormsby's Syracuse City Directory* (1853–54): 56; 1855–56, 19; *Boyd's Directory* (1874): 60, 135; *Daily Journal City Directory* (1866): 45; (1867): 62; (1869): 77; U.S. Census, Agriculture Schedule, 1860, 1870, 1880.

22. On Thomas: see U.S. Census, Population Schedule, 1850 (third ward 19th District, Milwaukee, Wisconsin): 323; "Liquid Manure Tanks," *CG* 14 (September 22, 1859): 187; *CG* 14 (October 27, 1859): 270. On Cain, see H. P. Smith and W. S. Rann, eds., *History of Rutland County Vermont* (Syracuse: D. Mason, 1886), 879. On Pierce, see Albert Annett and Alice Lehtinen, *History of Jaffrey New Hampshire* (Jaffrey, N.H., 1934): 599; Daniel Cutter, *History of the Town of Jaffrey* (Concord, N.H.: Republican Press Association, 1881), 197; Charles Hitchcock, ed., *Atlas of the State of New Hampshire* (New York: Comstock & Cline, 1877), 76; *CG* 18 (August 1, 1861): 78. Thanks also to Mrs. Robert A. Macready, Jaffrey Historical

Society; Marion Wood, Historical Society of Cheshire County; and David Proper, Deerfield, Massachusetts Libraries. On Hoxie, see: Orrin Guernsey and Josiah Willard, eds., *History of Rock County and Transactions of Rock County Agricultural Society* (Janesville, Wis.: W. M. Doty, 1856), 117; *History of Rock County Wisconsin* (Chicago: Western Historical Company, 1879), 693; *Combination Atlas Map of Rock County* (Chicago: Everts, Baskin, Stewart, 1873), 103 (an engraving of Hoxie's house); U.S. Census, Population Schedule, 1850 and 1860; Richard Perrin, *Historic Wisconsin Buildings* (Milwaukee: Milwaukee Public Museum, 1962), 57–59; Nancy Douglas and Richard Hartung, *Rock County Historic Sites and Buildings* (Janesville, Wis.: Rock County Bicentennial Commission, 1976). Thanks to Maurice J. Montgomery, Rock County Historical Society, for providing some of this information.

23. U.S. Census, Agriculture Schedules, 1850, 1860. Lee Soltow, *Men and Wealth in the United States, 1850–1870* (New Haven: Yale University Press, 1975), concluded that inequality and poverty in mid-nineteenth-century America were less pronounced in rural areas than in cities. He also found that wealth increased with age. Ohio calculations are from David Klingaman, "Individual Wealth in Ohio in 1860," in David Klingaman and Richard Vedder, eds., *Essays in Nineteenth-Century Economic History,* 177–190. Jeremy Atack and Fred Bateman, "Income, Inequality, & Age: The Rural North in 1860," *Journal of Economic History* 41 (March 1981): 85–94, offer a useful analysis of the correlation between property accumulation and age. See also Atack and Bateman, "The 'Egalitarian Ideal' and the Distribution of Wealth in the Northern Agricultural Community," *Review of Economics and Statistics* 63 (February 1981): 124–129; Donghyu Yang, "Notes on the Wealth Distribution of Farm Households in the United States, 1860," *Explorations in Economic History* 21 (January 1984): 88–102. 1860 figures for New York state are from Paul Gates, *Agriculture and the Civil War* (New York: Knopf, 1965), 375.

24. "M. W. H.," "Care of a Dairy," *AC* 10 (July 1843): 119; on Burr, see note 18. On Ellis, information comes from: D. H. Bruce, ed., *Onondaga's Centennial* (Boston: Boston History Co., 1897), 319; *Syracuse City Directory* (1857): 251; (1853): 7, 17, 54, 56, 97; *Ormsby's Syracuse Directory* (1853): 20; *Boyd's Directory* (1859): 103; (1874): 155; (1879): 326; *Daily Journal Directory* (1864): 133; (1866): 99; (1867): 126; (1869): 141; W. W. Clayton, *History of Onondaga County, New York* (Syracuse: D. Mason, 1878), 70; U.S. Census, Population and Agriculture Schedules, 1850.

25. On Lyman, see E. B. Huntington, *History of Stamford Connecticut* (Stamford, Conn.: Printed by the author, 1868), 461; *DAB* 6:516; *National Cyclopedia* 11:366; *The Philosophy of Housekeeping,* 14th ed. (Hartford, Conn.: S. M. Betts & Co., 1869). On Bedell, see W. A. Goodspeed and C. Blanchard, eds., *Counties of Potter and Lake, Indiana* (Chicago: F. A. Battey, 1882): 601.

26. Suel Foster, "Dwelling Houses," *PF* 15 (February 1855): 60.

27. S. B. Shaw, "Plan of a Cheap House," *AC* 8 (March 1841): 55. Information on Shaw is from the *New-England Mercantile Union Business Directory* (1849): 101. On the Berkshire agricultural society, see Jared van Wagenen, "Elkanah Watson, a Man of Affairs," *New York History* 13 (October 1932): 404–412.

28. Letter of William Verback, *AC* 6 (August 15, 1839): 119.

29. Solon Robinson, "A Cheap Farm House," *AA* 5 (February 1846): 57. Robinson's life before 1845 is documented in Herbert Anthony Kellar, ed., *Solon Robinson: Pioneer and Agriculturist* (Indianapolis: Indiana Historical Bureau, 1936).

30. *AC* 6 (August 1839): 117; *AC* 6 (November 1839): 164. These contests themselves were part of a time-honored tradition in progressive agriculture. On the evolution of the

system of competition for premiums, see Wayne Neely, *The Agricultural Fair* (New York: Columbia University Press, 1935). Solon Robinson, "A Cheap Farm House"; Solomon Jewett, *AC* 6 (August 15, 1839): 118; "H.A.P.," "Dwelling Houses," *AC* n.s. 3 (March 1846): 91.

31. "House-Building," *Moore's* 10 (April 30, 1859): 141.

32. See Glassie, *Pattern;* Peirce Lewis, "Common House"; Ernest Connally, "The Cape Cod House: An Introductory Study," *JSAH* 19 (May 1960): 47–56; Upton, "Pattern-Books"; Kniffen, "Building in Wood"; and Herbert Richardson, "Farm Plans and Building Types in Harrison Township, NJ," *Pioneer America Society Transactions* 3 (1980): 88–121; Allen Noble, *Wood, Brick and Stone: The North American Settlement Landscape* (Amherst: University of Massachusetts Press, 1984).

33. Biographical information on Lewis Falley Allen from Henry P. Smith, ed., *History of the City of Buffalo and Erie County* (Syracuse: D. Mason & Co., 1884), 701–702; *DAB* 1: 201; obituary, *Buffalo Express,* May 3 and 4, 1890; Truman C. White, *Our County and Its People* (Boston: Boston History Co., 1898); Allen, *American Short-horn Herd Book* (Buffalo: Jewett, Thomas, & Co., 1846). Thanks to Herman Sass, Buffalo and Erie County Historical Society, for sharing information on Allen, and to Dell Upton for information on Georgian era forms in the "Dutch" regions. On the Yankee influx into New York, see David Maldwyn Ellis, "The Yankee Invasion of New York," *New York History* 32 (January 1951): 1–18. Allen's comments and plans appear in the *Genesee Farmer* 1 (December 10, 1831): 388; *GF* 2 (February 4, 1832): 36; *GF* 2 (November 3, 1832): 348–350. For descriptions of traditional New World Dutch houses, see Marcus Whiffen and Frederick Koeper, *American Architecture, 1607–1976* (Cambridge, Mass.: MIT Press, 1981), 22; Barbara van Liew, *Long Island Domestic Architecture of the Colonial and Federal Periods* (Setauket: Society for the Preservation of Long Island Antiquities, 1974). For analysis of plans, see Allen G. Noble, "Variance in Floor Plans of Dutch Houses of the Colonial Period," *Pioneer America Society Transactions* 3 (1980): 46–56.

34. A. J. Downing, *Treatise on the Theory and Practice of Landscape Gardening,* 4th ed. (New York: G. P. Putnam, 1849), 372; *Cottage Residences* (1842. Reprint, Watkins Glen, N.Y.: American Life Foundation, 1967), 12–15, 33; *Rural Essays* (New York: G. P. Putnam, 1853), 210. For a biography of Downing, see George B. Tatum, *Andrew Jackson Downing, Arbiter of American Taste* (Ann Arbor: University Microfilms, 1949). See also J. W. Ward, "The Politics of Design," *Massachusetts Review* 6 (Autumn 1965): 661–689.

On pattern-books as a genre, see: Henry-Russell Hitchcock, *American Architectural Books* (Minneapolis: University of Minnesota Press, 1962); Michael J. Crosbie, "From 'Cookbooks' to 'Menus': The Transformation of Architecture Books in 19th-Century America," *Material Culture* 17 (1985): 1–23; Jack Quinan, "Asher Benjamin and American Architecture," *JSAH* 38 (October 1979): 244–270; Upton, "Pattern Books"; William B. O'Neal, "Pattern Books in American Architecture, 1730–1930," in Mario di Valmarana, ed., *Building By The Book,* Palladian Studies in America I (Charlottesville: University of Virginia Press, 1984), 47–64.

35. A. J. Downing, *The Architecture of Country Houses* (1850. Reprint, New York: Dover Publications, 1969), 24, 7, 136. Upton, "Pattern-Books," also notes a discrepancy between Downing's praise of rural life and his desire to raise farmers' taste. David Handlin in *The American Home: Architecture and Society 1815–1915* (Boston: Little, Brown, 1979), points out that Downing emulated genteel lifestyles in reaction to a childhood spent in poverty. Handlin also notes Solon Robinson's criticisms of Downing, but he is inconclusive about their meaning. Finally, Handlin sees *Country Houses* (with its expanded section on farm houses) as an attempt to meet the objections of the farmer class. The farmer-planners' own assessment of *Country Houses,* however, suggests that Downing was still unable to break out of his original mold.

36. Downing, "Hints on the Construction of Farm Houses," *AC* n.s. 3 (June 1846): 184–185.

37. L. F. Allen, "Farm Houses," *AA* 1 (January 1843): 342–343; "Rural Architecture," *AA* 1 (February 1843): 367–368. For favorable reviews of Downing's books, see "Rural Architecture," *GF* 11 (November 1850): 259; *AC* n.s. 2 (May 1845): 161–162; *AC* n.s. 8 (May 1851): 122.

38. L. F. Allen, "Farm Houses," *AA* 2 (October 1843): 245.

39. Allen, "Construction of Farm Cottages," *AA* 7 (June 1848): 183–188. Horatio Greenough was simultaneously directing similar criticisms at James Renwick's Smithsonian Institution building in Washington, D.C. See *Form and Function,* Harold Small, ed. (Berkeley: University of California Press, 1947).

40. Allen, "Construction," 184.

41. *Ibid.,* 185.

42. Allen, *Rural Architecture* (New York: Orange Judd, 1852), ix, 25, 60. John Kouwenhoven discusses Allen's book in *The Arts in Modern American Civilization,* 55–57. See also *Buffalo Architecture: A Guide* (Cambridge, Mass.: MIT Press, 1981), 100, 116, 264, 279.

43. *AC* 3rd ser. 7 (December 1859): 372; *PF* 15 (February 1855): 60–61. This process of incorporating pattern-book ideas has been incisively discussed by Dell Upton, "Pattern-Books."

44. Orson Squires Fowler, *The Gravel Wall and Octagon Mode of Building;* D. S. Curtis, "Octagon Houses," *CG* 11 (February 18, 1858): 114; *CG* 11 (January 14, 1858): 34. See also Carl F. Schmidt, *The Octagon Fad* (Scottsville, N.Y., n.p., 1958), and Schmidt and Phillip Parry, *More About Octagons* (n.d., n.p.). Norma Prendergast, in "The Sense of Home" (Ph.D. dissertation, Cornell University, 1981), devotes a chapter to Fowler. Kouwenhoven, *Arts,* 57–58, also discusses Fowler. H. T. Vose's article appeared in the *Cultivator* 3rd ser. 7 (July 1859): 214. (Vose erred in his page citation, but correctly identified the rule.)

45. Upton, "Pattern-Books."

46. *GF* 6 (April 23, 1836): 131.

47. Robert Leslie Jones, *History of Agriculture in Ohio to 1880* (Kent, Oh.: Kent State University Press, 1983), 230. For another perspective on architecture and social context, see Kevin Sweeney, "Mansion People: Kinship, Class, and Architecture in Western Massachusetts in the Mid-Eighteenth Century," *WP* 19 (Winter 1984): 231–255. Richard D. Brown, "Spreading the Word: Rural Clergymen and the Communication Network of 18th-Century New England," *Proceedings,* Massachusetts Historical Society, 94 (1982): 1–14, shows how ministers performed a mediating function in the colonial era, but later lost that position as other groups and institutions developed.

THREE

The Shape of Cooperation: The Farmstead as Workplace, 1830–1855

AMERICANS in the middle decades of the nineteenth century saw spectacular social and economic developments—vigorous new religious and reform movements emerged, cities grew rapidly, and industrial capitalism began to take shape. Change not only extended to families, but even to the spatial arrangement of their homes. In urban America, the gap between the worlds of work and domesticity began to widen. The nature of work for men and women diverged: men's work was removed from the house, and female-dominated home manufactures (such as spinning and weaving) declined. Men's work was now measured in units of time, contrasting to task-oriented domestic work. Moreover, men worked for cash in an economy where male-dominated cash exchanges were more important than barter. All of these changes accentuated the differences between men's and women's spheres. There developed a notion of home as a unique sphere reserved for women and separated from the competition, acquisitiveness, and stress of the work world. "Domesticity," which entailed devotion to bringing up children and thrifty housekeeping, took the place of the woman's direct economic contribution to the family livelihood. According to the "cult of domesticity," the wife and mother was entrusted with the responsibility of sanctifying and ennobling the home; under her guidance, the home sanctuary served as a counterbalance to the socially destructive effects of capitalism.[1]

In rural America, people were also beginning to re-evaluate their domestic space in response to changing patterns of household production. But because the demands of the new capitalist order upon rural households differed from those on urban households, the reshaping of domestic rural environments in the antebellum decades took a distinctly different turn. Progressive farm families began to alter traditional vernacular forms. The physical and economic interdependence of home and farm prevented the establishment of distinct boundary lines between women's and men's space, in contrast to the urban pattern. By examining the application of business principles to farming, the role of women in farm production, and farmhouse designs themselves, we shall trace the emergence of a different ideal of the nineteenth-century American home, one of rural domesticity.

This new ideal was taking shape at a moment of decisive change in agriculture, and was in fact intimately related to that change. In the eighteenth and early nineteenth centuries, the farm household had been the center of production; everyone worked together toward maintaining the family. As individual households were rarely able to provide for all their needs, exchange of labor and goods among neighbors supplied missing necessities for individual families, creating a close interdependence and a high degree of local self-sufficiency. Market forces operated within this context; people traded or sold surpluses in order to fill a need, not necessarily to accumulate capital.[2]

By the nineteenth century, this order was giving way to one based on competition, market orientation, capital accumulation, and profits. In the vanguard of the new order, progressive agriculturists preached the gospel of agricultural reform. Their mentality was in keeping with the times, as antebellum Americans set out to perfect everything from politics to eating habits to sexual mores. Like other reforms, those in agriculture had both conservative and radical implications. Some agricultural thinkers urged farmers to practice more intensive husbandry on smaller farms; this was at once a radical critique of prevailing land-extensive, soil-destroying techniques, and a scheme to protect the eroding (literally and figuratively) position of Eastern agriculture. But most reforming agricultural journalists stressed capitalism and technological innovation as the way of the future. They sought to make businessmen of farmers. Jesse Buel, a leading exponent of "The New Husbandry," counted profit-making and occupational prestige for farming among the goals of agricultural reform. In his widely circulated text, *The Farmer's Companion* (1839), Buel presented the notion of the businessman-farmer. He hoped to convert the "farmer who manages his business ignorantly and slothfully, and who produces from it just enough for the subsistence of his family" into a manager who "embrace[s] the principles and practice of business," so that "by the hope of distinction and reward" he would "triple the products of his labor." Agricultural re-

formers were apt to compare progressive farm management to the practice
of a merchant or broker. They especially admired the industrialist's achieve-
ment of efficiency through the division of labor; hence Lewis Allen's comment in 1847: "Let us, as our merchants, our mechanics, and our professional men have done, divide the realm of husbandry, and conquer success."
The farm as "manufactory" (where basic natural resources were transformed into food through scientific agriculture) became a popular analogy.[3]

Progressive agriculturists contrasted the old-fashioned, unsystematic,
semisubsistence farmer with his modern, innovative, market-oriented opposite, until the two types, "Farmer Slack" and "Farmer Snug," (Figure 3–
1) became stock formulas. Historians disagree whether the Farmer Slack
stereotype accurately portrayed the typical northern farmer, but literature
of progressive agriculture reveals that progressive farmers enthusiastically
accepted the market system and its possibilities for accumulating capital.
These journals abounded with advice on proper accounting for farmers, and
with correspondence arguing the profitability of various crops or tillage
methods. They also consistently featured exemplary accomplishments at
money-making.[4]

Under the emerging capitalist system, the processes and goals of farm
production had changed, but the farm household was still the center of
production. Progressive farm women were unequivocally incorporated into
this new farming system. A short notice in the *New England Farmer* of 1826
hailed an unnamed woman of Hampden County, Massachusetts, as a "profitable wife." This woman, it was claimed, managed a remunerative dairy by

Fig. 3–1. "Farmer Slack" (Left) vs. "Farmer Snug" (Right). 1857.

herself besides performing the regular housework. Eleven-year-old Eliza Ann Osborne of Brown County, Illinois, reported to the *Prairie Farmer* in 1847 that with the proceeds from her mother's butter alone ($50 in 1845, $33 in 1846) the family had been able to purchase a buggy. Women might also contribute to farm income by pursuing horticulture. The *Genesee Farmer* of 1856 cited a case in which a farm wife's interest in horticulture netted her family $800 in one year. Others touted the profits of a 10–15-acre garden located near a city. F. R. Elliott, an Ohio nurseryman, described the kitchen garden as first, a means of profit; second, a source of products for the family's comfort; and last, as an "innocent recreation." A writer for the *New England Farmer* expressed astonishment and admiration for a group of young women he had met on the way to market (a distance, he remarked, of 17 miles) with fresh-picked whortleberries to sell. He considered them excellent candidates for farmers' wives. As long as women worked in the kitchen garden, orchard, and dairy, they could make a substantial contribution to the family farm's financial success.[5]

A prudent wife could avert ruin by observing frugality in managing the husband's income, but agricultural journals also assigned to farm women a positive role in the farm's economy. Readers were told that "the prosperity of the farm depends largely on the proper performance of the duties of the wife. . . ." Farm women were especially urged to improve their dairies, because "however skilful, industrious, and prudent your husbands may be, their success in money making depends as much upon you as upon them."[6]

Letters and stories in the agricultural journals reveal that many farm women themselves shared this attitude. The *Prairie Farmer*'s editors noted in 1847 that farm wives sometimes subscribed to their paper in the hopes of prodding unenterprising husbands to pursue progressive farming. No doubt this represented a certain amount of wishful thinking, since editors always sought higher circulation levels. But the journals' awareness of their female readers was consistent and significant. In return, these women self-consciously portrayed themselves in their correspondence with the periodicals as a distinctive, productive group. A woman who signed her name as "Elizabeth" wrote to the *Ohio Cultivator* in 1845, remarking that "if by the term Lady, you mean one of those worthless parlor ornaments, then I shall not expect my communication to have a place in your 'Ladies' Department.' . . . I am a farmer's wife." Women of the western United States took pride in their contribution not only as farm wives but as pioneers. As one contributor (with a sneering reference to eastern "Ladies") wrote, "women of the west . . . do not sit like Turks on a divan." Another celebrated an active "western" woman who cooked for her family, knitted stockings for sale, rode out on horseback to visit friends far distant, and on the way home caught some game—all in one day, with a profit of $4 to show for her fast-paced industry.[7]

Women contributors moreover associated better management of the affairs in and about the house with agricultural improvement. If industry, economy, and neatness were practiced in the house, one declared, their influence would be seen all over the farm. Implicit in her statement was the notion that farm productivity might improve as a result of the farm wife's actions, and that Farmer Snug's farm was a product of both women's work and men's. Another "Young Farmer's Wife" recognized her stake in the farm when she wrote to the *Genesee Farmer* in 1847 that women who made their own butter enjoyed as much independence as did their husbands.[8]

These ideas had a solid basis in historical reality. Although a great diversity of agricultural conditions prevailed in the North, certain trends emerge fairly clearly. In the East, the 1830s witnessed a shift away from reliance upon wheat as farmers responded to the pressures of low-priced Western wheat, disease, pests, soil exhaustion, as well as the boon provided by the growth of urban markets close to home. Many turned to a more carefully managed mixed husbandry: hogs, grain, fowl, fruit, hay, and dairy products. In New York's Mohawk Valley, for example, dairy production increased by about one-third during the 1840s. By mid-century, the state's agriculture entered its most prosperous period, producing one-quarter of the nation's butter and half of its cheese. Centralization of production had not yet taken place, and much of New York's dairy output was produced at home by women. Women also seem to have supervised the kitchen garden and probably sold their produce in local markets.[9]

On the midwestern farming frontier of Iowa, Illinois, and Wisconsin, grains (especially wheat and corn) and livestock were emphasized, but typically farming still included a wide range of items, such as dairy products, hay, vegetables, and eventually fruit. On the frontier, women made a crucial contribution to initial farm-making, since they produced most of the household's food, clothing, and necessities such as soap. After the pioneer phase had passed, midwestern farm wives continued to participate both in the farm's commercial activities—cooking for harvest hands, occasionally working in the field, raising poultry, making butter, tending stock—and in more traditional subsistence activities such as dyeing textiles.[10]

Women in the 1840s and early 1850s continued to perform traditional tasks, but their products more often went to market. For farm women, then, the industrial age brought a continuation, not a decrease, in household manufactures. As Joan Jensen has pointed out, buttermaking, for example, had supplanted spinning and weaving in the Delaware Valley early in the nineteenth century, and similar patterns probably prevailed elsewhere. It is not clear whether farm women themselves controlled or even saw the cash income from their labors. Farm account books are ambiguous, especially where women's transactions are concerned. The records that have been analyzed indicate that in some households, women did receive the cash proceeds from dairying, poultry production, etc., while in others, husbands controlled all income. Nonetheless, women's role in farm production was economically significant; Nancy Grey Osterud has demonstrated that this role allowed rural women in the Nanticoke Valley (New York) to develop "strategies of mutuality" with men during the later nineteenth century that helped offset their legal and cultural disadvantages.[11]

When circumstances demanded, the usually well-defined lines between men's and women's work might become blurred. One woman, recounting the various "men's" tasks she had performed over the years, declared that "if ever I had a sphere, I must have lost it long ago." Isaac Roberts, a pioneer in agricultural education at the New York State College of Agriculture, remembered that on his family farm in the Finger Lakes region of central New York during the 1840s, life was "cooperative and whole-hearted." Roberts thought that stereotyping tasks according to sex was not the rule, although he noted that (after the initial settlement) the second generation of farm girls no longer worked in the fields. But farm day-books from the Nanticoke Valley show that farm women there performed traditional men's tasks far more regularly than they, or their husbands, perceived. And in Iowa, pioneer women diarists recorded plowing, planting, and harvesting.[12]

The blurred territorial boundaries of men and women were also evident in the terminology of the agricultural journals. In the *Genesee Farmer* of 1834, the importance of good breeds of stock was discussed under the heading "domestic economy," and the *New England Farmer* included a piece on sheep husbandry in its domestic economy column, suggesting that the term "domestic" was elastic enough to include activities which took place outside the home. In other instances, "Rural Economy" was even classed as a subcategory of "Domestic Economy." Domestic economy, then, was often a broad term involving both the farmer and his wife. This differed substantially from the urban middle-class understanding of the term, which applied exclusively to the home setting and to women only. The fluidity of descriptive phrases for the various branches of husbandry suggests that while farm men and women had well-defined separate responsibilities, all of their tasks were conceived as contributions to farm production and profits.[13]

Even the farm wife's role as mother held explicit economic significance. "Annette" agitated for a women's column in the *Genesee Farmer* with the claim that it would enable farmers' wives to rear generations of thinking farmers. This idea became common in the agricultural press, recalling the ideal of "republican motherhood" widely professed in the early days of American statehood, but with the more specialized goal of training progressive farmers. Concerned with the exodus of farm boys to the cities, agricultural writers emphasized the importance of educating children to become farmers and farmers' wives and not simply good citizens. Because no institutions then existed to provide this sort of education (the system of land-grant agricultural colleges was not established until the Civil War era), the task fell to the progressive farm mother. In this respect, her role in raising future farmers exceeded, ideologically at least, the influence of the urban mother, whose task for the most part, was moral development.[14]

These circumstances—the cooperative character of the farm, the drive for profit, and the promotion of systematic agriculture— form the context in which to view the farmhouse designs of the 1830s, 1840s, and 1850s. Farmer-planners, men and women alike, designed efficient houses and farmsteads in pursuit of the same goal: to facilitate production and, ultimately, to increase farm profits.

The businessman-farmer could implement the progressive philosophy of agriculture by following a system in every aspect of his work. Robert Sinclair of Maryland, in an 1828 article in the *New England Farmer,* urged the farmer to rise early, carry on regular inspections of his premises, and "have hands especially appropriated for each of the most important departments of labour . . . . Every means should be thought of to diminish labour." According to the *Genesee Farmer,* a "complete farmer" saved time scrupulously; he did not chat idly with his neighbors nor disdain punctuality in his business affairs. Moreover, a good farmer kept precise records of his crop yields, laborers' work, expenditures, and experiments.[15]

All of these virtues—regulation, system, record-keeping, profit-making, and labor-saving—contributed to the establishment of the most economically efficient farm possible. This ideal strongly influenced the spatial arrangement of farm buildings. Natural topography would present certain constraints, of course, but within those limits it mattered a great deal how the farm was set up. A first priority in "steading the farm" was to situate the house so as to reduce the amount of travel over the farm grounds. A correspondent of the *New England Farmer* wrote in 1828, "Nothing can be more preposterous, than to continue the old system of having the farmhouses placed in villages totally detached from the farm; a plan which originated, from the want of domestic security in feudal times . . . ." The writer explained that if the farmhouse sat in a corner of the farm lands, the most remote areas would be neglected and recommended a central location for the house, on a slightly hilly spot. Another writer, in an 1841 *Cultivator* series on farm buildings, suggested that the farmer consider where, when, and how his crops and animals would be moved about the farm, and that he take into account the amount of time and distance he would expend in traveling between the house, barn, and fields. The wise farmer, the author concluded, would build his house near the center of the farm. These attitudes reveal the transformation, most pronounced in New England, from a corporate village society, where farmers traveled to consolidated fields from their village homes, to a society of competitive, isolated, individual farmers.[16]

The ideal of isolated farmsteads was most fully realized on the western prairies, where pioneers dispersed from the very beginning of settlement. Thus correspondents of the *Prairie Farmer* also regarded a central location as the most appropriate site for a farmhouse. One contributor from Jo Daveiss County in Illinois advised prairie farmers to consider traffic patterns between house, field, water, and woodlot, and above all *not* to build their houses on the roadside.[17]

A central location not only reduced travel, it also "put it in the power of the farmer to see what is going forward in every direction." The idea that a farmer should be able literally to oversee his domain may have come from the English tradition in farm planning, since American agricultural reformers often took their cues from English predecessors. Readers of the early nineteenth-century English handbook, *The Complete Grazier*, for example, were advised that "the window of the keeping-room, should look full upon the grand avenue to the yards, cattle, etc., and, if possible . . . full into the farm-yard." An English writer, Henry Stephens, whose *Book of the Farm* was published in the United States in 1847, offered a similar prescription: "Perhaps the best situation for the house is on one side of the farm-yard, with the common parlor and kitchen opening onto it." Stephens particularly stressed the need for keeping an eye on the hired hands. An architectural solution to the requirement for efficiency, then, lay in visual and spatial continuity between the farmhouse and the farm grounds proper. The farmer could supervise several activities simultaneously, and could ensure that his hired hands did not shirk. Moreover, domestic space blended with the farm grounds visually and physically, because the farmhouse was envisioned as a base for business operations.[18]

Placing the house at the farm center had social ramifications for the farmer's everyday life. A pattern of commentary emerged in which correspondents insisted that progressive farmers should avoid the inevitable social encounters fostered by proximity to public roads. "L.A.M." of Lansing, New York, in an 1839 article sarcastically commented upon the farmer who built his house directly on the public highway: "The owner likes to see every thing that passes by, and all that is said too." Lewis F. Allen, writing in 1842, extended the case for building away from the road: the farmer, conveniently situated in the center of his farm, could "let the travelled highway go where it may, and there [in his house] he awaits the call of the public, attending solely to his own domestic affairs . . . hieing out from his domicil when occasion demands it . . . ." The curious farmer would thereby be prevented from pursuing his desire to "know as it occurs, every thing of public import as well as of private rumour." A central location for the house would save time for productive pursuits which would otherwise be spent in idle gossip. Progressive planning was intended to reinforce systematic work values rather than social amenities.[19]

The progressive farmer's systematic habits were supposed to influence architectural planning in other ways. For example, the farmer was exhorted to have a "place for everything," particularly in the orderly storage of farm implements. Ideally, the farmer would build a separate toolshed or even a fully equipped workshop so as profitably to pass stormy days (see Figure 3–1).[20]

Whether or not the farmhouse was in the exact physical center of the farm, farmhouse and farmstead space were always closely tied together, as seen in actual farm layouts. Cyrus Bryant, for instance, built a barn about 1855, a decade after he finished his house in Princeton, Illinois. He chose to place the barn on the kitchen side of the house, just off-center from a direct linear connection. Between house and barn was an orchard. E. C. Bliss of Chautauqua County, New York, published a plan of his farm in 1849 (Figure 3–2). The farmhouse was embedded in farm work spaces: orchard, bee house, smokehouse, fruit patch, vegetable garden, hog house, and corncrib. A large poultry yard was placed beyond the cattle sheds. A closer examination of the plans shows that a large proportion of the farmhouse proper was given over to farm production. The kitchen, flanked by a well-room and sink-room, directly faced the entrance to the vegetable garden. A cheese and churning room was aligned with the path to the barnyard, and a 30' × 38' cellar provided a bake room and food storage facilities. Clearly, Bliss's layout integrated all farm production activities, whether they occurred within the house or without.[21]

Between house and field a variety of activities took place. Ellen Chapman Rollins remembered in *New England Bygones* that the orchard "almost always started from the back-door of the farm-house." She went on to describe the orchard in summer: "the bare-armed women, spreading their linen to bleach; pans scalding in the sunshine; the bee-hives; the grindstone; the mowers whetting their scythes; and other loose-lying debris of farm-

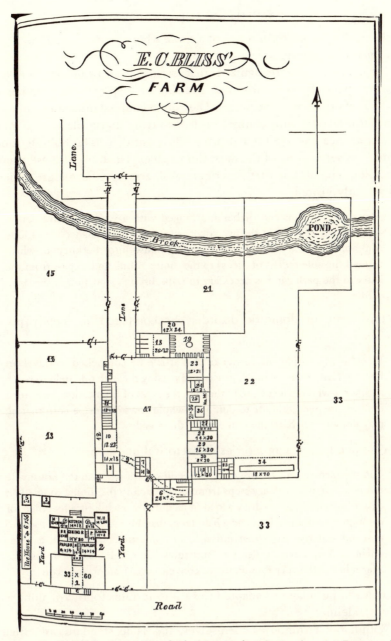

Fig. 3–2. E. C. Bliss's Farm, Westfield, New York (1849), plan. (1) Front yard. (2) Dwelling house. (3) Smoke and Ash house. (4) Bee house. (5) Water closet. (6) Carriage house and Horse barn. (7) Corn barn. (8) Hog and Pig house. (9) Tunnel. (10) Open shed. (11) Stable. (12) Passage. (13) Garden, vegetable. (14) Calf yard. (15) Peach and Pear orchard. (16) Reservoirs. (17) Barnyard. (18) Horse barn. (19) Storeroom. (20) Cider press. (21) Sheep yard. (22) Sheep and Poultry yard. (23) Open shed. (24) Stable for oxen. (W) Machine house. (25) Circular saw. (26) Horse power Hay loft. (27) Stable. (28) Threshing floor. (29) Bay. (30) Passageway. (31) (labelled 13 on picture) Stable. (32) Poultry house. (33) Orchard. (34) Sheep shed.

work." Rollins's description was of a space where women's and men's work met on common ground.[22]

Farmer-designers recognized that system and order applied to all branches of husbandry, from cattle-raising to soap-making, whether pursued out of doors or in the house. They often coupled discussions of convenient farm layouts with counsel on labor-saving house plans. The Albany *Cultivator*'s lead article for February 1852, entitled "The Sub-Division of Farms," presented one of the most thorough explanations of these planning principles. The author first described an ill-arranged farmhouse which he had recently visited.

> The rooms . . . instead of being arranged with a view to convenience, appeared to have been thrown together according to chance. . . . [T]he common entrance was through the woodhouse into the kitchen, which formed the sole means of access to the dining room; and to pass from the latter to the parlor it was necessary to walk through a portion of the open yard.

To this scene of domestic disorder, he compared an ineptly planned farmstead:

> How far . . . would the reader of this article be compelled to travel, to find the farmer who is in the practice of passing through one field to reach another—who must cut a road through the grass of his meadow, to enter a field of ripened grain, or to demolish whole rows of unripe corn that he may draw to his barn the contents of the meadow.

He continued by posing a series of rhetorical questions:

> Can the farmer travel more easily a needless furlong, than the housewife can take five unnecessary steps from the kitchen to the dining room? Is it easier for the farmer to draw a load of manure over a hill fifty feet high, or through a mudhole a foot and a half deep, than his partner within doors to descend and rise from that nuisance in domestic arrangement, a cellar kitchen? A moment's reflection must show that a well planned division of a farm lies at the very foundation of convenience, system, and economy.[23]

Examples of farm layouts adapted to various terrains followed, along with a set of guidelines.

Within the farmhouses themselves, the same standards of efficiency were applied to women's work, as shown by the house plans sent to the agricultural papers from 1830 to 1855 by both men and women. Their interest in time- and labor-saving arrangements prompted a spurt of experimentation in domestic design.

Progressive farm wives systematized their work with a rigor similar to that encouraged for the farm as a whole. Housewives had long been urged to practice rigorous economy, to save time, to keep careful accounts, and to put everything in its proper place. The agricultural periodicals in the 1820s and 1830s were filled with such exhortations, which took on more coherence and detail with time. Following Catharine Beecher's lead, "E.S." gave "Hints to Country Housekeepers" in the *American Agriculturist* for 1846. She recommended that the farm housewife be "regular and systematical": upon rising, she must "inspect the dairy, poultry-yard, kitchen, and garden. . . . Every member of the family . . . should have a regular task to perform . . . the whole family should be ready to take their seats when the coffee is placed upon the breakfast-table." "H.L.Y." urged *Michigan Farmer* readers to "see that every step counts. Do everything at the proper time." A woman writing under the signature "Old Lady" described her efficient home in detail, adding that "On a farm, as in a bee-hive, all should be workers, and the drones sent off," and that efficiency was the goal: "if from careful management of time, you save one hour a day, either from unnecessary sleep, pleasure, or ignorance, you will gain in five years, seventy-five days and two hours for profitable improvement of mind or means."[24]

Like Beecher, the farm women extolled "method," a comprehensive approach to work that unified the unconnected series of hints favored by their predecessors. In their view, the woman who worked as hard as everyone else but only accomplished half as much "had no method." Such unfortunately disorganized farm wives lacked "system and tact, forethought and calculation"; they traveled many times to the cupboard instead of once. They were advised to adopt system and order so as to "accomplish the most that can possibly be done in a given length of time."[25]

This concern for efficiency was expressed spatially in farmhouse plans. In 1843 Matilda W. Howard of Zanesville, Ohio, became one of the first women to publish a plan in the agricultural press. It is not clear whether the house was actually built, but even if it remained a dream, the careful thought invested in it reveals much about the progressive farmhouse ideal. Mrs. Howard began her long letter of explanation in the *Cultivator* by declaring that:

> having been much interested in the plans of farmhouses and cottages, from time to time given in the *Cultivator,* I have been induced to send you the accompanying plan of a farm cottage, which I projected some three or four years since. It may be thought by some, that a female is stepping out of her department, when she attempts planning houses. I do not think so, inasmuch as females are the parties most concerned in these arrangements.

Mrs. Howard, like her agriculturist house-designer colleagues, had learned about house design the hard way. "This plan," she explained, "was predicated upon a six years' residence in a farm house, which . . . was as convenient as most houses of that class, but when the '*labor-saving*' principle was applied, it was found very defective." In particular, Mrs. Howard desired a dairy contiguous to the house proper: "Without this, I consider a farm house incomplete . . . from the experience I have had in this matter, I am induced to shrink at the very thought of going out in the hot sun three or four rods from the house, as many times in the day as is necessary to go to the dairy." She also appealed for a cooperative approach to house design: "If men would oftener consult their wives in these matters, I presume they would . . . reap their reward for any fancied compromise of dignity, in additional *peace and quiet.*"[26]

Her plan (Figure 3–3) was a detailed, sophisticated solution to her requirements. The main block smoothly incorporated the wing containing dairy and wood house; a direct, covered passageway connected kitchen and dairy. The ice house, which projected away from the house proper, probably to avoid the house's heat, abutted the dairy, providing necessary cool temperatures. An ingenious cool-storage closet was built into the dairy, thereby fully exploiting the cool space. A number of remarkable devices— sink, pump, and boiler—occupied the kitchen area. These were unusual for a farmhouse of the 1840s, and their logical, efficient placement was still more unusual. Finally, a small bathing house projected from the kitchen; it was equipped with a "faucet for warm water."[27]

The principal living and working areas were contiguous to one another; from the kitchen, the dining/sitting room could be reached either directly or in passing by the pantry. The sleeping room adjoined the kitchen. Efficiency was prime among Matilda Howard's intentions.

Mrs. Howard's plan also expressed the division of labor on the farm by portraying the interlocking of household and farmstead. Her husband had suggested "that to complete the arrangement of the farm buildings, the barn, carriage house, granary, piggery, etc., should be erected in the rear, so as to form a hollow square." Although the responsibility for design related to the keeping of livestock (Mr. Howard was a stock breeder) and the storage of field crops was clearly assigned to the farmer, there was no abrupt break between the house/dairy and the other buildings: the kitchen faced the outbuildings, as Mrs. Howard was closely involved with the production of milk, cheese, and butter, and she understood the care of milch cows, even if she was not directly involved with their management.[28]

Another aspect of the plan yields more intriguing information about the farm's spheres of labor. The rear entranceway was equipped with a sink (r)

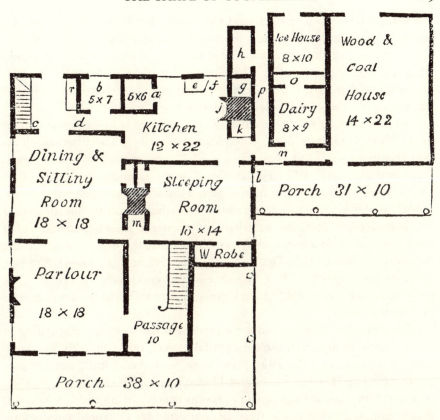

Fig. 3–3. Matilda Howard, design for a farmhouse in Zanesville, Ohio (1843), plan. (a) Dairy utensil room. (b) Storeroom and pantry. (c.d.) Cellar door. (c) Sink. (f) Pump. (g) Boiler. (h) Bathing house. (i) Fireplace. (k) Oven. (l) Window to floor, opens as a door. (m) Book closet. (n) Covered passage. (o) Closet. (p) Passage. (r) Sink.

for the purpose of "preventing the necessity of farm hands, and others, going to the kitchen to wash." This measure suggests that farm workers washed in the rear entranceway prior to entering the large dining room to eat. Because all of the hands likely came to the farmhouse to eat, the house functioned as a vital locus within the workplace. Moreover, the rear entrance stood in marked opposition (social and spatial) to the front entrance, which opened onto the parlor. Family and workers would enter at the same place, while the front door usually served to admit people such as clergy, non-family visitors, business callers, and all other outsiders. The overall effect of the plan thus was to divide the house into two parts, one oriented toward the farm, the other to the public. This suggests that the most important division on the farmstead was not between home and work, between the sexes, or between laborers and employers, but between the farm as a whole (including laborers) and the public. In this sense the public and private sectors of the home were well-defined, but in a manner different from that prescribed by such urban-oriented pattern-book writers as A. J. Downing, who treated the entire home as an asylum, enveloping it within a protective landscape and obscuring private work areas.[29]

Another, similar plan submitted by Mrs. Howard won the first premium of the New York State Agricultural Society for 1848. This plan and elevation (Figures 3–4, 3–5), with its center hall, was more formal and stylish than the earlier one. A library was added, on the same axis with the parlor. In the work portion of the house, Mrs. Howard now appended a "wash room" to the kitchen, while retaining the other features. She improved efficiency by relocating the pantry directly between the kitchen and dining room (instead of in a passageway) and by placing the dairy storage nearer the dairy (compare (a) in Figure 3–3 to "pantry" in Figure 3–5). She emphasized the importance of a "good cellar for good farmers." Finally, she proposed a hot-air central heating system, again exhibiting her awareness of new technologies.

Once Matilda Howard had set a precedent for women participating in the dialogue on design in the agricultural papers, others quickly followed. Mrs. James Ellis won the 1846 New York State Agricultural Society premium with her "Design for a Farm-House." Her plan (Figures 3–6, 3–7) repeated Mrs. Howard's grouping of rooms into two main clusters: kitchen, milk room, and wood house were all connected by a covered passageway. Mrs. Ellis placed the milk room within the kitchen to "save time and labor . . . as it is very unpleasant passing to and from the 'piazza'."[30]

Convinced that the kitchen was indeed the most important room in the house, farmhouse planners applied their imaginations to efficient kitchen design. Their ideas included not only careful placement of auxiliary rooms (the woodshed, milkroom, etc., as in Howard's and Ellis's plans) but a detailed analysis of movement within the kitchen itself. Anticipating Catharine Beecher by several decades, they experimented with the kitchen's furnishings; some plans were surprisingly detailed, down to the placement of small appurtenances.

In 1847, Solon Robinson of Crown Point, Indiana, presented one of several plans which featured a "Real farmer's kitchen" (Figure 3–8). He regarded the kitchen as the "grand desideratum of every farm house." Farmer-planners had little esteem for designers who neglected this room. When in 1850 a plan of a suburban residence designed by architect William McConnell appeared in the *Genesee Farmer,* the editors disapprovingly noted its inadequate kitchen: "The kitchen is the business room, and we

Fig. 3–4. Matilda Howard, design for a farmhouse in Zanesville, Ohio (1848), elevation.

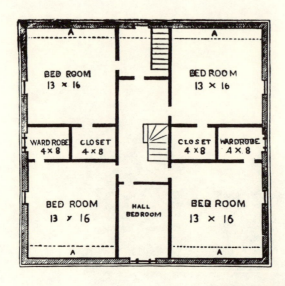

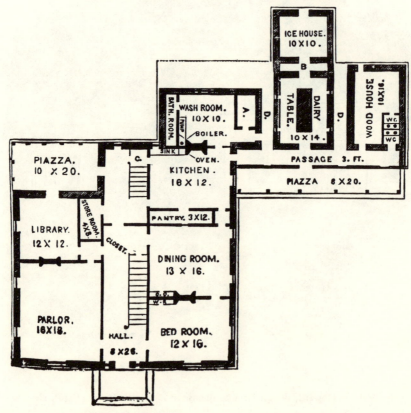

Fig. 3–5. Matilda Howard, 1848 design, plan. (Above) Second floor. (Below) Ground plan. (A) Storeroom. (B) Not labeled, probably a cold closet. (C) Closet. (D) Passages. (c.c.) Closet, probably china closet. (w.r.) Wardrobe.

Fig. 3–6. Mrs. James Ellis, design for a farmhouse in Onondaga, New York (1847), elevation.

think should be the most commodious one in the house." In view of the editors' promotion of the farm as a business enterprise, their choice of the term "business" in reference to the kitchen seems especially significant.[31]

In 1849 the *Cultivator* published a plan for a "Working Woman's Cottage" contributed by a "Farmer's Wife" from Clarence, New York. Designed with the "working family" in mind, this plan (Figure 3–9) conformed to the same general configuration set out by predecessors. But note this woman's attention to detail regarding the arrangement of her workplace:

> As you enter the kitchen from the woodhouse first comes the cooking stove, and fire place, next the closet (K) for kettles and many other things not fit to be put in the pantry; next if you wish, the shelf for the water pail to stand on; the sink, with a shelf at the left hand to put the dishes on, then the pantry door, with a space between that and the cellar door.[32]

Her ability to visualize kitchen arrangements probably came from long experience in the kitchen, and her intent was clearly to minimize motions in doing everyday chores.

In 1847, "Old Lady" urged readers of the *American Agriculturist* to take notice of the "Economy of Labor-saving Utensils in a Kitchen or on a Farm." Arguing that time was "equally valuable" as money, she recom-

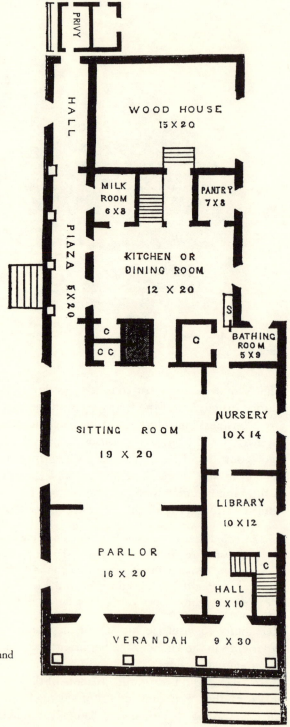

Fig. 3–7. Ellis design, ground plan.

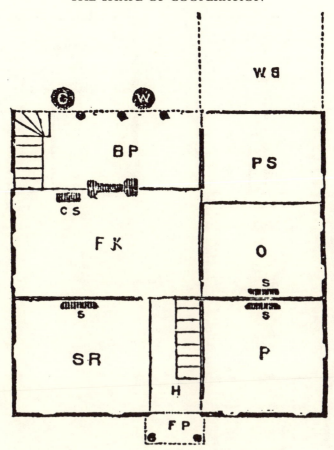

Fig. 3–8. Solon Robinson, plan for a farmhouse in Crown Point, Indiana (1847). (BP) Back porch. (C) Cistern. (CS) Kitchen stove. (FK) Farmer's kitchen. (FP) Front porch. (H) Hall. (O) Old folks' bedroom. (P) Parlor. (PS) Pantry and Storeroom. (S) Stoves. (SR) Sitting room. (W) Well. (WS) Woodshed.

mended judicious investment in such devices as the modern "sausage-chopper, that noiseless friend to the farmer's wife, that will silently do in two hours what it would take a man a whole day to accomplish." She also described the "wood-shed into which the kitchen shall open, where a space can be portioned off for barrels and boxes that are to be receptacles for all sorts of things that the women should have in use close to the scene of their labors." A row of barrels would contain soap, soap fat, water, chicken feed, compost, and pig slop all "under the mistress's eye." With these arrangements, the "Old Lady" promised that soap would "practically make itself" and that the chickens and pigs could be fed without wasted steps. The

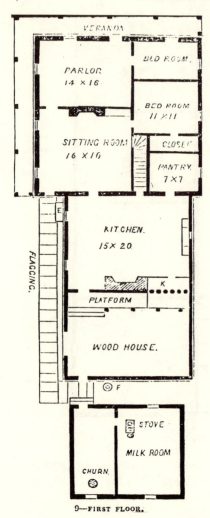

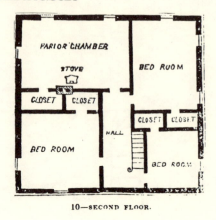

10—SECOND FLOOR.

9—FIRST FLOOR.

Fig. 3–9. Anonymous plan for a "working woman's cottage" in New York State (1849). (Left) First floor. (Right) Second floor.

orderly arrangement of such receptacles on the ground level instead of in cellar storage may foreshadow the coming of more complex kitchen cabinetry.[33]

In *Moore's Rural New Yorker* of 1859, a Cambridge Valley, New York farmer-schoolteacher described a house he and his family had built in the mid-1850s. Declaring that the house "suited the presiding genius of my household," he proceeded to describe the work room. "It contains a sink on one side, shelves on two sides with drawers, and cupboards underneath for spices, bread, etc., besides recesses for flour and meat barrels." Water and wood stood a step away. Here the storage containers for meat and flour have been moved right into the kitchen. The arrangement of sink, shelves, and recessed storage may anticipate the famous "cooking form" publicized by Catharine Beecher a decade later.[34]

Enthusiasm for new technology abounded among these farmhouse planners. The "Old Lady" investigated new machines for aiding in such chores as churning butter. The farmer-schoolteacher designed a set of innovative, built-in work and storage areas. (Most conventional kitchen furniture of the period came in the form of movable free-standing chests.) Perhaps most remarkable, Matilda Howard envisioned a water heater, pump, and sink in her kitchen, along with a hot-air central heating system in the basement. This would have been most unusual, because few private homes, even in cities, had either central heating or indoor plumbing before about 1845.[35]

Perhaps the most important technological innovation of the era affecting domestic work was the stove. Heating stoves such as the famous Franklin stove had been available since the eighteenth century, but in the early nineteenth century improved ironmaking technology stimulated a burst of experimentation with both cooking and heating stoves. The new cookstoves not only had ovens for baking, but also were fitted with boiler holes to admit pots. This latter development speeded the elimination of open-hearth cookery and its attendant equipment. As one historian has put it:

> The pleasant old fireplace with its swinging crane of well-filled pots and kettles, hearth spiders with legs, and bake kettles and tin bakers to stand before the blazing logs and bake custard pies in, all went down at once and disappeared before this stove without so much as a passing struggle.

The reasons were not hard to find. Mass production in specialized factories made cookstoves affordable to most families, and the stoves used far less fuel than the open hearth. They also made cooking less difficult physically, for they reduced the stooping and heavy lifting demanded by open-hearth cooking, and brought with them new, lighter pots, pans, and other cooking utensils. Heating stoves also developed rapidly in this era; they became smaller as well as more efficient. As a result, they also allowed more flexibility in house planning, for they eliminated massive chimney stacks. Progressive farmhouse planners, like Solon Robinson or the Wisconsin woman whose plan appears in Figure 3–10, readily incorporated this new technology into their designs.[36]

Together, the farmer's essays and plans reveal the salient attributes of work spaces in progressive farmhouses before 1855. First, house and farm grounds overlapped, reflecting the woman's active partnership in the farm enterprise. Second, farmers applied businesslike efficiency to their houses and farmsteads. Third, they investigated new devices to aid in saving labor.

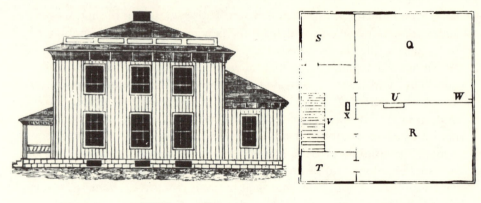

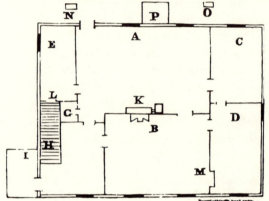

Fig. 3–10. Anonymous woman's design for a farmhouse in Wisconsin (1853). Plan and Elevation. (Below left) *Ground Floor:* (A) Kitchen. (B) Parlor. (C,D) Bedrooms. (E) Pantry. (F) Hall (not labeled). (G) Closet. (H) Stairs. (I) Porch. (K) Fireplaces and stove. (L) Cellar entrance. (M) Book closet. (N) Well. (O) Cistern. (P) Cellar entrance. (Right) *Second Floor:* (Q,R) Bedrooms. (S) Chamber. (T) Closet. (U) Chimney. (V) Stairs. (W) Garret entrance. (X) Garret ladder.

Thus, at mid-century the progressive farmhouse retained the unity of home and work that had characterized preindustrial American households. Yet by combining the older ideal with modern values of acquisitiveness, innovation, science, and system, progressive farmers thoroughly transformed this unity. Thus the progressive farmhouse ideal was as much representative of its time as the urban or suburban model of the home as asylum; it represented a rural version of American domesticity.[37]

The unity of work and home ran counter to some new developments in American cultural life, especially the idea of the home as asylum. A leading proponent of the idea was Catharine Beecher, eldest daughter of the illustrious family. She published plans in successive editions of her enormously popular *Treatise on Domestic Economy* (1841 to the 1850s), in *Harper's Magazine* (1864 and 1865), and in her most famous work, *The American Woman's Home* (1869). Beecher's biographer, Kathryn Kish Sklar, has revealed the richness and complexity of Beecher's life and thought. Sklar has placed Catharine Beecher squarely among the influential figures of the nineteenth century who contributed to the ideology of domesticity. A member of the urbanizing middle classes, she not only articulated but shaped their aspirations. Among the central tenets of her thought was that the home should be "an oasis of noncommercial values in an otherwise acquisitive society." Women would contribute to national unity through self-sacrifice: "By removing half the population from the arena of competition and making it subservient to the other half, the amount of antagonism the society had to bear would be reduced to a tolerable limit." Domesticity (and therefore domestic work) took on moral significance—housekeeping would be "ennobled by sentiment." Consequently, Catharine Beecher regarded labor-saving as a means to form character in children, enhance women's moral power in the home, and ultimately, to regenerate society. To her, regulation was "the essence of a perfect character." In the ideal household that Beecher imagined, work would assume a significant role in character formation. Miss Beecher prized efficiency for practical reasons, but above all of its moral effects.[38]

Prescriptions regarding the cultivation of fruit trees provide a telling comparison between Beecher's perspective and that of the progressive farm women. Fruit culture was viewed by farmers as an avenue for profit, or at least as a source of the family food supply. Miss Beecher, by contrast, thought of fruit cultivation as a "refining source of enjoyment," which doubled as a means of Christian charity, since the grower could supply the neighborhood's poor from her harvest. The orchard, she supposed, would acquire the character of a "small Eden," the antithesis of commercial greed. Whereas Beecher viewed horticulture as part of a scheme which would allay the socially destructive effects of capitalism, farm wives, imbued with acquisitiveness themselves, saw the orchard simply as one component of the farm's "manufactory."[39]

A comparison of house plans by Beecher and the progressive farmers reveals more about their distinctive points of view. In the early 1840s, Beecher designed plans according to her version of domesticity: they usually consisted of a nursery, kitchen, dining room, and parlor. Bed presses (recesses just large enough to contain a bed, with doors) allowed for multiple use of space. The plans reflected Beecher's assumptions about the preeminence of child rearing. For example, in Figure 3–11, the nursery and child's room are together on the second story, separated from the kitchen and parlor/dining room. In contrast, when the farmers' plans contained nurseries, they occupied proportionally less space and usually appeared nearer the kitchen.

With respect to technological innovation, the farmers' designs appear to be as fully imaginative as Beecher's. Some of her plans incorporated sinks,

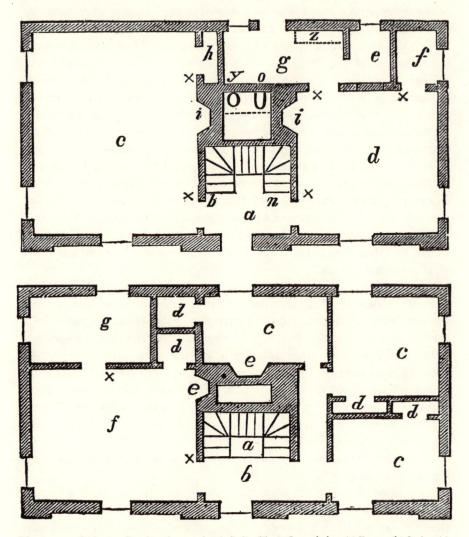

Fig. 3–11. Catharine Beecher, house plan (1848). (Top) *Ground plan:* (a) Entry. (b) Stairs. (c) Parlor. (d) Kitchen. (e) Closet. (f) Pantry. (g) Sinkroom. (h) Closet. (i) Fireplaces. (n) Cellar door. (o) Oven. (y) Furnace. (z) Sink. (Bottom) *Second story:* (a) Stairs. (b) Passage. (c) Bedrooms. (d) Closets. (e) Fireplaces. (f) Nursery. (g) Room for young children.

but not within the kitchen proper. Matilda Howard's pump, boiler, and bathing room resembled the arrangement in Beecher's *Treatise,* but Howard's fixtures were all in the kitchen, while Beecher separated the sink from the pump and boiler. Beecher's original plans mention closets for utensils, but do not depict the placement of kitchen appurtenances. Her most original ideas would come in the 1860s; in the forties and fifties the farmer-designers occupied an equal rank among leaders in architectural innovation.[40]

Incorporating the profit motive into their homes allowed progressive farmers' wives the satisfaction of contributing to the farm enterprise, but not without a heavy penalty. These women were asked to do substantially more work than their city counterparts: they had to look after the family as well as laborers, keep house, raise poultry, tend the dairy, and perform numerous other tasks. As standards of gentility reached rural areas, more housework may have been added to their list of duties. While farm women made important contributions to the family's income, they did not do so without complaint. Charges of drudgery had always appeared in the farm journals, but they increased significantly after about 1855. In response, efficiency in house design was turned to new purposes.

NOTES

1. Mary Ryan, *Cradle of the Middle Class: The Family in Oneida County, New York, 1790–1865* (Cambridge: Cambridge University Press, 1981); Nancy Cott, *The Bonds of Womanhood: "Woman's Sphere" in New England, 1780–1835* (New Haven: Yale University Press, 1977); E. P. Thompson, "Time, Work-Discipline, and Industrial Capitalism," *Past and Present* 38 (1967): 56–79; Barbara Welter, "The Cult of True Womanhood," *AQ* 18 (Summer 1966): 151–174; Gerda Lerner, "The Lady and the Mill Girl," *American Studies* 10 (Spring 1969): 5–15; Kirk Jeffrey, "The Family as Utopian Retreat from the City: The Nineteenth Century Contribution," *Soundings* 55 (Spring 1975): 21–42; William Bridges, "Family Patterns and Social Values in America," *AQ* 17 (Spring 1972): 3–11; Clifford Clark, "Domestic Architecture as an Index to Social History," *JIH* 7 (Summer 1976): 35–56.

2. Michael Merrill, "Cash is Good to Eat: Self-Sufficiency and Exchange in the Rural Economy of the United States," *Radical History Review* 4 (September 1976): 42–71; Christopher Clark, "Household, Market, and Capital: The Process of Economic Change in the Connecticut Valley of Massachusetts, 1800–1860," Ph.D. diss., Harvard University, 1982; Robert Mutch, "Yeoman and Merchant in Pre-Industrial America," *Societas* 7 (Autumn 1977): 279–302; Bettye Hobbs Pruitt, "Self-Sufficiency and the Agricultural Economy of Eighteenth-Century Massachusetts," *WMQ* 3rd ser. 41 (July 1984): 333–364.

3. Jesse Buel, *The Farmer's Companion* (Boston: Marsh, Capen, Lyon, and Webb, 1839), 14, 276. Attempts to raise the farmer's status are chronicled in Paul Johnstone, "In Praise of Husbandry," *Ag. History* 11 (April 1937): 80–96; and Richard Abbott, "The Agricultural Press Views the Yeoman, 1819–1859," *Ag. History* 42 (January 1968): 35–44. Allen, letter, *AA* 6 (June 1847): 181–183; "The Farm as a Manufactory," *GF* 14 (January 1853): 9; Jason Smith, "Farmers and Manufacturers," *GF* 14 (October 1853): 314. Charles Hammond, "Where the Arts and Virtues Unite: Country Life Near Boston, 1637–1864," Ph.D. diss., Boston University, 1982 and Tamara Thornton, "The Moral Dimensions of Horticulture in Nineteenth-Century America," *New England Quarterly* 57 (March 1984): 3–25, chronicle the gentleman farmer's life and thought.

4. *GF* 9 (October 1848): 248–249; *AA* 10 (December 1851): f.p.; James Smeallie, letter, *AC* 4 (July 1836): 85.

The extent of innovative behavior and outlook among nineteenth-century farmers is a matter of debate. Clarence Danhof argues, in *Change in Agriculture: the Northern United States, 1820–1870* (Cambridge, Mass.: Harvard University Press, 1969), 277–280, that the number of "rational, market-oriented farmers" who were willing to innovate was small. David Danbom, *The Resisted Revolution: Urban America and the Industrialization of Agriculture, 1900–1930* (Ames: Iowa State University Press, 1979), 39, 41, 70–71, 88, 142, argues that farmers in general resisted innovations introduced by the Country Life Movement. See also Earl Hayter, *The Troubled Farmer 1850–1900* (De Kalb: Northern Illinois University Press, 1968).

Other historians have attempted to approach the question by determining the characteristics of innovative farmers. See Allan Bogue, *From Prairie to Corn Belt: Farming in the Illinois and Iowa Prairies in the Nineteenth Century* (Chicago: University of Chicago Press, 1963), 212–214; Mildred Throne, "Book Farming," *Iowa Journal of History* 49 (April 1951): 117–143; Gould Colman, "Innovation and Diffusion in Agriculture," *Ag. History* 42 (July 1968): 173–187; Richard Wines, "The Nineteenth-Century Transition in an Eastern Long Island Community," *Ag. History* 55 (January 1981): 50–83.

Most of these writers treat innovativeness and conservatism as opposite poles, but this is not necessarily the case. Leo Marx, in a paper given at a conference on "Rural Improvement and Reform," Bethel, Maine, October 1985, pointed out that farmers may have accepted innovation in order to stay in their traditional occupation. Robert Gross, "The Great Bean-Field Hoax: Thoreau and the Agricultural Reformers," *Virginia Quarterly Review* 61 (Summer 1985): 483–497, shows that New England's agricultural reformers had conservative social goals.

A related question, the timing and significance of the beginnings of market-oriented agriculture in the United States, has also been debated extensively by historians. A convenient summary can be found in Winifred Rothenberg, "The Market and Massachusetts Farmers, 1750–1850," *Journal of Economic History* 41 (June 1981): 283–315. Percy Wells Bidwell, in "The Agricultural Revolution in New England," *American Historical Review* 26 (July 1921): 683–703, first outlined the transition from self-sufficiency to commercial agriculture, citing 1820 as a pivotal time. Danhof, in "The Farm Enterprise: The Northern United States, 1820–1860s," *Research in Economic History* 4 (1979): 127–191, shows that subsistence and market farms existed simultaneously in the same region, and that the line between the two types was not always clear. Robert Gross, in "Culture and Cultivation: Agriculture and Society in Thoreau's Concord," *JAH* 69 (June 1982): 42–62, has suggested that Henry Thoreau's criticism of Americans' acquisitive values be viewed as a reaction to his neighbors' market orientation. Others have questioned Bidwell's claim that market activity did not increase until 1820. See George Rogers Taylor, *The Transportation Revolution* (New York: Rinehart, 1951); "American Economic Growth before 1840," *Journal of Economic History* 24 (December 1964): 427–431; James T. Lemon, "Household Consumption in Eighteenth-Century America" *Ag. History* 41 (January 1967): 59–71; Rodney Loehr, "Self-Sufficiency on the Farm," *Ag. History* 26 (April 1952): 37–41.

James Henretta, in "Families and Farms: Mentalité in Pre-Industrial America," *WMQ* 3rd ser. 35 (January 1978): 3–33, argues that farmers acted primarily out of loyalty to family and communal values, not from profit motives. He points to the persistence of the term "surplus" to show that capitalistic values did not hold sway in the early nineteenth century. In the same vein, Christopher Clark, in "The Household Economy, Market Exchange, and the Rise of Capitalism in the Connecticut Valley, 1800–1860," *Journal of Social History* 13 (Winter 1979):

169–191, suggests that initial involvement of farmers in capitalistic ventures grew out of family need, but that the very fact of market involvement changed farmers' priorities and values. See also Merrill, above note 2.

The assumed opposition between family and profit-making is artificial; in an economy increasingly dominated by cash exchange, it may have been to a farm family's advantage to accumulate money.

5. "A Profitable Wife," *NEF* 5 (December 21, 1826): 164; *PF* 7 (May 1847): 156; "The Wife's Influence," *GF* 17 (April 1856): 127; "Profits of a Garden," *AA* 6 (March 1847): 89; F. R. Elliott, letter, *GF* 6 (May 1845): 67; "Female Industry," *NEF* 12 (August 28, 1834): 51. See also *MF* 13 (May 1855): 145–146.

6. "Ladies' Saloon," *OC* 1 (January 1, 1845): 5; address to the Essex County Agricultural Society, *GF* 1 (October 1840): 152.

7. *PF* 7 (April 1847): 133; "Elizabeth," "Letter from a Farmer's Wife," *OC* 1 (February 1, 1845): 21; *PF* 7 (March 1847): 84; "Western Women," *PF* 1 (March 1841): 24.

8. "Elizabeth," "Letter"; "Young Farmer's Wife," *GF* 8 (May 1847): 124.

9. Percy Wells Bidwell and John Falconer, *History of Agriculture in the Northern United States, 1620–1860* (1925. Reprint, New York: Peter Smith, 1941); Paul Wallace Gates, *The Farmer's Age: Agriculture, 1815–1860* (New York: Holt, Rinehart, & Winston, 1960); Joseph Schafer, *Social History of American Agriculture* (New York: Macmillan, 1936), 135–136; David Maldwyn Ellis, *A History of New York State* (Ithaca, N.Y.: Cornell University Press, 1967), chapter 22; David Ellis, *Landlords and Farmers in the Hudson-Mohawk Region* (New York: Octagon Books, 1967), chapter 6; Neil Adams McNall, *Agricultural History of the Genesee Valley, 1790–1860* (Philadelphia: University of Pennsylvania Press, 1952), chapter 10; Gates, "Agricultural Change in New York State, 1850–1890," *New York History* 50 (April 1969): 115–141; Russell Anderson, "New York Agriculture Meets the West," *Wisconsin Magazine of History* 16 (December 1932): 163–199; Neil McNall, "King Wheat in the Genesee Valley," *New York History* 27 (October 1946): 426–441; Eric Brunger, "Dairying and Urban Development in New York State 1850–1900," *Ag. History* 29 (October 1955): 169–174; Yasuo Okada, "The Economic World of a Seneca County Farmer, 1830–1880," *New York History* 66 (January 1985): 5–29; Eric Lampard, *The Rise of the Dairy Industry in Wisconsin* (Madison: State Historical Society of Wisconsin, 1963), especially the first two chapters; Robert Leslie Jones, "The Dairy Industry in Ohio Prior to the Civil War," *Ohio State Archaeological and Historical Quarterly* 56 (January 1947): 46–70; Fred Bateman, "Improvement in Dairy Farming 1850–1910: A Quantitative Analysis," *Journal of Economic History* 28 (June 1968): 255–273; Clarence Danhof, "The Farm Enterprise: The Northern United States, 1820–1860," *Research in Economic History* 4 (1979): 127–191; Richard Wines, *Fertilizer in America: From Waste Recycling to Resource Exploitation* (Philadelphia: Temple University Press, 1985); Howard S. Russell, *A Long, Deep Furrow: Three Centuries of Farming in New England* (Hanover, N.H.: University Press of New England, 1976); Robert Leslie Jones, *A History of Agriculture in Ohio to 1880* (Kent, Oh.: Kent State University Press, 1983); Jeremy Atack and Fred Bateman, *To Their Own Soil: Agriculture in the Antebellum North* (Ames: Iowa State University Press, 1987).

10. Allan G. Bogue, *From Prairie to Corn Belt;* Gilbert Fite, *The Farmers' Frontier, 1865–1900* (New York: Holt, Rinehart, & Winston, 1966); Everett Dick, *The Sod-House Frontier* (Lincoln, Neb.: Johnsen Publishing Co., 1954); Gates, *The Farmer's Age;* Glenda Riley, *Frontierswomen: The Iowa Experience* (Ames: Iowa State University Press, 1981); Joanna Stratton, *Pioneer Women: Voices From the Kansas Frontier* (New York: Simon and Schuster, 1981); Mary W. M. Hargreaves, "Women in the Agricultural Settlement of the Northern Plains," *Ag. History* 50 (January 1976): 179–189; Angel Kwollek-Folland, "The Elegant Dugout: Domes-

ticity and Moveable Culture in the United States, 1870–1900," *American Studies* 25 (Fall 1984): 21–37; Christine Stansell, "Women on the Great Plains," *Women's Studies* 4 (1976): 87–98; Jacqueline Reinier, "Concepts of Domesticity on the Southern Plains Agricultural Frontier, 1870–1920" in John Wunder, ed., *At Home on the Range* (Westport, Conn.: Greenwood, 1985).

11. Joan Jensen, "Churns and Butter-Making in the Mid-Atlantic Farm Economy, 1750–1850," *Working Papers, Regional Economic History Research Center* 5 (1982): 60–100; Jensen, "Cloth, Butter, and Boarders: Women's Household Production for the Market," *Review of Radical Political Economics* 12 (Summer 1980): 14–24; Jensen, *Loosening the Bonds: Mid-Atlantic Farm Women, 1750–1850* (New Haven: Yale University Press, 1986); John Mack Faragher, *Women and Men on the Overland Trail* (New Haven: Yale University Press, 1979); Faragher, *Sugar Creek: Life on the Illinois Prairie* (New Haven: Yale University Press, 1986); and "History From the Inside-Out: Writing the History of Women in Rural America," *AQ* 33 (Winter 1981): 537–557; Nancy Gray Osterud, "Strategies of Mutuality: Relations Among Women and Men in an Agricultural Community," (Ph.D. diss., Brown University, 1984).

12. "Woman's Sphere—What Mrs. Jone's [sic] said about it," *OC* 7 (January 1, 1851): 15; Isaac Phillips Roberts, *Autobiography of a Farm Boy* (Albany, N.Y.: J. B. Lyon, 1916): 24–25; "The Farmer's Wife," *CG* 16 (September 13, 1860): 179; Osterud, "Strategies," III: 1, 2; Riley, *Frontierswomen*, 85.

13. "Domestic Economy," *GF* 4 (April 16, 1834): 127; "Domestic Economy," *NEF* 12 (March 19, 1834): 282.

14. "Annette," letter, *GF* 1 (March 1840): 48; "Annette," letter, *GF* 1 (May 1840): 76; "Qualifications for Farmers' Wives," *MF* 1 (December 15, 1843): 163; Ruth Bloch, "American Feminine Ideals in Transition: The Rise of the Moral Mother, 1785–1815," *Feminist Studies* 4 (June 1978): 101–127; Linda Kerber, "Daughters of Columbia: Educating Women for the Republic, 1787–1805," in Stanley Elkins and Eric McKitrick, eds., *The Hofstadter Aegis: A Memorial* (New York: Alfred A. Knopf, 1974), 36–60.

15. Robert Sinclair, "Importance of Knowledge to Farmers," *NEF* 7 (September 5, 1828): 52; "The Character of a Complete Farmer," *GF* 3 (January 19, 1833): 19.

16. "Farm Buildings," *NEF* 7 (September 19, 1828): 69; "Farm Houses," *AC* 8 (October 1841): 157. Lewis Mumford, in *Sticks and Stones: A Study of American Architecture and Civilization* (New York: Boni and Liverright, 1924), argued that the New England village represented the "common spirit" of "corporatism" which was subsequently lost in the "diaspora of the pioneer" (chapter 1). Later, J. B. Jackson echoed Mumford, characterizing the isolated farm settlement pattern of the nineteenth century as a departure from the old New England ideal of the village as "superfamily." See his essays, "The Westward-Moving House," *Landscape* 2 (Spring 1952): 10–18, and "Jefferson, Thoreau, and After," in Ervin Zube, ed., *Landscapes: Selected Writings of J. B. Jackson* (Amherst: University of Massachusetts Press, 1970): 5–43.

17. "W," "Situation of Farm Buildings," *PF* 12 (January 1852): 19.

18. "Farm Buildings," *NEF* 7 (September 19, 1828): 69; Lincolnshire Farmer, *The Complete Grazier,* 4th ed. (London: Baldwin, Cradock, and Joy, 1816), 92; Henry Stephens, *The Book of the Farm,* 2 vols. (New York: Greeley & McElrath, 1847), 155. On the significance of English agricultural reform to America, see Rodney Loehr, "Influence of England upon American Agriculture 1775–1825," *Ag. History* 11 (January 1937): 3–16. On English agricultural reform and its architecture, see John Martin Robinson, *Georgian Model Farms* (New York: Oxford University Press, 1983).

19. "L.A.M.," "Farm Buildings," *GF* 9 (January 12, 1839): 12; Lewis Allen, "Farm Buildings," *AA* 1 (July 1842): 116. These views of the farmstead invite comparison to A. J. Down-

ing's ideal of the secluded country house. Downing's ideal country house was placed deep within a carefully planned, graded series of concentric circles of landscaping. Each bush, tree, and hedge was intended to screen the house and family from the public gaze; a primary goal of landscaping was privacy. In contrast, efficiency was the progressive farmer's main motive in removing his house from the roadway. The most commonly cited drawback of roadside life was not that company intruded upon the farmer's private life, but that casual visiting wasted his precious time. Farmers were assured, in fact, that their neighbors and friends would find them easily. The contrasting interests of working farmers and country gentlemen are again in evidence: both wanted to control public access to the house, but they had very different reasons for doing so.

20. "A Talk on Orderly Farming," *AA* 16 (December 1857): 283; *GF* 2 (December 22, 1832): 401; Allen, "Farm Buildings," *AA* 1 (April 1842): 117.

21. Correspondence with Joel Nelson, Jr.; *Bryant Association Reunion of 1897*, 69, 72, 80. Charity B. Robinson (b. 1848) remembered that she had attended the barn raising as a child. There are of course more complexities to farm layouts than can be discussed here. For some insight as to the influence of ethnic and regional tradition, see Stewart McHenry, "18th Century Field Patterns as Vernacular Art," in Dell Upton and John Michael Vlach, eds., *Common Places: Readings in American Vernacular Architecture* (Athens, Ga.: University of Georgia Press, 1986), 107–124.

22. E. H. Arr, [Ellen Chapman (Hobbs) Rollins], *New England Bygones* (Philadelphia: J. B. Lippincott, 1880), 11–12.

23. "The Sub-Division of Farms," *AC* n.s. 9 (February 1852): 65–66.

24. "E.S.," (Ethel Stone?), "Hints to Country Housekeepers," *AA* 5 (June 1846): 194; "H.L.Y.," "Economy in Housekeeping," *MF* 14 (April 1856): 117; "Old Lady," "Economy of Labor-Saving Utensils in a Kitchen or on a Farm," *AA* 6 (May 1847): 158.

25. "Half Housewife," *CG* 2 (December 15, 1853): 384; "Martha," "Hints to Farmers' Wives," *AC* 10 (December 1843): 199; Mrs. M. P. A. Crozier, "Farmers' Wives," *Moore's* 8 (May 23, 1857): 168.

26. Matilda Howard, "Plan of a Farm-House," *AC* 10 (April 1843): 69.

27. Ibid.

28. Ibid.; "M.W.H.," "Care of a Dairy," *AC* 10 (July 1843): 119.

29. Norma Prendergast, "A Sense of Home," Ph.D. diss., Cornell University, 1981; J. W. Ward, "The Politics of Design," *Massachusetts Review* 6 (Autumn 1965): 661–689.

30. Mrs. James Ellis, "Design for a Farm-House," *AA* 6 (June 1847): 184–185. Jensen, *Loosening the Bonds*, 133, notes that Esther Lewis rearranged her own home in a very similar way.

31. Solon Robinson, "A Cheap Farm-House," *AA* 6 (July 1847): 216–218; *GF* 11 (February 1850): 44.

32. "Working Woman's Cottage," *AC* n.s. 6 (January 1849): 25.

33. "Old Lady," "Economy of Labor-Saving Utensils," *AA* 6 (May 1847): 158.

34. "H.K.F.," "Experience in Building," *Moore's* 10 (November 19, 1859): 374. On earlier forms of kitchen cabinetry, see Donna C. Hole, "The Kitchen Dresser: Architectural Fittings in Eighteenth and Early Nineteenth Century Anglo-American Kitchens," *Petits Propos Culinaires* 9 (October 1981): 25–37.

35. Robert Bruegman, "Central Heating and Forced Ventilation: Origins and Effects on Architectural Design," *JSAH* 37 (October 1978): 143–161; Eugene Ferguson, "An Historical Sketch of Central Heating 1800–1860," in Charles Peterson, ed., *Building Early America: Contributions Toward the History of A Great Industry* (Radnor, Pa.: Chilton Book Co., 1976);

Benjamin L. Walbert, "Infancy of Central Heating in the United States 1803–1845," *APT Bulletin* 3 (1971): 76–85; Samuel Edgerton, "Heating Stoves in Eighteenth-Century Philadelphia," *APT Bulletin* 3 (1971): 14–104; May N. Stone, "The Plumbing Paradox: American Attitudes toward late Nineteenth Century Domestic Sanitary Arrangements," *WP* 14 (Autumn 1979): 283–311.

36. William J. Keep, "Early American Cooking Stoves," *Old-Time New England* 22 (October 1931): 78; Ruth Schwartz Cowan, *More Work for Mother: The Ironies of Household Technology from the Open Hearth to the Microwave* (New York: Basic Books, 1983). Cowan's argument that the stove created more work for women minimizes the extent to which purely physical demands were reduced by domestic technology. See also Thomas Hubka, *Big House, Little House, Back House, Barn: The Connected Farm Buildings of New England* (Hanover and London: University Press of New England, 1984); Susan Strasser, *Never Done: A History of American Housework* (New York: Pantheon, 1982).

37. David Handlin, in an article about "Efficiency and the American Home," *Architectural Association Quarterly* 5 (October/December 1973): 50–55, argues that not until the twentieth century, when they applied the ideas of Frederick W. Taylor, did American house designers become overtly concerned with efficiency. The farmer-planners' work suggests that a tradition of crude time-motion analysis preceded Taylorism. Moreover, none of the features described by Handlin seems especially new in the twentieth century.

38. Kathryn K. Sklar, *Catharine Beecher: A Study in American Domesticity* (New Haven: Yale University Press, 1973), 156–167.

39. Catharine Beecher, *Treatise on Domestic Economy* (Boston: Marsh, Capen, Lyon, & Webb, 1848), 256, 251.

40. Ibid., 276–278.

FOUR

The Spheres Diverge: Work on the Progressive Farmstead, 1855–1885

Work, work, work,
Is ever the farmer's song,
There's never a time to stop and think,
Be the evenings ever so long.

Yes work, work, work
Till your hands are hard and rough;
Work, and wring, and scrape,
Till your finger nails wear off.

And then sit down and write
Of the joys of a farmer's life;
'Tis, Oh, to be a slave,
Or a modern farmer's wife.

Oh no, the men are not to blame,
For they do all they can;
But then there are a hundred things
That are beyond a man.

They do *their* work, then go to sleep.
No "yeast" is on their minds;
If all the babies wake and weep,
It ne'er disturbs a man.

It's work, work, work,
Yes, cook, and weed, and hoe,
Till our ladylike and dimpled hands
Are not as white as snow.

I would that I were dead,
And buried in a row,
Under a fragrant cabbage head,
And at my feet a hoe.

But I can't die, I have no time,
'Twould take a day or two,
And stop the plow,
So I must wait
'Till the busy time is through.

This poem, submitted to the *Prairie Farmer* in 1876, appeared under the pen name "Hail Columbia." It applied to farm women the idea of Thomas Hood's famous "Song of the Shirt" (1843). (Hood's popular verse denounced the severe overwork endured by seamstresses working in mid-century predecessors to sweatshops.) A generation earlier, its sentiments would have been unusual, but by the mid-1870s they were common. From New England westward, progressive farmers' wives were voicing their dissatisfaction with a life they had come to view as filled with drudgery. The next episode in the history of the progressive farmhouse will show how, in the period from 1855 to 1885, changes in the progressive farmstead's work world contributed to its physical transformation.[1]

Farmer-designers from the 1830s to the early 1850s arranged their houses for efficiency, enabling women to contribute their full measure to the farm economy. The ideal of the efficient farmhouse drew support from wives who valued their role in farm production. After about 1855, the ideal of the "profitable farm wife" gave way to another image—that of a worker whose primary tasks more often consisted of services to the family—child nurture, cooking, sewing, cleaning—rather than participating in the farm's production for market.

Several developments were responsible for this change. There was a heightened awareness of drudgery. On progressive farmsteads everywhere, the rapid mechanization of field work brought into sharp relief the manual nature of women's work. Specialization removed the production of some farm commodities from women's hands. Middle-class urban values began to compete with farm wives' already wavering loyalties to farm work; even if her farming duties lessened, the progressive farm wife found herself scrambling to meet new standards of housekeeping, gentility, and child rearing.

Thus as progressive farm families grew more prosperous, the farm wives experienced the paradoxical burden of more work.

These economic and social changes brought with them a new spatial arrangement on the farmstead: people were sorted out by class and by gender. Laborers' quarters lightened the burden associated with boarding hired help, afforded privacy for the farmer's family, and reinforced growing class divisions. Men and women planners tended to isolate and specialize the kitchen; the "business center" of earlier decades became the exclusive domain of the woman. The kitchen's location began to change as planners stressed the desirability of a sunny position, perhaps overlooking a roadway instead of facing the back as was customary. The farmhouse remained the site of experiments to improve efficiency, but these experiments now focused on the internal dynamics of the kitchen. The primary purpose of efficiency was no longer to serve the farm, but to preserve the farm wife. This chapter will explore these architectural responses to changing circumstances of rural life in the northern states during and after the Civil War period.

Complaints about farm wives' drudgery first increased noticeably in agricultural journals late in the 1840s. In the *Genesee Farmer* of 1847, "A Farmer's Wife" explained why young women refused to marry farmers. Farmers' daughters could well see that "as their fathers' lands increase, so does [sic] their mothers' cares." What rational girl would choose a life of unremitting labor? "No class of women toils harder," the writer warned. Ironically, she linked prosperity not to increased leisure for women (as in the cities) but to increased work. In the 1840s and 1850s, these charges met with spirited refutations from defenders of farm life, but thereafter the chorus of complaints escalated while defenses ebbed.[2]

Why did the progressive farmers' wives, supposedly the most privileged of rural classes, begin to see their lives as monotonous rounds of hard work? There are several reasons. Prominent among these was the rapid development of agricultural technology. Earlier generations of farm men and women had worked with simple tools. Farmers sowed their seed by the ancient broadcast method and they walked behind the slow-moving moldboard plow. Women milked the cows, cared for pigs and poultry, tended the kitchen garden, and did all housework by hand. Moreover, where technological innovations were concerned, domestic and field work seemed to equally benefit. This was the era of the new-model kitchen stove.[3]

During the mid-1850s and later, improvements in horse-powered farm implements (especially the plow, reaper, mower, thresher, and seed drill) increased yields while reducing labor requirements. For most farmers, the Civil War years marked the turning point in the shift to more mechanized farming, but the trend was well in evidence by the mid-1850s. By that time, the reaper was widely used in northern Illinois and southern Wisconsin. In Ohio alone 10,000 reapers had been sold by 1857.

During the Civil War, conscription disproportionately affected rural areas in the North, and high farm prices at home and overseas encouraged increased production. Farmers responded by planting more acres and investing in machinery. By 1864, three-quarters of farmers owning over 100 acres possessed a reaper or mower. In the Midwest, where wheat was the principal crop, farmers usually bought reapers, while in the East where hay occupied most cultivated land, they used a mower (a simpler variation of the reaper). These devices reduced labor requirements drastically. Work which formerly required five men could now be done with two. The farmer did not necessarily curtail his work hours when the reaper came, but the amount he could produce in a day rose quickly.[4]

The new agricultural technology enhanced the progressive farmer's dominant position in rural society because it increased capital requirements for farming, and thereby also increased the poorer farmer's competitive disadvantage. Moreover, because fewer people could manage more acres, successful farmers began to add to their holdings and farm size grew. One farmer's experience with his new mowing machine gave an indication of the widening gap between the well-to-do progressive agriculturist and his poorer competitors and hired hands. Daniel Edwards, a successful farmer and lumberman in Little Genesee, New York, had fared well enough to build a new house, and in 1858 he sent the plan to the *Genesee Farmer*. About the same time, he also acquired a new mower. We can never know what motivated a group of neighborhood boys to dump the machine into a pond, but it is possible that Edwards's prosperity and innovative habits inflamed resentment among his less fortunate neighbors.[5]

The benefits of the new agricultural technology were unequally distributed in another way: the most effective machines were found in the men's sphere of the fields. As early as 1847, a woman writing to the *Ohio Cultivator* observed this imbalance: "Of one thing we are certain, that their [men's] 'improvements' do not lessen our cares." Mechanization magnified the division in farm households everywhere. In 1867 the Chicago-based *Prairie Farmer* ran a series of front-page features on "The Kitchen." The lead article asserted that "We need machines and implements for both [kitchen and farm]. Genius has done but little comparatively for the former as for the latter. . . . While the farmer must have the best seed plow, the farmer's son the best riding cultivator, the farmer's wife must too often be compelled to use some worthless old stove." Protests continued to stream into the farm papers in the 1860s and 1870s. One contributor to the *Genesee*

Farmer (1861) argued with eloquence: "The intelligent, wide-awake farmer procures every implement which will lighten his labor, thinking that 'time saved is money earned.' Why not the same for the care-worn wife? The men walk off to talk to their friends about the crops, the weather, our next President, the tyranny of the slaveholders, etc. . . . little thinking that the wife at home is as great a slave to the small steel needle." In *Moore's* in 1860 and 1861, staff writer "H.T.B.," in his essay on "Labor-Saving Indoors—Women's Rights," declared that while reapers and other machines reduced men's labor by half, "Floors are swept with the same weeds tied to the end of a stick, and by the same persistent swing of the arms, as when our mothers were young. . . . Electricity, and steam, and water-power, do not condescend to household affairs—they have been subsidized by man."[6]

Farm writers' portrayals of the contrast between kitchen and field technology were accurate. Certainly new aids to women's work existed: water pumps, sewing machines, lightweight cutlery and cookware, kitchen ranges, new types of butter churns, washing machines, and a variety of small gadgets were available in the post-Civil War period. These tools undoubtedly saved work, but their impact could not be compared with changes wrought by, for example, the reaper, because they were applicable to more limited tasks, and because many patent devices were imperfectly developed.

The most onerous of farm women's tasks still involved substantial manual labor. Even the improved cookstove required hauling wood and careful attention to fire building. Laundering entailed heating and carrying gallons of water, and food had to be processed from its rawest form. Women usually milked the cows, baked bread daily, kept a kitchen garden, and preserved vegetables and fruit. Making butter was still done by hand churning. Domestic cheese manufacture demanded exacting and strenuous labor. Much of the family wardrobe was hand-sewn. Farm women cooked and cleaned for the hired hands as well as for the family, and so it is possible that, as farms expanded, the burden for well-to-do, progressive farm wives was actually greater than for their neighbors who hired fewer hands.[7]

Poetry in the agricultural press expressed the contrast especially vividly. "A. Zalia's" "Help for Housewives," published in *Moore's* in 1874, was a startling, utopian vision of the ultimate in household conveniences.

> The day had been a long and weary one,
> And, when at last its tiresome hours were run,
> I sat me down in twilight calm to rest;
> And ponder o'er my troubled life, unblest.
> "From morn till night," I said, in fretful tone,
> "Tis endless toil, and thankless moil, alone;

"Nobody cares how many steps I take!
Nobody thinks my back is like to break!
Nobody sees that I am old and worn!
Nobody knows my heart with grief is torn!
Tis everybody for himself alone,
And I must slave till I'm but skin and bone."

Thus speaking to myself in sad dismay,
My weary frame upon the couch I lay,
And o'er my wretched lot I dropped a tear,—
When, suddenly, my heart stood still with fear!
For, looking round, I saw a marvelous change
On things anear; the very walls looked strange.

"Why, what is this?" I cried, in great amaze;
"The house is mine; and yet where're I gaze
Not one familiar object do I see!
I'm sore distressed! What can the meaning be?"
As if in answer to my query, there
Appeared a sprightly dame, who asked me where

I wished to go. "Sit down and rest awhile,
You've lost your way," she said, with friendly smile,
And shoved an easy chair. Confused, I turned
Me round, and said—my cheeks to crimson burned—
"There must be some mistake; I thought, till now,
This house was mine,"—She made a stately bow,

And muttered to herself—"The woman's mad!"
Then, quick regaining her composure, bade
Me follow her; she'd show me her domain
And soon convince me I must be insane
To think the house could e're belong to me!
Then turned about, with quiet dignity.

And to the kitchen, quick, she led the way.
"You must excuse the room, 'tis washing day
With us," she said. I gave a hasty glance,
Then started with surprise, to see advance
A something, half-way twixt a brush and broom,
That, without aid, began to sweep the room!

My hostess answered, now my questioning look.
Into her hand the queer machine she took:
"This sweeper is, I fancy, new to you."
Thereat she turned it round, and showed to view

A tiny door within the handle. "See,
She said, "we wind it with this little key.

"We set the works for any hour we please,
And, at the stated time, with perfect ease,
Our good machine comes out and sweeps the floor."
I sighed, and said, within myself, "No more
Would arms grow lame, nor feeble backs give out,
If in each house this sweeper walked about."

"We've all the last improvements," then she said,
"Here is our wash-room." As I turned my head,
She opened wide a door, and just within,
I saw a large and intricate machine.
And, as I looked by some strange power unseen,
The clothing went in soiled—AND CAME OUT CLEAN!

The astonished woman is shown a dining room where hot food is truck-ed in on a miniature rail system before she is awakened:

"You've been asleep an hour or more. I tried
To keep the babies still, but Georgie cried,
And all attempts to hush him were in vain;
So do wake up! There's all the milk to strain!"
'Tis ever thus; things are not what they seem
We're sure to wake and find it all a dream!

"A. Zalia" inherited her lively interest in labor-saving machinery and house design from a previous generation, but her poem utterly lacked their optimism. Matilda Howard, the "Old Lady," and the "Farmer's Wife" had used household aids to save time and labor, and probably felt that house-hold technology would keep pace with field technology. "A. Zalia," by contrast, envisioned dream machines which would rescue her from break-down. By the early 1870s, progressive farm wives agreed that the dramatic mechanization of agricultural production had left the farm household be-hind where technology was concerned, sharpening the differences between the house and the farm proper.[8]

Women's stories and letters in the farm journals soon began to link menial labor to physical breakdown, making still more explicit the message in the poem. In 1873, a *Prairie Farmer* column traced a progressive farm couple—according to the author, a representative pair—from their modest beginnings through middle age, lucidly depicting the evolution of drudgery. The paths of husband and wife begin as parallels, but soon diverge: after five years, he "had added more land to his possessions, and better farming implements . . . and is able to have an occasional hired hand, who boards in the house of course, his washing and ironing done there. . . . *She* has two or three babies . . . their modest vegetable and flower gardens are made by herself; she coddles the early lambs and feeds the pigs, and milks the cows, from which she makes butter. . . . She raises troops of chickens, and ducks and turkeys for market . . . withal she must keep herself, her house and household decently clean, or the 'neighbors will talk,' and so she does it. She is 25 years old, and looks 40; *but her husband is growing rich*" (his italics). The pattern continues, and after twenty years, the husband has reached a healthy, prosperous middle age, while his wife "is gray, and wrinkled, and thin; pain is her most constant companion." One hot August day, after feeding the hands, washing, and ironing, she collapses and dies. The author asked angrily, "Where does the responsibility lie, of deaths like this?"[9]

At the same time agriculture was being mechanized, it was also becoming increasingly specialized, which also affected the farm wife's duties. Following the Civil War, northern agriculture underwent significant changes, forced by more intense competition, massive rural migration to the cities, and (between 1873 and 1879) economic depression. The farmers who survived tended to possess better lands, but often also employed superior methods. Urban markets proved the key to survival for some, particularly for progressive farmers who actively sought new markets and willingly changed their husbandry. Dairy farming, horticulture, and truck farming was expanded and intensified. A much greater urban area was able to receive the products from a particular dairy region because of railroad connections. This prompted farmers to breed cows specifically for milk production and to pay more attention to feed and shelter; between 1870 and 1900 Connecticut farmers managed a fivefold increase in fluid milk production. Dairying also became important in Wisconsin and northeastern Iowa. Close to the cities, market gardens were expanded into truck farms where farmers raised a variety of vegetables. Less perishable potatoes and onions became important crops further from the cities. Farm-grown hay provided energy for the cities' transportation systems. The fruit industry gained hold in New York, Ohio, Pennsylvania, Michigan, and Illinois, especially in the Great Lakes region. In the emerging Corn Belt, corn and hog production dominated, but the *Prairie Farmer* noted that the region's farmers also specialized in stock feeding, hay production, and even fruit growing. In the newer territories of Minnesota and the Dakotas, spring wheat prevailed, while in Kansas and Nebraska, farmers relied more upon corn, winter wheat, and sorghum.[10]

The gradual specialization of northern farms often entailed removal of some tasks from women's supervision, most notably in dairying. In 1851, Jesse Williams of Rome, New York, established the nation's first cheese factory. During the next decade, the factory movement faltered, but during the war the number of cheese factories mushroomed from about sixty to more than four hundred. Farmers delivered milk to the factory, usually a few miles distant, in the morning and evening. At the factory, a half dozen employees supervised production of cheese from the milk of hundreds of cows. By 1870 over eight hundred cheese factories operated in New York state alone, and Wisconsin was beginning to compete strongly in the industry. In the 1880s, creameries, which centralized butter production, appeared as well. They never supplanted home-produced butter in the nineteenth century, but they did make inroads, especially near city markets. Thus the new cheese and butter factories removed manufacturing of these commodities from the individual farm family and home. Moreover, as farmers specialized in dairying, they incorporated the care and improvement of stock into their sphere of responsibility.[11]

The expansion of large-scale commercial truck farming and fruit growing, stimulated by the canal and railroad transportation booms, challenged the family orchard and market garden. The orchard owner or truck farmer hired male laborers and immigrant women and children to cultivate and pick his crops. The family orchard or garden did not disappear, but large-scale commercial operations probably accounted for an increasing proportion of market sales in the cities. Admonitions to farm wives to take up vegetable and fruit culture for profit must have seemed less and less relevant. In 1865, Mrs. H. C. Johns of Decatur, Illinois, advised in an essay on "The Farm Home" that "if women and children can give [the vegetable garden] some time and labor, it is well; but it should no more be left to them . . . than should the cultivation of the corn and potatoes." Even where farm wives continued to make products for cash income, their contribution, when compared to the enlarged yields and capital investment of the main farm, must have seemed less crucial to farm profit in the 1860s and 1870s than in 1840.[12]

Even farm women's traditional job of feeding poultry and swine seemed to be changing. As early as 1857, the *Michigan Farmer* noted that the "spread of agricultural knowledge" had stimulated farm men to appropriate the care of "squealing pigs." It continued, "the excitement about poultry, took many a man into the hen-yard who never before had considered eggs or chicken worthy of his notice, except when they appeared on his table."[13] Work which originally was assigned to women was now arrogated to men; a "de-feminization" of agriculture had begun. This trend probably occurred first among progressive farm families.[14]

Specialization, unlike mechanization, might mean relatively less farm work for some progressive farm wives, yet the cries of drudgery persisted, even growing more strong. To understand why, we must look to the cultural changes beginning to affect rural society in the post-Civil War era. Women correspondents now more often mentioned tasks such as sewing, cleaning, and cooking as women's work. This change did not simply mean a different kind of work, it meant more work, because it came during a period of rising standards of housekeeping. Mrs. E. P. Allerton, addressing the Wisconsin Dairy Association in 1875, alluded to new cultural standards of housekeeping when she explained why the dairy factory system was a "blessing to the farmer's wife." She believed that "Life on the farm, as well as everywhere else, grows more and more complicated," explaining that

> Upon the farmer's wife the new conditions press heavily. So many things are expected of her, which were not in the good old simple days. Our grandmothers scrubbed floors on their hands and knees, but there was usually but little floor to scrub. . . . Formerly, "dressing up" was reserved for special occasions. Now the farmer's wife who sends her daughter to the village school, must keep her fit for church all through the week.

The dairy factory system would allow the farm wife "a little blessed idleness," relieving her from the necessity of "performing the various functions of milk maid, house maid, and dairy maid,—yes, and nurse maid, also at the same time." Leading dairymen X. A. Willard and W. H. Comstock agreed that "the old system of family cheesemaking has done more to injure the health of our wives and daughters than any other cause." Significantly, Comstock hailed the factory system as "an enterprise which relieves and benefits our families, and makes the home-circle more useful and more pleasant. . . . There let social virtues, domestic culture, and natural refinement sow their most precious seeds."[15]

Ironically, even the domestic technology available played part in increasing women's housework. A good example is the vaunted sewing machine. When the Wheeler and Wilson and Grover & Baker machines first appeared, farm journalists hailed them as precious labor-saving and health-preserving devices. But the optimism soon turned to dismay, for the machines simply made possible hitherto unimagined elaborations in the farm family's apparel. By 1873, one woman admitted in the *Prairie Farmer* that her home sewing had increased since she acquired her sewing machine. She enjoyed making "side-plaits, box-plaits . . . puffs, flounces, and ruffles" for her daughter, even if it did take more time than the simpler sewing of an earlier day.[16]

Standards of eating went up too. An "amateur housekeeper" from

Howell, Michigan, in 1883 scolded her fellow farm wives for yielding to their families' demands for "cookies. I think them an invention of the 'Evil One' to which farmers' wives are joined like Ephraim's idols." But more and more women apparently did elaborate and diversify their families' diets. If the appearance of multi-course menus in the farm journals is evidence of a trend, progressive farm wives were plying their families with oysters, pudding, neck of veal, and curried rabbit.[17]

An engraving of 1888 from *Moore's* (Figure 4–1) illustrates the new priorities assumed by farm women in the latter decades of the century. The engraving shows the beneficial effects of the creamery upon the farmer's family life. The "creamery patron" (lower right) is shown in her family sitting room, mending clothes and watching over her small children, performing morally crucial domestic services instead of economically productive tasks. This split could be seen even in the arrangement of the farm periodicals: the "domestic economy" section became the woman's page or household column, more explicitly divided from the farm news and more narrowly addressed to home economy and to women. As the century waned, progressive farm wives had begun to abandon the acquisitive, productive role their mothers had filled as "profitable farm wives" in favor of a new ideal which stressed service to their families.[18]

Many women correspondents to the agricultural journals expressed deep ambivalence about this transition. These sentiments burst onto the pages of journals with startling intensity beginning about 1860. The issue was most often put in the form of anxious questions: "What is woman worth?" In the 1860s and 1870s women from New England to Nebraska shared a troubling problem: they worked hard for their families, but could not count on their husbands to compensate them. Many spoke of feeling humiliated, dependent, "indignant," and embarrassed to have to ask for money or to run up a debt at the village store. In the *Country Gentleman* in 1866, "One of the Wives" asked plaintively, "Do Farmers' Wives Pay?" She listed the tasks of cooking, washing, mending, and churning, and wondered, "If there is any standard by which the value of her services can be rightly estimated, we would like to know it." Farm wives, she thought, should not feel guilty when asking their husbands for money. Her questioning attitude contrasted sharply with the confident assumptions of the preceding generations of farm women.[19]

Such queries invariably met with animated response from progressive farm wives in the rural North. One woman, calculating the cash price of her labor, arrived at a total of $300 per year. Another pointed out that farmers willingly paid wages to their "helps," and yet "[a wife] does the work of several servants and only takes the board of one . . ." In her autobiography

Fig. 4–1. "Creamery pictures" illustrating the advantages of factory dairy production (1888).

Harriet Connor Brown wrote, "I've often thought that a considerable part of that $10,000 [the selling price of the Browns' farm] surely belonged to me." There was a unanimous feeling that farm women earned, but seldom received, a share of the farm's cash income. In effect farm wives sought an approximation of wages for services rendered, not a return for products grown or manufactured. They understood that their labor supported the farm enterprise, but at the same time, the ideal of the "profitable wife" no longer seemed to characterize the new progressive farm wife and the anti-materialist urban ideal of womanhood.[20]

Few women could offer solutions that would get more money into their hands. One woman from Utica, Michigan, urged farm wives to "insist upon it as our right, that we have an income, be it much or little, but in proportion to the general income of the business in which our husbands may be engaged." Another regarded such a solution as unrealistic; "[the wife] is perfectly powerless without her husband's concurrence," she wrote. And one despairing farm wife could only advise young women to choose the "frying-pan" of "single blessedness" to the "fire" of unpaid toil.[21]

It is not clear whether the wives of progressive farmers ever had complete access to the cash proceeds of their farm labor. But they had probably managed to control at least some of the income from such exclusively female endeavors as butter-making, and they had always been able to link their work with the farm's economic fortunes. As the nature of their work changed, they faced a new difficulty—dealing with the broader culture's definition of housework as outside the domain of the capitalist economy. Sometimes they rejoiced in their new freedom from being "mere dollar-making machines," and they always took pride in their roles as mothers and homemakers, but they also realized with regret that the economic value of housework was not recognized. Accustomed to considering their labor as economically productive, they argued for some form of remuneration. Significantly, as cash was more important in the industrial economy, the lack of it was correspondingly more painful.

The cumulative effect of these new cultural values and experiences was evident in the farm press. For example, columnists now urged the farmer's wife to avoid overzealous pursuit of her duty. The responsibilities of motherhood provided justification for this. In a melodramatic warning entitled "But One Mother," *Moore's* in 1871 painted a dark scene of the consequences of overwork: drudgery leads to collapse; without the mother's influence, the farmer turns to drink and ruins his family forever. The *Prairie Farmer* put it more bluntly. "God has given the wife a family to care for, and no one else in all the world can care for it as she can, and it is her duty to take such care of herself that she may live as long as possible to care for them."[22]

True to their tradition, the journals offered advice to overworked housewives. A persistent theme was that the farmer and his children ought to help the wife accomplish her duties—to "help with the washing, dinner, and dishes." The *Michigan Farmer* illustrated this with an amusing story. It portrayed "careless Raymond," the farmer who wears out one wife with his inconsiderate behavior. His second wife refuses to consent to being a slave, and goes on strike. One day Raymond, having neglected to fill the wood-pile, sits down to table to find that his meal has not been cooked: "there were potatoes just as they had been dug . . ." These imaginative tactics naturally convert him to "industrious Raymond." Numerous pieces echoed this trend, explaining "How to Train a Husband," or "Woman's Rights to a Woodpile."[23] As with all prescriptive demands, these trends are problematic to interpret. Urging farmers to share the burden of housework is perhaps more indicative of the widening divergence between men's and women's spheres on the farm, rather than an indication that farm men were actually willing to help out in the house.

Some contributors advocated a still more decisive departure, recommending "Rest for Farmers' Wives," urging the farm wife to abandon unnecessary tasks and instead to cultivate her God-given mental faculties. An emphasis upon self-improvement replaced self-sacrifice. One writer in the *Prairie Farmer* thought that farm women owed no apology for pursuing the "non-paying employment" of music, botany, and ornamental horticulture. Another wrote that "Women's Rights on the Farm" included the "social privileges" of lectures, concerts, and drama; she warned that "the round of household tasks cannot and does not satisfy the heart of a woman . . . the longing for a higher life." By the 1870s and 1880s, farm writers even explained how to "Take a Vacation."[24]

The fictional "Mrs. Capable" summarized these attitudes in the 1872 issue of *Rural Affairs:* "If you think yourself worth the least of all your husband's possessions, you can start out a drudge and end your career in broken health or early death. You can be the one to jump when anything is wanted. You can wait on the 'men folks' so obsequiously that they will grow very particular." Mrs. Capable related how her sons and husband helped with her work, and concluded that "while the woman and the family are in some instances degraded into mere dollar-making machines, the direct aim of all economy has been to promote and leave room for the social, mental, moral and religious."[25]

Such messages had become clichéd formulas by the 1870s. The shift away from the farm's overall operations toward child rearing, self-improvement, and strictly house-related work was probably accelerated by exposure to city ways. By the 1880s, the farm population was rapidly being outstripped by the urban population. Information on city life reached the progressive farm, oriented as it was to urban markets, by a variety of means. Lower postal rates, new subscription systems, club plans, and direct selling to local booksellers all allowed urban-based publications to reach rural markets.

These publications might find a place in a personal library or in one of a growing number of private or public circulating libraries, reaching a still wider audience after arriving in the rural community. One writer defending "country life" in the 1880s in Michigan noted that in his neighborhood, families of education and refinement had made their personal libraries and collections of periodicals available to others. He recalled borrowing back issues of *Harper's* and the *Atlantic*. Lending libraries (often operating on subscriptions of users) had existed even on the frontier, and in many communities had become stable fixtures.[26]

Other contacts were more direct between urban and rural life. Railroads allowed farm families to visit the city, and relatives or friends who had migrated to urban areas might write about their experiences in letters home. "All who have visited Chicago," said the *Prairie Farmer* in 1867, "have doubtless observed how handy the water is in the kitchen—turn a faucet and the water is at hand." Though she may have remained convinced of the city's iniquity, the progressive farm wife could not help but be impressed that, for example, her city counterpart could buy bread at a baker's. By the 1870s, the city dweller could obtain cheap oleomargarine, and a milk vendor might come to the door—there was no need to keep a cow. The urban housekeeper, if she were able to afford it, could also choose from a variety of canned goods produced by the burgeoning food preservation industry. She might also purchase ready-made clothing. Urban department stores dramatized the appeal of consumerism. To a farm wife, city life must have seemed leisurely in comparison with her own. One writer believed that a disproportionate number of the female insane were farmers' wives; she explained that the "lady of the house" in "many branches of business . . . finds several hours each day when she can be neatly and tastefully dressed, and spend in reading, writing, walking, or conversation." Farm wives, she alleged, lacked these necessary diversions.[27]

Finally, the middle-class ideal of "true womanhood," which exalted values of domesticity, built upon the image of women as nurturers, bearers of culture and refinement, and exemplars of Christian morality. This cult of true womanhood ascribed to women qualities of submissiveness, moral purity, and aesthetic sensibility. Self-improvement and child nurture assumed heightened importance as religious activities. Benevolent activity (moral reform societies, children's aid, or temperance reform) was regarded as an appropriate extension of the domestic sphere. Women also dominated middle-class evangelical Protestantism, participating in the Sunday School movement and in missionary activity at home and abroad. Although the previous generation had not fully subscribed to this idea, by the 1860s and 1870s rural women apparently found it more appealing as their economic role in the farm family changed.[28]

Another dimension to the transformation of the progressive farm woman's orientation involves the transition from one generation to the next. The younger generation of well-to-do farm girls in the 1850s and 1860s had likely been exposed to new cultural values through education. By the post-Civil War period, many young women were being sent to female academies and seminaries after grammar school. Jared Van Wagenen and Isaac Roberts both recalled that well-to-do farm families often sent their children to boarding school, and some of the farmer-designers' biographies reveal their participation in founding local academies.

The content of young women's seminary studies undermined the ideology of the progressive farm wife. The academies offered intellectually demanding, but nondomestic, subjects such as Greek and Latin, mathematics, history, and literature, as well as music, painting, and dance. The Academic Department of the Home Cottage Seminary in Clinton, New York, for instance, offered in 1856 a "comprehensive course in Mathematical and Philosophical Science, History, and Literature" and also the "Extra Studies" of "Ancient and Modern Languages, Drawing, Painting, Music, Etc."[29]

If the farm journals' condemnation of the evils of female education is any gauge, these young women faced a severe conflict in values when they returned to the farm after a term or two at boarding school. They had acquired new tastes, perhaps for music or for natural philosophy, but at home they had to divide their attention between these interests and the more prosaic work of a farmer's daughter. It is small wonder that they were confused and discontented, and perhaps became agents of change within the progressive farm household.[30]

Changes on the farm itself, awareness of urban lifestyles, and selective acceptance of prevailing images of middle-class womanhood all combined to make farm women dissatisfied with their lot. Mechanization in the field pointed up drudgery in the house. Agriculture became specialized, removing essential farm production from women's domain. These developments sharpened the distinction between the farm and the home. Information and expectations about home and family were transmitted to rural areas from the increasingly dominant urban culture, accelerating the change in function and expectations of home. The rural culture of the progressive farm family showed unmistakable signs of change.

What directions did these new ideas take where the progressive farmer's house was concerned? An example from the beginning of the period offers some clues. In 1855–56 Harry B. Hart, prosperous farmer, merchant, and postmaster of Rush, New York, built a new frame house at a crossroads (Hart's Corners), about 25 miles from the city of Rochester. Though in 1855 Hart had not fully shifted to mechanized intensive farming, he spent a large sum, $300, on lime fertilizer, and valued his farm implements at $195, well above the state average.[31]

From the road, his neighbors saw an unpretentious structure (Figure 4–2), its idiosyncratic Greek Revival styling decidedly old-fashioned. Today its exterior, although altered (the second floor has been raised, and the porch extended), still gives much the same impression. Two plain clapboard blocks, asymmetrically fenestrated and awkwardly joined, are bounded with heavy columns. In keeping with the heavy corner columns, the first-story windows are surrounded with thick moulding which extends to the foundation. Externally, the Harry Hart house is a rather ordinary vernacular building, one that evidently grew with the household.

But the documentary record shows that Harry Hart spent a substantial amount—$3,000—for the house, even bringing cobblestones from the shores of Lake Ontario for the foundation. Visitors to the house might also have noticed that the interior arrangement combined familiar formulas with newer ideas (Figures 4–3, 4–4). Many vernacular designers made outside stylistic innovations and left traditional interior plans intact, but Harry Hart did the opposite; he fashioned an innovative "premium plan" behind a stylistically dated exterior. Especially with regard to work spaces, the Hart plan represented a transitional stage in the evolution of the progressive farm family's home.

In the kitchen, some practices established during the previous decades were continued. In introducing his plan, Hart kept to the ideal of incorporating women's voice into house design: "I am of the opinion that the interior plans for, or arrangement of, most of our farm houses are too hastily matured or in many instances left to architects and builders, without consulting the FARMER'S WIFE, who, of all others, should know, and does know, more about the real comfort and conveniences of a good farm house than a score of those who make high pretensions in these matters." Also in keeping with the times, Hart emphasized the necessity for saving steps: "if only one step be saved in going to and returning from the kitchen to the cellar, the pantry, the dining-room, the cistern, etc., how many will it save in a day, a month, a year?" To this end, he placed "dish and wash sinks" in kitchen and washroom; in the pantry, he put "a large *dish cupboard* and *six smaller ones* . . . numerous *drawers,* a *cooling shelf,* and four *flour chests.*"

But other aspects of the kitchen space signaled a turn to newer ideas. One was semantic: Hart chose to call his kitchen the "cook-room," giving it one specific function. Cook-room and dining room were separated by a stairway and passage, cutting the kitchen off from living areas. Access to the kitchen was also limited—it could not be entered from the veranda, as could the living room and dining room. Hart also called attention to an outbuilding in which he had installed a "cauldron kettle, a good fire-place, etc., in which we can do all of what is usually called dirty work, without even

Fig. 4–2. Harry B. Hart house, Rush, New York (1855–56), photographed in 1986.

the scent of grease about the dwelling," differentiating between genteel and "dirty" work and specializing the kitchen's functions even further. He believed the kitchen should be in a "*pleasant* part of the house—unlike too many cook-rooms which have more of the aspect of a prison than a place for lovely woman to dwell in." Although he did not put the kitchen in a sunny spot—it was on the northeast side—he did give it three windows. The reference to "lovely woman," too, may indicate a growing preoccupation with the notion of the "true woman" and ideas of an appropriate environment for her.

Hart's provisions for the hired help also pointed in a new direction. In each of five state and federal census years (1850, 1855, 1860, 1865, 1870) at least two and as many as four men and women hired hands resided in the Hart household. Of eighteen hired helpers in this period, fourteen were foreign-born, from England, Germany, Switzerland, and Canada, and the Hart plan shows that spaces were created specifically for them. Hart himself explained that a good plan should spare the farm wife such indignities as "having the shins of a dozen stalwart men (especially in the morning) to step over, or pass around to get to the cook-stove, and as many eyes scanning the movements of the already half-faint cook, while she is preparing the meal!"

Fig. 4–3. Harry Hart house, elevation (1859).

Fig. 4–4. Harry Hart house, plan. (Left) *First Floor:* (A) Parlor. (B) Bedroom. (C) Living room. (D) Nursery. (E) Dining room. (F) Cook room. (G) Pantry. (H) Hall. (J) Washroom. (K) Wood house. (P) Bedroom. (a) Closets. (b) Sinks. (Right) *Second Floor:* (A, B, C, D, E, F) Chambers. (G) Hall. (H) Closets. (I) Storeroom. (K) Sleeping rooms.

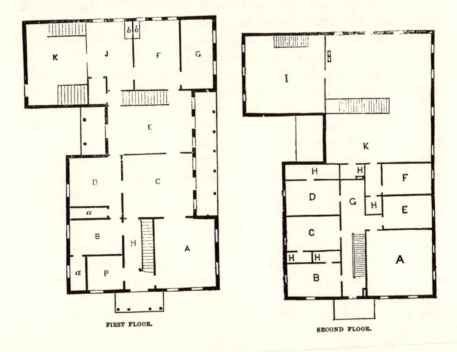

FIRST FLOOR.

SECOND FLOOR.

Evidently his wife preferred having a secluded spot to cook in, and the staircase from the employee's quarters (K) landed at the juncture of the dining room and washroom, away from the kitchen. Sleeping quarters were also arranged to keep hired help and family apart: bedroom "F" and "Sleeping-Room K" were accessible only from the back stairs.

Harry Hart's house contained a transitional set of work spaces, retaining established ideas of efficiency. But it also set off farm laborers from the family, and isolated and specialized the kitchen, allowing more privacy for Mrs. Hart as she worked. The house forecast transformations: as the ideal of the "profitable farm wife" broke down, the house forms which had suited that ideal also changed.

Different arrangements emerged which reflected a search for architectural responses to new attitudes. One solution to the problem of farm women's drudgery lay with separate laborers' quarters. The idea of cottages for workingmen had been advanced in England years earlier by such reformers as J. C. Loudon. A. J. Downing carried on this tradition in *Country Houses* (1850). His descriptions of "working-men's cottages," however, seldom specified the sort of workingmen who would occupy them. Agricultural reformers, however, adapted a generalized concept of the workingman's cottage specifically for farm laborers.[32]

By the mid-1850s, articles favoring separate housing for farm workers appeared frequently in the agricultural press. The first issue of *Rural Affairs* (1855) featured a long essay on laborers' cottages. Even the well-to-do farmer's wife, the author argued, "is closely preoccupied from earliest dawn to dark, with a constant and laborious round of baking, boiling, stewing, and roasting . . . of washing, scrubbing, ironing, and an endless routine of other labors." No wonder that the country woman appeared "bent down and furrowed with premature old age, while the merchant and mechanic's wife, and the city resident, . . . free from this grinding burden, remain at the same period of life, straight, vigorous, blooming and active." Throughout the century progressive farmers and their wives continued to see the laborer's cottage as an architectural solution to the evils of drudgery. One woman summarized her feelings this way: "Is it not enough for the wife to rear her own children, and please her own husband, without taking upon her tired shoulders the responsibility of pleasing other mens' wives?"[33]

It is difficult to know exactly how many farmers housed their hands separately, but the numbers were significant. The limited census data on farmer-designers tend to confirm this trend. In 1850, twelve of the seventeen farms for which data are available housed laborers, but by 1880, only one of six families housed farm laborers, although the census indicates that these farmers did pay wages to laborers. Among farmer-designers' plans,

the second-story layout indicated more and more the segregation of workers. It became more common to place workers' sleeping quarters over an
auxiliary wing (usually the kitchen), cutting them off from bedrooms obviously intended for the family.

Diaries and memoirs give more evidence of changing attitudes. In 1866
Henry Dey, a farmer living near Geneva, New York, wrote in his diary that
he built housing for his farmhands at a cost of $212. Isaac Roberts related
that he built hired hand housing during his tenure at the Iowa Agricultural
College in the 1870s. Thomas M. Atkeson of West Virginia became a
leader of the national Grange, and in his autobiography he recorded that in
the 1870s he did away with the practice of boarding hired men because "I
felt that their presence at the table broke into the privacy of our family
life."[34]

Atkeson's remarks suggest that laborers' cottages were not only a remedy for overwork; they also gave privacy to the farmer's family. This concern
had first surfaced in the mid-1850s, when *Rural Affairs* charged that "the
great mass [of hired men] care little for either cleanliness or culture. They
throng the farm-house at noon and in the evening, and often on the Sab-
bath, so that the wife and daughters have little or no seclusion for conversation, study, or writing, for it is next to impossible to prevent in an ordinary
farm-house a pretty thorough intermixture of individuals of all sorts and
sizes." *Moore's* justified its presentation of three laborers' cottages by claim-
ing that through this means, "the home circle may be kept more sacred."[35]

The preoccupation with family privacy stands in contrast to the earlier
attitudes of farmer-planners. Matilda Howard and her contemporaries did
not worry that laborers in the farmhouse would infringe upon the family's
sanctity. Few of the farmer-planners of the 1840s and 1850s stressed privacy as a requisite for farmhouse design. The earlier emphasis upon the
removal of the house to the center of the farmstead had served to keep the
farmer concentrated on his work, not to prevent unwelcome intrusions into
his family's private life. This tendency toward privacy in the progressive
farm family was part of a broader trend in nineteenth-century America
(especially among the middle classes) toward separating the nuclear family
from the work world. Concepts of privacy had always existed and were
always associated with family and home, but as the worlds of work and
domesticity diverged and as corporate ideals of society gave way to competitive individualism, lines between public and private became still more
clearly defined.[36]

To account for the rising interest in segregating laborers from the farm
family we must also consider the changing fortunes of the laborer. A young
man starting in the 1840s and 1850s as a farm worker could look forward to

advancing on the "agricultural ladder"; he might accumulate enough money to start a farm of his own. Moreover, he would likely be the son of a neighboring family. After mid-century, as capital costs of farm-making rose, the possibility of someday owning a farm became more remote. Farmers' sons and daughters took to the city in search of fortune, and immigrants more often took their places as farm laborers. Harry Hart's household exemplified this trend. Official and informal accounts contrasted the competent, versatile, resourceful Yankee hired hand of the previous generation to the immigrant bunglers (as they were perceived) then available. D. G. Mitchell, a popular writer, expressed the opinions of many employers when he mourned the passing of the American-born hired man, "the most indefatigable and industrious of farm workers," and contrasted him to the "rawest and most uncouth of Irish and Germans" then available.

As agriculture intensified, especially in the truck-farming regions, farmers thought of labor as simply a factor in costs; this businesslike attitude rendered the relationship between the farmer and his hand still more impersonal. In the agricultural press, letters began to appear which chastised farmers for treating their hired hands coldly and unsociably; as one put it in the *Prairie Farmer* of 1875, "they [the landlords] do not seem to know there is anyone living in that small house . . . [as if] it might disgrace them to associate with anyone who was so poor while they are so rich."[37]

Clearly, class divisions were reflected spatially as the progressive farm family sought more privacy. A trend toward privacy was evident within the farmhouse and family itself, as well. Farmhouse plans from the mid-1850s onward give evidence of this attitude. A plan submitted to the *Cultivator* by H. Huffman of Richland County, Illinois (1858), presaged this trend (Figure 4–5). Huffman wrote in his accompanying letter that he intended to simplify "all the business of a house" that was "transacted" in livingroom, diningroom, and kitchen. He added, "To visitors and stranger I assign the front door, which will take them to any apartment except the sanctum sanctorum, or kitchen." Huffman retained the usual pattern of a front parlor with rear kitchen, and compared the house to a "business"; but his explicit characterization of the kitchen as a "sanctum sanctorum" implied an unprecedented preoccupation with some sort of privacy in that room.[38]

Other plans reflected similar concerns. In 1856, J. J. Thomas, a prosperous central New York farmer, noted that his kitchen (Figure 4–6) was "rendered inconspicuous by . . . intervening stairs." This arrangement was similar to Harry Hart's. C. W. Spalding of St. Louis sent a plan to the *Cultivator* in 1861 with the request that the editors criticize it and offer suggestions. They complied, publishing a slightly altered version of his plan (Figure 4–7). They explained, "To avoid the inconvenience or evil of mak-

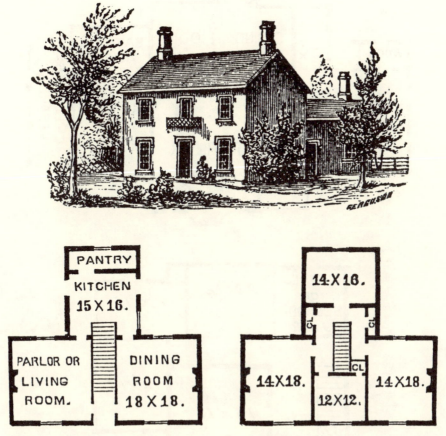

Fig. 4–5. H. Huffman, design for a farmhouse in Richland County, Illinois (1858). Plan and elevation. (Left) First story. (Right) Second story.

ing the pantry a passageway from the dining room to the kitchen, the shelves are all closed, thus shutting out sight, dust, and all intruders." Further, "This . . . excludes sight from one room to the other in a more perfect manner."[39]

Some farmer-planners, then, were beginning to show interest in cutting off the kitchen from other rooms both visually and physically. In 1859 one writer noted that "a hall will give your men folks a fair chance to come in and sit down while awaiting their meals, without having to find their way through wood-house, cook-room and kitchen, which is always a source of annoyance and often disturbs the equanimity of the presiding genius of the household."[40]

Isolation of the kitchen was a move toward establishing separate spaces

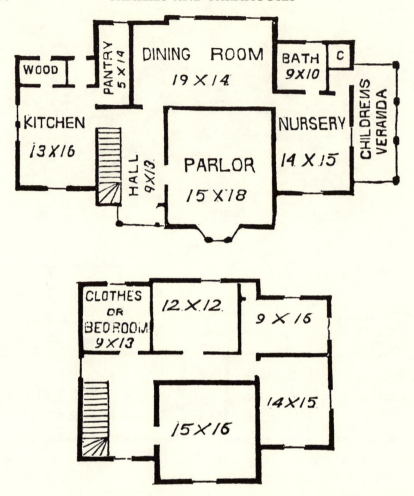

Fig. 4–6. J. J. Thomas, Gothic country house, plan (1856). (Above) Ground floor. (Below) Second floor.

for men and women in the farmhouse. The idea of privacy in the kitchen eventually extended from the exclusion of male hirelings from the kitchen to all "men folk" including husbands and sons. In 1871 *Moore's* ladies' column "visited" Mrs. Pelle Tyler, a model farm wife in Pennsylvania. Mrs. Tyler had planned her own farmhouse, placing the kitchen out of the flow of traffic because it was "likely to be invaded by masculines, and how much pleasanter it is to do one's labor without too much inspection." Her use of the term "invasion" bespeaks more than a simple desire to keep hired men out of the kitchen: she thought of her kitchen as an area designed exclusively for women. Kitchen work, she implied, ought to be invisible. Mary Wager-Fisher, ladies' columnist for *Moore's,* later advised women not to "allow anybody to use the kitchen as a place to 'stand around in'," and a "Grandmother" reminisced about the old-time gatherings around the kitchen stove, but concluded that it was well that those days were gone, as crowds around the stove had impeded the kitchen work.[41]

Even the design process seemed to become more segregated. By 1895, for example, over one-third of the *American Agriculturist's* prize-winning plans were designed exclusively by women. This trend also became evident in farm-journal fiction. "Nellie Bestway," subject of a short story in the

Fig. 4–7. C. W. Spalding, plan for a house in St. Louis, Missouri (1861).

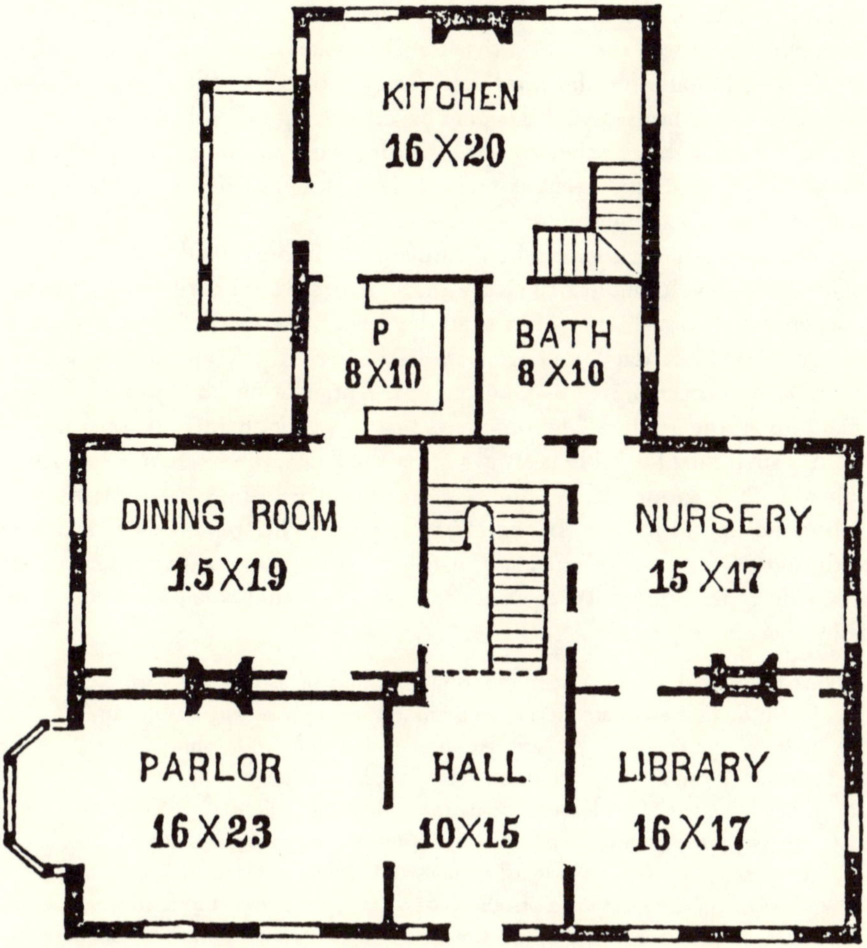

Michigan Farmer, is invited by her husband to design their home because (he says) "I expect you are going to run this part of the domestic machinery. I should hate to have you attempt the job of bossing around my barn and sheds—and—well, what's sass for the goose is sass for the gander." "Nellie" carries this separation out in her planning. She deliberately makes her cellar too small for the supply of root crops for the animals, thus reinforcing the shift in livestock care to the man's domain. Further, her kitchen door "can't be left open." This allows the kitchen worker, Nellie, a "coolness, quietness—undisturbedness—that is at once inviting and refreshing," emphasizing kitchen privacy.[42]

This trend to private kitchens followed a pattern long apparent in urban middle-class homes, but in farmer-designers' plans, segregation of the kitchen was never taken as far as it occasionally was in urban housing; for example, none of the farmer-designers ever planned a basement kitchen. Farm wives accepted the notion that the sights and sounds of kitchen work ought to be hidden, but did not themselves renounce kitchen work. Moreover, in country houses kitchens may have been cut off and their workings shielded from sight of other rooms, but they were not literally invisible in the same way that city kitchens were. Privacy for the country kitchen was compatible, for example, with a roadside view.[43]

Specialization of the kitchen's functions accompanied and complemented the development of privacy there. More planners removed dining to a separate room (Henry Hart used the term "cook-room" instead of the broader term "kitchen"). George Cattell of Harrisville, Ohio, sent a plan to the *Genesee Farmer* of 1858 (Figure 4–8). Anticipating objections to "the smallness of the kitchen," he observed that "its convenience to the dining-room is such, that the table is always set in the latter, the kitchen being used only as a cook-room." B. W. Steere, a nurseryman from Adrian, Michigan, elaborated upon this idea. In the 1860s and 1870s he frequently sent plans to the agricultural periodicals, and in 1874 *Rural Affairs* featured a number of his designs, along with an essay. Steere advocated small kitchens. His essay reveals why.

> As small kitchens have been mentioned, it may be as well to say that the intention in these plans is to have them too small for setting a table, and if there is any probability of undertaking such a thing, they should be still smaller. If there is any one thing better calculated than another to weaken digestion, mar the pleasure of eating, grate upon delicate nerves, and harrow up the feelings generally of persons of some degree of culture and refinement, it is to sit down to meals in a room impregnated with the odors of cooking, cabbage or potato water, and the greasy liquid in which meat or fish was cooked; on the other side perhaps a sink or shelf,

Fig. 4–8. George Cattell, plan for a farmhouse in Harrison County, Ohio (1858). (1) Entrance. (2) Parlor. (3) Family bedroom. (4) Dining room. (5) Kitchen. (6) Bathroom. (7) Porch. (8) Passage. (9) Pump. (10) Oven. (11) Fireplace. (12) Ash house. (13) Wood house. (14) Coal house.

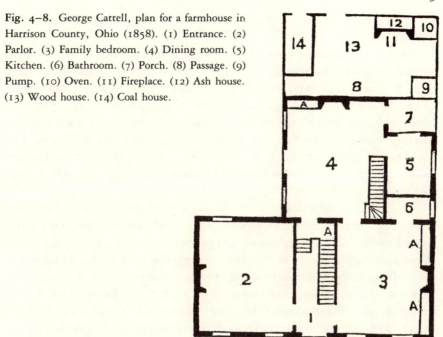

containing the endless list that will accumulate in cooking, of dirty dishes, pans, spiders, skillets . . . and what not, that in the hurry to have the meal at the exact minute, must be tossed into the nearest catch-all. Oh, what a place for that social and intellectual feast—that warm commingling of the feelings and affections which in some families can occur only at meal time.[44]

Steere associated kitchen work, and all its sights and smells, with lack of refinement. His concern for refinement and culture in dining suggests that some farm families took notice of the standards of decorum being fashioned in middle-class culture at large, in particular the increasing significance of the family meal as a symbolic ritual. The census of 1870 shows that Steere sold $1,000 worth of market produce, far more than most farmers in his neighborhood, which perhaps indicates that Steere catered to urban markets, and thus was tuned in to the currents of fashionable behavior. In fact, progressive farmhouse designers were beginning to think of eating as an activity requiring a separate space. In the 1830s and 1840s, only 30 percent of the plans had separate dining rooms, but by 1900, 70 percent possessed a specially designated room for eating. Progressive farm families even branched into suggesting appropriate topics of dinner conversation. In 1876, a *Prairie Farmer* feature on "Talking at Table" prescribed uncon-

troversial, happy topics; other suggestions in the same vein soon followed.[45]

As the separation of cooking and eating spread among the progressive
farmer-designers, the size of kitchens decreased. In the 1840s, the average
farmer-designer's kitchen was 240 feet square; by the 1890s, it had shrunk
to 187 square feet. This suggests that the kitchen was becoming the locus of
fewer different activities, and also perhaps frequented by fewer people,
whether workers or visitors. For the lone kitchen worker, a smaller kitchen
could save steps simply because of the dimensions, but it also implied the
restrictive cultural value that the kitchen was the domain of a single, female
worker.

The pages of agricultural journals give tantalizing clues as to what was
taking place in these smaller kitchens. Women often concurred in the move
toward specialization as well as toward privacy. For example, in 1884, "Mrs.
F." emphatically insisted, in a letter to *Moore's,* that "my kitchen is my work-
room. It is used neither as the family sitting-room nor as the dining room."
In *Farm Homes: Indoors and Out* (1881), Mrs. E. H. Leland included an
especially vivid illustration of the close interaction between notions of privacy and specialization. She described the modest house of a young, prom-
ising farmer couple. Upon first examination, the plan (Figure 4–9) seems
remarkably open and unspecialized, but Mrs. Leland's description shows
how the inhabitants rigorously divided the space:

> The cook-stove retires with the modesty of true merit toward the end of
> the apartment . . . everything pertaining to kitchen-work is kept a myste-
> ry until the time for tea approaches, when the bright woman opens a
> cupboard here, pulls out a drawer there, whisks off the ornamental roof of
> the retiring cook-stove, and presto!—what was a few moments ago a quiet
> sitting-room with its workbasket, open book, and rocking-chair is now an
> animated kitchen . . . While the bright woman spreads her table she arch-
> ly invites you to take a book from the library and find a seat in the
> conservatory until called for . . .

Even though the "bright woman" uses the same space for many purposes,
she keeps them strictly separated: the kitchen remains invisible until
needed, and when it is in use, the cook preserves her privacy by dispatching
the guest to the other end of the house.[46]

A rise in the number of articles and plans devoted solely to kitchens
reflected the changing purposes of the room and increased specialization of
women's work. Cabinetry became more elaborate, and more kinds of kitch-
en furnishings, especially tables, appeared. Probably the rise of the large

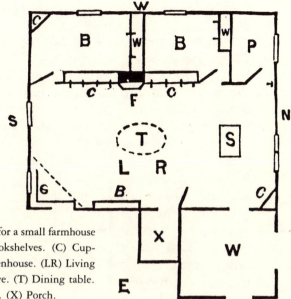

Fig. 4–9. E. H. Leland, plan for a small farmhouse (1881). (B) Bedroom and bookshelves. (C) Cupboards. (F) Fireplace. (G) Greenhouse. (LR) Living room. (P) Pantry. (S) Cookstove. (T) Dining table. (W) Woodshed and Wardrobe. (X) Porch.

Midwestern mail-order houses made such furnishings more accessible to rural families. Three examples hint at this trend.[47]

Laura E. Lyman's 1867 plan (Figure 4–10) typified many plans and descriptions in the agricultural periodicals of the 1860s and 1870s. Mrs. Lyman began by describing how her husband kept the farm gates and outbuildings in good repair. "Now I am determined," she wrote, "to equal him in my department if I can . . . Why should I not map out my domain, especially as it is a realm I love to call my own?" She arranged the work table, sink, pump, stove, and pantry, so as to "keep my work in one end of the kitchen. My wood, water, provisions, and stove are so near to each other that a step or two will bring me within reach of everything I need." She thought she could accomplish "twice as much in an hour as I could in mother's kitchen." Mrs. Lyman's reference to her kitchen as her "domain" or "realm" implies a degree of boundedness and specialization absent from earlier descriptions. Efficiency now applied to the confines of one room, not to the farmhouse as a whole, as before, when the range of women's farm work was wider.[48]

L. D. Snook's 1876 engraving (Figure 4–11) exemplified the elaborate kitchen cabinetry which began to appear later in the century. A work table is shown adjacent to the pantry; a pump, sink, shelf, and cupboards face the

A is the principal door opening on the north side, *B* another door leading into the old house; *C* the bed-room door, and *D* leads into the wood-house. There are two windows on the south side, between which stands my work table, and one on the north, throwing light on Edward's business desk, which occupies the corner between the doors *A* and *B*. At the right of *B* is my dining table, over which hangs a fruit picture, which I painted when I was a school girl. At the window on the left of my work table Edward has fasten-ed a couple of shelves, where I can have my gera-niums, and they are blooming now in that sunny ex-posure. *S* is my stove, standing just midway be-tween the sink and the pantry.

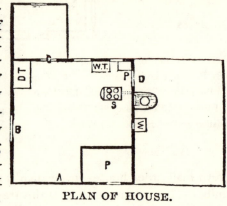

PLAN OF HOUSE.

Fig. 4–10. Laura Lyman, plan for a kitchen (1867). (A, B, C, D) Doors. (DT) Dining table. (P) Pump. (S) Stove. (W) Sliding door to wood house. (WT) Worktable.

window. The cupboards, Snook informs the reader, would store kettles and pots; the cabinet is for china storage. The stove (not depicted) is supposed to be near the work table.[49]

Mrs. R. W. Springmire of Johnson County, Iowa, in 1885 described to readers of the *Prairie Farmer's* women's column "one of the most conve-nient arrangements I have ever seen for dining-room and kitchen" (Figure 4–12). This two-sided cabinet opened into both rooms, with a passage for "victuals." The elegantly finished dining room side was for the storage and display of such items as table linens, and the plain kitchen side for dirty dishes. Again, the physical separation of genteel and "dirty" functions is evident. Yet, as Mrs. Springmire observed, it still "save[s] a great many steps."[50]

The interest in saving steps, so much in evidence earlier in the century, persisted—even the cabinetry descended from earlier experiments. But the rationale for labor-saving had changed. Efficiency in the kitchen no longer

Fig. 4–11. L. D. Snook, design for a kitchen (1876). (B) Dish rack. (E) Sink. (F) Bracketed shelf. (H) China closet. (K, P) Closets.

Fig. 4–12. Mrs. R. W. Springmire's design for connecting kitchen and dining room (1885). (Left) Dining room cupboard opening into kitchen. (Right) Kitchen cupboard opening into dining room.

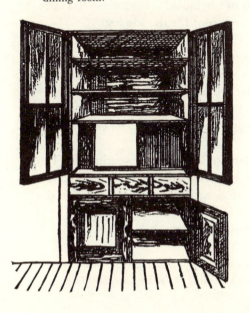

served chiefly to increase farm production; it now served the purpose of reducing household drudgery so that women could be healthier.[51] Snook observed in 1870 that the most important reason for kitchen convenience was to preserve the mother's health: "duty to herself is duty to her children." Mrs. D. W. Case, Dodge County, Wisconsin, agreed. "Give us wives better and more convenient houses, and pay less money to the doctor."

A piece on "Improving Your Old-Fashioned Kitchen" (1884) summed up the transformation. "Mary Edwood" portrayed the traditional country kitchen as the family living room. Guests entered there, the family gathered there, and all the while the kitchen work went on, making the kitchen the "business center of the farm." An earlier generation had used exactly the same phrase in a positive way. "Mary Edwood" however condemned the arrangement, recommending that the wide-awake farmer cast away this anachronism, and instead entertain the family and guests in the sitting room, equipping the kitchen with proper work tables, closets, and pump. In this way, the wife could prepare a "better meal, in quicker time," than in a crowd.[52]

During this period of transition planners began to relocate the kitchen, moving it to a sunny place, or orienting it toward the public highway, or both. In 1857 Lewis Lorenzo Pierce, a carpenter from East Jaffrey, New Hampshire, presented a plan to the *American Agriculturist*. He explained its unorthodox arrangement: "It brings the kitchen to the front and pleasant part of the house, where in my opinion, it should always be, instead of placing it in some isolated part of the L. How foolish it is for a man to labor and toil for years to accumulate means to build a homestead . . . and then doom himself and his family to the rear of the block!" (Figure 2–18) Harry Hart, too, had recommended a "pleasant" spot for the kitchen.[53]

These opinions spread during the Civil War era. In the 1863 *Genesee Farmer,* for example, a farmer's wife complained that "the kitchen may be wherever there is room for it, with a view from curtainless windows of barnyard or wood-pile. . . . No wonder women look careworn." Another writer in the *American Agriculturist* (1868) insisted that the farm wife "is fairly entitled to a cheerful outlook from her window . . . where pigs and poultry do not intrude."[54]

In succeeding years, farmhouse plans reflected these sentiments. The convention of front parlors and rear kitchens still predominated, but a significant number of plans experimented with new orientations for the most heavily used rooms. L. D. Snook's 1869 plan in *Moore's* (Figure 4–13) placed the kitchen (right) along the front axis of the house:[55]

> The plan or idea of having the kitchen situated in one of the rear rooms of the house, or in such a position that a direct view of the highway from the

Fig. 4–13. L. D. Snook, design for a farmhouse in Yates County, New York (1869).

kitchen window is impossible. [sic] Within the kitchen walls the house-wife is compelled to spend a great portion of her time in the prosecution of domestic duties. Who is able to give good reasons to excuse this old-fogy style of architecture? Ask the tens of 1000's of American farmer's wives, who spend a great portion of their lives in the daily monotonous labor of kitchen duty, and as far as my observation extends, their almost unanimous answer would be . . . If I were ever . . . to have the planning of another house, the kitchen would occupy a front and sightly position, and not be . . . secluded . . . from an immediate view of the moving panorama of highway travel.

During the 1870s and 1880s, house plans more commonly featured kitchens facing some sort of public view. S. Goss's plan of 1871 replied to those readers who had requested a kitchen from which "the main road could be seen." Other plans are similar. The ground plan and elevation of a "$6,000 Farm House" in *Moore's* (1870) put the main axis of the building parallel to the road (Figures 4–14, 4–15). This design shows how visual subordination and isolation of the kitchen was compatible with a roadside

Fig. 4–14. (Above) Anonymous design for a "$6,000 farmhouse" (1870). Elevation.

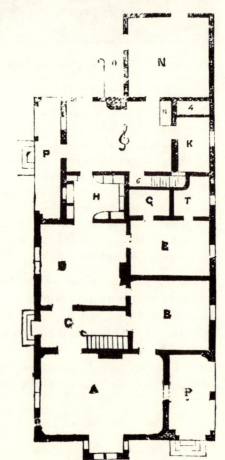

Fig. 4–15. (Right) "$6,000 farmhouse" plan. (A) Parlor. (B) Library. (C) Hall. (D) Living room. (E) Bedroom. (F) Bath (mislabeled 'T'). (G) Closet. (H) Pantry. (I) Kitchen. (K) Storeroom. (M) Woodshed. (N) Kitchen sink. (O) Outside stairs. (4) Cistern. (6) Back stair. (P) Porches.

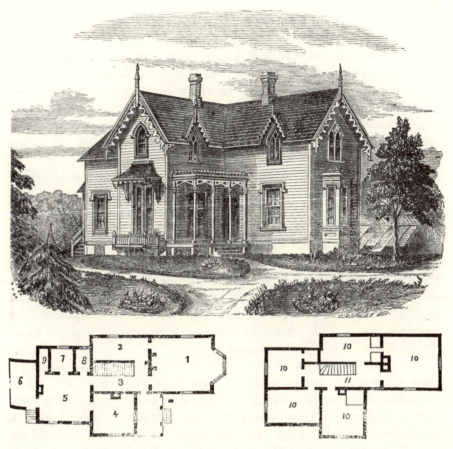

Fig. 4–16. Edgar Sanders, design for a house in Lake View, Illinois (1866). Elevation and plan. (Left) *Ground Plan:* (1) Parlor. (2) Library. (3) Hall. (4) Living room. (5) Dining room. (6) Kitchen. (7) Pantry. (8) Closet for children's clothes. (9) Stairs. (Right) *Chamber Plan:* (10) Chambers. (11) Hall.

location. The kitchen wing (at the left in the elevation) is clearly subordinated to the main block, and the pantry (H) separates kitchen from living room. At the same time, the kitchen faces outward, as does the main part of the house. Edgar Sanders, a florist from Lake View, Illinois (Figure 4–16), in 1866 built a Gothic cottage "arranged to suit two fronts, being on a prominent corner lot." The kitchen, dining room, and living/sitting room all faced the road and shared a southern exposure. The privacy envisioned for the kitchen, then, was internal, not privacy from outside.[56]

Other planners also paid more attention to the house's orientation. L. L. Pierce's 1865 plan was "drawn to face east, to bring the kitchen on the south side, so as to receive the sun all day in the short days of winter, which

makes it healthy, saves fuel and makes it warm and pleasant for the cultivation of flowers, etc." Mrs. Leland, in *Farm Homes,* devoted close attention to
this issue: windows, she declared, let "heaven" in, allowing glimpses of the
world outside. She contrasted a "House Without Sunlight" to a "Well
Lighted House" (Figure 4–17). Another plan in her book, by a "young
farmer's wife," received special praise for its cheerful, sunny rooms. She
had "dreamed it out upon paper until she had cheerfulness and utility
successfully combined." The plan gave a winter kitchen south and east
exposures, and the summer kitchen windows on north, east, and south.[57]

Warney Wilson's house in Beverly, Ohio, shows how one farmer carried
out these ideas. Wilson, a dairyman and nurseryman, built his house in 1870
on "an elevated piece of ground, with fine views . . . of the Muskingum
River" (Figure 4–18). He pointed out that "the sun visits each room in the
course of the day" and in fact, the kitchen faced east to catch the morning
sun. He also swung it around to face the roadside (Figure 4–19). A corridor
between washroom and pantry carefully cut off the kitchen from the dining
room. In keeping with the growing class separation on the farm, Wilson had
hired hands to look after his dairy herd and he provided for separate quarters for them (F on the second-story plan).[58]

An 1875 atlas engraving of Wilson's house shows how women's work
space was changing (Figure 4–20). The veranda (M on the plan) served as an
extension of the kitchen. Trees were planted between kitchen and road,
perhaps to allow a screened view of the road. Straight through the kitchen
and to the back of the house, the well, cistern, and coal house defined the
boundaries of the housewife's more arduous work. I use the term "boundaries" here because the continuum between house and field apparently was
broken on Wilson's farm. His description indicates that the house was
surrounded not by a pasture lot for his herd (which occupied 1¼ acres and
was bordered with nut trees), but by "garden, ¾ acre; lawn 1 acre; orchard, 2
acres . . . protected by [an] evergreen windbreak." The orchard, more formal and elaborate than its predecessors of an earlier generation, no longer
formed an integral part of the household space. Mrs. Wilson, whether she
looked from her kitchen to front or to back, would gaze upon carefully
designed "grounds," not open fields. Even the dairy cows were framed by
nut trees.

Perhaps the Wilson farmstead was the realization of a dream expressed
by "Beatrix" in the *Michigan Farmer:* "the squealing of pigs and the lowing
of cattle are pleasant to the ear of their owner; they remind him of the clink
and rustle of gold and greenbacks . . . but then cash value is the same if they
are kept at a respectful distance." "Beatrix's" ideal was a "high and long

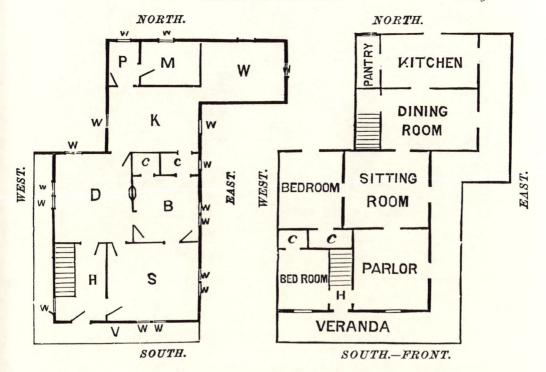

Fig. 4–17. E. H. Leland, comparison of a plan for a house with sunlight to one without sunlight (1881). (Left) "A well-lighted house." (B) Bedroom. (D) Dining room. (H) Hall. (K) Kitchen. (M) Milk room. (P) Pantry. (S) Sitting room. (V) Veranda. (W) Wood house. (c) Clothes press and bathroom. (w) Windows. (Right) "House without sunlight."

trellis, covered with grape vines . . . shutting off the view of all save well-shingled roofs and painted weather-boards."[59]

By 1885, the social class filtering and ideas on spatial reorientation had reached a point where a consensus on progressive farmhouse design had developed, especially regarding the kitchen's position. When the *Prairie Farmer* sponsored a house-design competition in that year, most of the respondents distinguished between cooking and eating space and between servants and family, if indeed they had servants at all. Moreover, all gave the kitchen more than one outlook and most, like M. L. Gould of Polk County, Nebraska (Figure 4–21), gave it a "cheerful outlook" fronting the road.

Relocation of the farm kitchen signified an important reorientation of aspects of northern farm life in the post-Civil War period. Most obvious, the shift in kitchen location confirmed a change from the old cooperative

Fig. 4–18. Warney Wilson house, Beverly, Ohio (1870), photographed in 1985.

Fig. 4–19. Warney Wilson house, plan (1873). (Left) *Ground Plan:* (A, L, M) Verandahs. (B) Hall. (C) Parlor. (D) Dining room. (E) Library. (F) Kitchen. (G) Pantry. (H) Storeroom. (I) Coal room. (K) Washroom. (N) Cistern. (O) Well. (b) Bath. (c) Closets. (f) Back stair. (p) Pump. (s) Shelves. (t) Sink. (Right) *Chamber Plan:* (A) Hall. (B, H, K) Bedrooms. (C) Closets. (D) Linen closet. (E) Attic stairs. (F) Servant's bedroom. (G) Garret. (R) Roof.

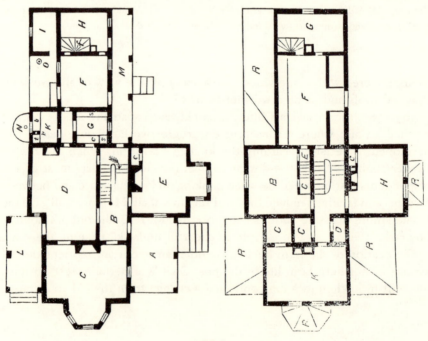

Fig. 4–20. Warney Wilson house, elevation (1875).

Fig. 4–21. M. L. Gould, plan for a farmhouse in Polk County, Nebraska (1885). (Left) First story. (Right) Second story.

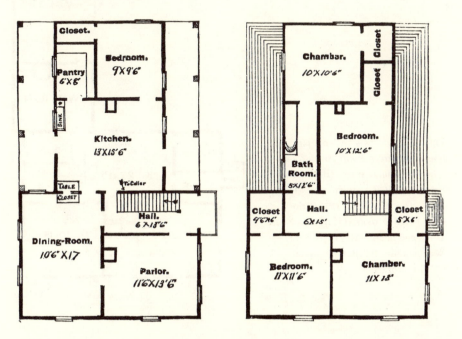

ideal, in which the women's sphere—the kitchen, dairy, and poultry yard—faced and even overlapped the men's world of barnyard and fields. The earlier image of the farm as a cooperative "bee-hive" no longer applied. Earlier, Lewis Falley Allen had recommended that "one side and adjoining the house, should be the garden, the clothes-yard, and the bee-house, which last should always stand in full sight, and facing the most frequented room, say the kitchen." His plan (Figure 4–22) fulfilled his prescription. By the 1870s, farmer-planners had rejected this in favor of an attractive view,

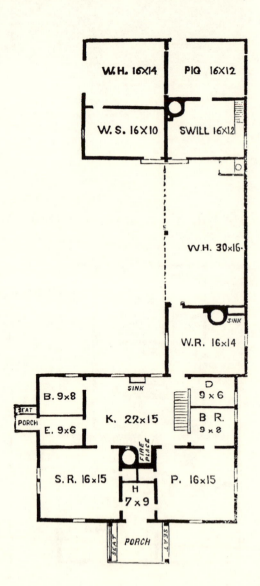

Fig. 4–22. Lewis Allen, farm-house plan from *Rural Architecture* (1852). Ground floor. (B, D, E) Pantries. (B.R.) Bedroom. (H) Hall. (K) Kitchen. (P) Parlor. (S.R.) Sitting room. (W.H. 30 × 16) Wood house. (W.H. 16 × 14) Wagonhouse. (W.R.) Washroom. (W.S.) Workshop.

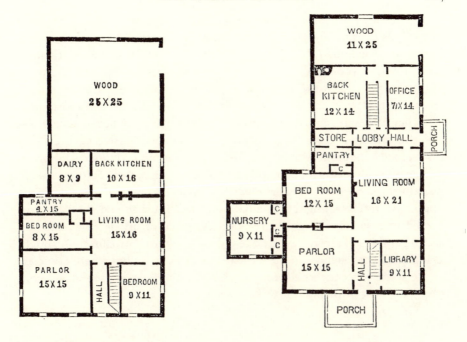

Fig. 4–23. Alteration of a farmhouse plan (1860). (Left) Before. (Right) After.

suggesting that farm women sought contact with the outside society, with passers-by on their way to and from town. Social contacts broke up the monotony of household work. Looking out from the kitchen wing, they tried to forget the farmstead that lay beyond.[60]

About 1860, *Rural Affairs* published an article about the "alteration of an Old House" in Lamoille County, Vermont. "Before" and "After" plans (Figure 4–23), reveal the increasing separation between the worlds of work and family. The "after" plan eliminates the dairy room altogether, indicating perhaps that dairying was shifting to the man's domain. A "lobby" intervenes between kitchen and living room, reinforcing the notion of the kitchen's isolation. A nursery and a library are incorporated—evidence, perhaps, of growing concern with child nurture and self-culture. Finally, an office occupies a small space across from the kitchen. The office, although rare, deserves notice because it represents an extreme in the separation of home and business. *Rural Affairs* praised the office as "a room which every country and city resident should have, who wishes to avoid doing business in the parlor or settling accounts among the kitchen dishes." The office (later more frequently adopted) constituted another challenge to the old notion of the kitchen as a "business room."[61]

The progressive farm family's work culture and work space changed primarily as a result of industrialization and urbanization. Particularly where gender was concerned, the division of labor on the progressive farmstead more closely approached that of urban middle-class families. House plans reveal the physical form that new expectations assumed. Laborers were removed; the farmhouse kitchen was isolated, specialized, and reoriented. Efficiency in design, applied by earlier generations to the house as a whole, now concentrated upon the kitchen. Although progressive agriculturists still regarded the farm woman's domestic work as an economic support to the farm, values of womanhood associated with urban culture gained strength among progressive farm families. Where work was concerned, the progressive farmer-designers' mediation between urban and rural cultures seemed to result in a large degree of acceptance of urban forms and values.[62] But the influence was not one-sided. The term "urbanization" might be applied to the changes in the farmstead's work areas, but where domestic leisure space was concerned, rural designers would make a significant contribution to the reshaping of urban vernacular.

NOTES

1. "Hail Columbia," "Work, Work, Work," *PF* 47 (January 29, 1876): 35. For an earlier poetical "Complaint of the Farmer's Wife," see *MF* 13 (January 1855): 20. These poems were probably inspired by Thomas Hood's popular "Song of the Shirt" (1843) reprinted in Miriam Schneir, ed., *Feminism: The Essential Historical Writings* (New York: Vintage Books, 1972), 58–61.

2. "Farmers' Daughters," *GF* 8 (March 1847): 76; "The Farmer's Wife," *AC* n.s. 6 (September 1849): 281. The equation of increased prosperity with increased labor was common. See, for example, Mrs. H. C. Johns, "The Farmer's Home," *Transactions,* Illinois State Board of Agriculture 6 (1865–66): 293. See also Ruth Schwartz Cowan, *More Work for Mother* (New York: Basic Books, 1983).

3. *MF* n.s. 1 (December 3, 1859): 350.

4. Paul W. Gates, *The Farmer's Age* (New York: Holt, Rinehart, & Winston, 1960), 166; Robert Leslie Jones, *History of Agriculture in Ohio to 1880* (Kent, Oh.: Kent State University Press, 1983), 269; Howard Russell, *A Long, Deep Furrow* (Hanover, N.H.: University Press of New England, 1976), 421; Ephraim Perkins, notices in the *PF* 8 (February 1848): 62, and *PF* 8 (August 1848): 204; sales figures, *PF* 9 (July 1849): 212.

The general literature on mechanization of agriculture is extensive. Leo Rogin's study of *The Introduction of Farm Machinery* (Berkeley: University of California Press, 1931) remains an essential source. More recent studies include Paul David, "The Mechanization of Reaping in the Antebellum Midwest," in Henry Rosovsky, ed., *Industrialization in Two Systems* (New York: Wiley, 1966); Robert Ankli, "The Coming of the Reaper," in Gerald Nash, ed., *Issues in Economic History* (Lexington, Mass.: D. C. Heath, 1980), 191–198; Alan Olmstead, "The

Mechanization of Reaping and Mowing, 1833–1870," *Journal of Economic History* 35 (June 1975): 327–352; William R. Baron and Anne Bridges, "Making Hay in New England: Maine as a Case Study, 1800–1850," *Ag. History* 57 (April 1983): 165–181; Clarence Danhof, *Change in Agriculture: The Northern United States, 1820–1870* (Cambridge: Harvard University Press, 1969), chapters 8 and 9; Wayne Rasmussen, "The Civil War: A Catalyst of Agricultural Revolution," *Ag. History* 39 (October 1965): 187–194; and "The Impact of Technological Change on American Agriculture 1862–1962,"*Journal of Economic History* 22 (December 1962): 578–591; Paul Gates, *Agriculture and the Civil War* (New York: Knopf, 1965); Fred Shannon, *The Farmer's Last Frontier: Agriculture, 1860–1897* (1945. Reprint, White Plains, N.Y.: M. E. Sharpe, 1971), chapter 6. The reaper may be the most literal occurrence of the "Machine in the Garden." Leo Marx's book of that title (New York: Oxford University Press, 1964) deals primarily with literary sources in studying the relationships between technology and the pastoral ideal in American thought. If the agricultural periodicals are an accurate indicator of sentiment, the farmers who bought reapers and mowers did not express the ambivalence about technology which Marx finds pervades the literary sources.

5. Farmers were also beginning to pay cash for fertilizer, another capital expense not previously required. See Richard Wines, *Fertilizer in America: From Waste Recycling to Resource Exploitation* (Philadelphia: Temple University Press, 1985). Information on Edwards is from Harold Benson, "The Mowing Machine that Disappeared," unpublished manuscript, courtesy of Bill Greene, Jr., Historian, Allegany County Museum, Belmont, New York.

6. "Mary," "Advice to a Young Housekeeper," *OC* 3 (April 15, 1847): 61. "In the Kitchen," *PF* n.s. 20 (November 2, 1867): 273; "P," *GF* 22 (March 1861): 60; "H.T.B.," "Labor-Saving Indoors," *Moore's* 11 (December 8, 1860): 390. See also Mrs. J. L. Trowbridge, "Relations of Women to the Labor and Duties of Agriculture," Wisconsin Dairymen's Association *Report* 3 (1875–76): 38–40. Other statements of the disparity abounded. Examples include: "Only One Pair of Hands," *PF* 57 (February 7, 1885): 90–91; "Farmer's Daughter," *MF* 12 (July 1854): 211; "Domestic Helps," *MF* 3rd ser. 12 (November 29, 1881): 7; "From a Farmer's Daughter," *MF* 12 (June 1854): 180–181.

A few dissenting views did appear. See, for example, the story "John Merrill's Theory," in which a woman's health is saved by patent devices (*PF* n.s. 18 (September 22, 1866): 190).

7. Sarah McMahon, "A Comfortable Subsistence: A History of Diet in New England, 1630–1850," (Ph.D. diss., Brandeis University, 1982). William Bowers, *The Country Life Movement* (Port Washington, N.Y.: Kennikat Press, 1974), 126; Susan Strasser, *Never Done* (New York: Pantheon, 1982); Ruth Schwartz Cowan, *More Work for Mother*. Dorothy Brady, in "Relative Prices in the Nineteenth Century," *Journal of Economic History* 24 (June 1964): 145–203, makes a number of stimulating but largely unsubstantiated statements about the labor-saving value of various small implements; further basic research is necessary. On the physical effects of cheesemaking, see the *Annual Report*, New York State Cheese Manufacturers Association 1–2 (1864): 23, 67.

8. "A. Zalia," "Help for Housewives," *Moore's* 23 (April 8, 1871): 227. The reference to an implied central kitchen may have been drawn from the widely publicized discussions of "cooperative housekeeping." See Dolores Hayden, *The Grand Domestic Revolution: A History of Feminist Designs for American Homes, Neighborhoods, and Cities* (Cambridge, Mass.: MIT Press, 1981), section 3. See also Judith McGaw, "Women and the History of American Technology," *Signs* 7 (Summer 1982): 798–829.

9. "Farmer's Wives," *PF* 44 (April 26, 1873): 131. For a very similar story, see *MF* 3rd ser. 12 (May 3, 1881): 7. This view of the physical effects of overwork is discussed by Joan

Brumberg, "Zenanas and Girlless Villages: The Ethnography of American Evangelical Women," *JAH* 69 (September 1982): 347–372.

10. General trends in northern agriculture from 1850 are described in several works. See especially Fred Shannon, *The Farmer's Last Frontier,* chapters 6, 11, 12; Gates, *Agriculture and the Civil War;* Margaret Pabst, *Agricultural Trends in the Connecticut Valley 1800–1900,* Smith College Studies in History, vol. 26 (Northampton, Mass.: The Department of History of Smith College, 1941); Gates, "Agricultural Change in New York," *New York History* 50 (April 1969): 115–141; Margaret Beattie Bogue, "The Lake and the Fruit: The Making of Three Farm-Type Areas," *Ag. History* 59 (October 1985): 493–523. On western agriculture, see Allan Bogue, *From Prairie to Corn Belt: Farming in the Illinois and Iowa Prairies in the Nineteenth Century* (Chicago: University of Chicago Press, 1963), 239; Walter Prescott Webb, *The Great Plains* (Boston: Ginn and Co., 1931); Gilbert Fite, *The Farmer's Frontier 1865–1900* (New York: Holt, Rinehart, & Winston, 1966).

11. Thomas W. Pirtle, *History of the Dairy Industry* (1926. Reprint, Chicago: Mojonnier Brothers, 1973); Fred Bateman, "Improvement in American Dairy Farming, 1850–1910: A Quantitative Analysis," *Journal of Economic History* 28 (June 1968): 255–273; H. E. Erdman, "The Associated Dairies of New York as Precursors of Agricultural Cooperatives," *Ag. History* 36 (April 1962): 82–90; Eric Brunger, "Dairying and Urban Development in New York State, 1850–1900," *Ag. History* 29 (October 1955): 169–174; Loyal Durand, Jr., "The Migration of Cheese Manufacturing in the United States," *Annals,* Association of American Geographers 42 (December 1952): 263–283; and "Historical and Economic Geography of Dairying in Northern New York," *Geographical Review* 57 (January 1967): 24–48; Eric Lampard, *The Rise of the Dairy Industry in Wisconsin* (Madison: State Historical Association of Wisconsin, 1963).

12. Mrs. H. C. Johns, "The Farmer's Home," Illinois State Agricultural Society *Transactions* 6 (1865–66): 297; Blake McKelvey, "The Flower City: Center of Nurseries and Fruit Orchards," Rochester Historical Society *Publications* 18 (1940): 121–169; U. P. Hedrick, *A History of Horticulture in America to 1860* (New York: Oxford University Press, 1950), chapter 10. The labor force of fruit- and vegetable-growing operations are described in *Moore's* 60 (September 1, 1900): 589; and *Moore's* 22 (October 22, 1870): 265.

13. "A Word of Advice," *MF* 15 (April 1857): 117–118.

14. For a discussion of the "de-feminization" of agriculture in western Europe, see Bengt Ankarloo, "Agriculture and Women's Work: Directions of Change in the West, 1700–1900," *Journal of Family History* 5 (Summer 1979): 111–120. Corlann Bush, "The Barn is His, the House is Mine: Agricultural Technology and Sex Roles," in George Daniels and Mark Rose, eds., *Energy and Transport* (Beverly Hills: Sage Publications, 1982), 235–259, has found a similar transformation in Idaho in more recent times. Bush documents the transition as it relates to the replacement of horse-powered machinery by gasoline-powered tractors. The findings here suggest that a similar change was already taking place in the horse-power era, as farm women participated less in actual production, but more heavily in support services such as boarding harvest hands.

15. Mrs. E. P. Allerton, "Dairy Factory System—a Blessing to the Farmer's Wife," Wisconsin Dairymen's Association *Report* 3 (1875): 18; *Annual Report,* New York State Cheese Manufacturers' Association 1–2 (1864): 67.

16. "Mrs. Homespun," *PF* 44 (January 4, 1873): 3; *PF* n.s. 3 (April 21, 1859): 233; Faye Dudden, *Serving Women: Household Service in Nineteenth-Century America* (Middletown, Conn.: Wesleyan University Press, 1983). "Children's Fashions," *MF* 3rd ser. 12 (October 18, 1881): 7; Mrs. M. E. Woodford, "The Fashionable Lady's Lament," *PF* 47 (January 15, 1876): 19.

17. "Amateur Housekeeper," "Domestic Bondage," *MF* 3rd ser. 14 (May 8, 1883): 7;

household column, *PF* 64 (June 3, 1893): 10; Merrill K. Bennett and Rosamond Peirce, "Change in the American National Diet, 1879–1959," *Food Research Institute Studies* 2 (May 1961): 95–121.

18. Figures on creamery centralization are from Eric Brunger, "Changes in the New York State Dairying Industry," Ph.D. diss., Syracuse University, 1954. A "Word to Farmers' Daughters" [*AA* 47 (June 1888): 229] exposed the disadvantages of this transition for farm women, who, the author argued, "have to contend for existence under the pressure of a severely restricted area of usefulness." The author's solution, however, was based on the false assumption that prices for home-made goods were high.

19. "One of the Wives," "Do Farmers' Wives Pay?," *CG* 28 (November 29, 1866): 354–355. For more responses see *CG* 29 (March 21, 1867): 195; *CG* 29 (April 11, 1867): 242; *CG* (April 18, 1867): 259–260; *CG* (May 2, 1867): 290.

20. J. P. Smith, "My Opinion," *MF* 3rd ser. 12 (February 1, 1881): 7; For further discussion of the issues involved, see: "J.M.J.," "Husbands and Wives," *PF* n.s. 7 (May 23, 1861): 334; *MF* 3rd ser. 12 (March 15, 1881): 7; *MF* 3rd ser. 12 (March 29, 1881): 7; *MF* 3rd ser. 12 (April 5, 1881): 7; *MF* 3rd ser. 12 (April 19, 1881): 7; *MF* 3rd ser. 12 (May 3, 1881): 7; *MF* 3rd ser. 12 (June 21, 1881): 7; Harriet Connor Brown, *Grandmother Brown's Hundred Years* (New York: Blue Ribbon Books, 1929), 175.

21. "A Farmer's Wife," "To Farmers' Wives," *MF* n.s. 1 (January 1, 1859): 15; "Claims of Farmers' Wives," *MF* n.s. 1 (December 3, 1859): 390; "Myrtle" of Oneida County, "Does It Pay to Be A Woman?," *CG* 29 (April 4, 1867): 227. See also: "Farmer's Wife," "Claims of Farmers' Wives," *MF* n.s. 1 (December 24, 1859): 414. Some women dissented from the complaints about drudgery, blaming farm women themselves for lacking "faculty." See "C.A.B.," "Learning How to Live," *PF* 44 (May 31, 1873): 171. Significantly, by the late 1880s and early 1890s, the women's columns were running features on ways to make money, perhaps an indication of lost skills. See "Housekeepers' Club," *PF* 60 (August 25, 1888): 552.

22. "May Maple," "But One Mother," *Moore's* 24 (July 8, 1871): 19; "C.A.B.," "Learning How to Live," *PF* 44 (May 31, 1873): 171. The capable housewife came under increasing criticism as drudgery became a concern. See "A Chapter on Housekeeping," *MF* 15 (August 1857): 247–248; "Mrs. Hiram Jones," *PF* n.s. 3 (January 27, 1859): 60; Mrs. Gage, "My Neighbor Mrs. C.," *PF* n.s. 5 (March 28, 1860): 203.

23. "Grace," "Voice from within the Treadmill," *PF* 44 (August 9, 1873): 259; William Coggeshall, "Easy Warren," *MF* n.s. 2 (March 10, 1860): 78; "How to Train a Husband," *PF* 53 (July 8, 1882): 214; "Woman's Rights to a Woodpile," *PF* 44 (January 4, 1873): 2. "Let the Boys Help," *PF* 48 (January 20, 1877): 19; "Housework on the Farm," *MF* 3rd ser. 12 (February 15, 1881): 7; "Another County Heard From," *MF* 3rd ser. 12 (March 29, 1881): 7; "My Labor-saving Husband," *Moore's* 11 (March 10, 1860): 79, "Thoughtlessness of Men," *Moore's* 11 (April 30, 1860): 286.

24. Marie Estelle, "It Don't Pay," *PF* n.s. 17 (February 10, 1866): 58. "The Wifely Rights Which Daisy Desires," *MF* 3rd ser. 12 (May 31, 1881): 7. "Take a Vacation," *MF* 3rd ser. 12 (August 20, 1881): 7; "Mrs. Franklin's Economies," *PF* 60 (August 18, 1888): 540. Daniel Rodgers, *The Work Ethic in Industrializing America* (Chicago: University of Chicago Press, 1978), 102–106, discusses the emerging notion of the vacation.

25. "Housekeeping Economy," *Rural Affairs* 6 (1870–72): 200–209.

26. On the subscription system, see John William Tebbel, *A History of Book Publishing in the United States,* 5 vols. (New York: R. R. Bowker, 1972–1981), 1: 206, 239. Edgar Martin, *The Standard of Living in 1860* (Chicago: University of Chicago Press, 1942), chapter 11, points out that the invention of electrotype in 1850 spurred a great increase in the output of books. Frank

Luther Mott's *History of American Magazines,* 5 vols. (Cambridge: Harvard University Press, 1938–68), provides a context for the figures on agricultural periodicals found in A. L. Demaree, *The American Agricultural Press 1819–1860* (New York: Columbia University Press, 1940). Vernon J. Brown, "Country Life in the Eighties," *Michigan History* 17 (Spring 1933): 175–191.

27. "In the Kitchen," *PF* n.s. 19 (December 21, 1867): 386; "Farmer's Wives and Daughters," *CG* 28 (September 27, 1866): 210; "How Women Become Insane," *MF* n.s. 3 (October 26, 1861): 365.

For a provocative assessment of the familial links between rural and urban cultures in an earlier era, see Richard Bushman, "Family Security in the Transition from Farm to City, 1750–1850," *Working Papers,* Regional Economic History Research Center 4 (1981): 26–61. On factory-produced foodstuffs, see Strasser, *Never Done;* Dudden, *Serving Women;* Earl Hayter, *The Troubled Farmer* (De Kalb: Northern Illinois University Press, 1968), chapter 4; Edgar Martin, *The Standard of Living in 1860.* Three articles investigate the spread of urban amenities to rural areas. See T. D. S. Bassett, "A Case Study of Urban Impact on Rural Society: Vermont, 1840–1880," *Ag. History* 30 (January 1956): 28–35; Richard D. Brown, "Emergence of Urban Society in Rural Massachusetts," *JAH* 61 (June 1974): 29–52; Jack S. Blocker, "Market Integration, Urban Growth and Economic Change in an Ohio County 1850–1880," *Ohio History* 90 (Autumn 1981): 298–317.

28. The body of literature on the cult of domesticity is extensive. A list of major contributions begins with Barbara Welter, "The Cult of True Womanhood," *AQ* 18 (Summer 1966): 151–174. Nancy Cott, *The Bonds of Womanhood: "Woman's Sphere" in New England, 1780–1835* (New Haven: Yale University Press, 1977), and Mary Ryan, *Cradle of the Middle Class: The Family in Oneida County, New York, 1790–1865* (New York: Cambridge University Press, 1981), elaborate on the nature and meaning of nineteenth-century domesticity. Kathryn K. Sklar, *Catharine Beecher: A Study in American Domesticity* (New Haven: Yale University Press, 1973), is a biography of a major theoretician of domesticity. Carroll Smith-Rosenberg, *Religion and the Rise of the American City* (Ithaca, N.Y.: Cornell University Press, 1971); Keith Melder, "Ladies Bountiful," *New York History* 48 (July 1967): 231–254; and Joan Jacobs Brumberg, *Mission for Life* (New York: Free Press, 1980), contribute to explanations of evangelical culture. Ann Douglas, *The Feminization of American Culture* (New York: Knopf, 1977), approaches the question mostly through literary figures. For indications of farm women's interest, see Gail Hamilton [Mary A. Dodge], "Farmers' Homes and Wives," *PF* 43 (May 4, 1872): 139; "Farmers' Wives," *PF* 45 (April 25, 1874): 134; "House vs. Home," *MF* 3rd ser. 13 (February 5, 1882): 7.

29. Jared Van Wagenen, *Days of My Years* (Cooperstown, N.Y.: New York State Historical Association, 1962); Isaac Phillips Roberts, *Autobiography of a Farm Boy* (Albany, N.Y.: J. B. Lyon, 1916), 52; Thomas Woody, *History of Women's Education in the United States,* 2 vols. (New York: Science Press, 1929), 2: 415. See also Barbara Miller Solomon, *In the Company of Educated Women* (New Haven: Yale University Press, 1985); *Home Cottage Seminary Catalog,* Clinton, New York, 1856.

30. *Moore's* 32 (September 18, 1875): 195; *Moore's* 32 (December 4, 1875): 371; *Moore's* 30 (April 3, 1874): 225; *Moore's* 33 (February 5, 1876): 63; *Moore's* 33 (January 8, 1876): 31; *Moore's* 33 (March 18, 1876): 191. An example of the common critique of women's education can be found in Mrs. Gage's "Housekeeper's Diary," *PF* n.s. 3 (February 17, 1859): 108.

31. *Monroe County Directory 1869–70* (Syracuse, 1869), 265; *History of Monroe County New York* (Philadelphia: Everts, Ensign, & Everts, 1877), 258; U.S. Census, Population and Agriculture Schedules, 1850, 1860; Agriculture Schedule, 1870, 1880; New York State Census,

1855, 1865; *Atlas of Monroe County New York* (New York: F. W. Beers, 1872), 105, 112; communication with Katherine W. Thompson, Rush Town Historian.

32. Mark Girouard, *Life in the English Country House* (Harmondsworth, U.K.: Penguin, 1980) points out that the English gentry began to segregate servants quite early.

33. "Working Men's Cottages," *Rural Affairs* 1 (1855–57): 25–27; *CG* 38 (June 5, 1873): 366. David Schob, in *Farm Hands and Plow Boys* (Urbana: Univeristy of Illinois Press, 1975), mentions that laborers were housed in separate cottages as early as 1819, but that the practice grew more popular in the 1850s.

34. David Smith, "Middle Range Farming in the Civil War Era: Life on a Farm in Seneca County in 1862," *New York History* 48 (October 1967): 353–363; Isaac Phillips Roberts, *Autobiography of a Farm Boy*, 154; Thomas and Mary Atkeson, *Pioneering in Agriculture* (New York: Orange Judd, 1937), 98. David Maldwyn Ellis, in his *History of New York State* (Ithaca, N.Y.: Cornell University Press, 1967), mentions that in the later nineteenth century, the hired man usually boarded with the farm family if he were single, but that there were many tenant houses too. Anne Gertrude Sneller, *A Vanished World* (Syracuse: Syracuse University Press, 1964), 40, 285, on the other hand, recalls that the hired men and women were always "part of the family and treated as such."

35. "Working-Men's Cottages," *Rural Affairs* 1 (1855–57): 25–26; M. Hill, "Laborers' Cottages—Farmers' Wives," *GF* 19 (January 1858): 16; *Moore's* 20 (February 27, 1869): 133.

36. The family as asylum is discussed by Christopher Lasch, "The Discovery of the Asylum," in *The World of Nations* (New York: Knopf, 1973), and *Haven in a Heartless World* (New York: Basic Books, 1977); Mary Ryan, *Cradle*; Kirk Jeffrey, "The Family as Utopian Retreat from the City," *Soundings* 55 (Spring 1972): 21–42; and David Rothman, *The Discovery of the Asylum* (Boston: Little, Brown, 1971).

37. D. G. Mitchell, *My Farm of Edgewood* (New York: Charles Scribner, 1863), 74; "Farmers and Their Hands," *PF* 46 (February 6, 1875): 41. Different regions experienced this development at varying times. Robert Gross, "Culture and Cultivation: Agriculture and Society in Thoreau's Concord," *JAH* 69 (June 1982): 42–62, suggests that in Concord, paid labor replaced family labor as early as the 1820s. In Illinois, according to David Schob, *Hired Hands and Plowboys*, attitudes regarding hired labor began to change during the 1850s. Gates, in *Agriculture and the Civil War*, chapter 8, detects significant change by the Civil War period. Susan Geib, "Changing Works," (Ph.D. diss., Boston University, 1981), documents the disappearance of informal labor exchanges. Lawanda Cox's compelling figures demonstrate the crystallization between 1865 and 1900 of these new patterns in agricultural labor. See Lawanda Cox, "The American Agricultural Wage Earner, 1865–1900," *Ag. History* 22 (April 1948): 95–114, and "Tenancy in the United States, 1865–1900," *Ag. History* 18 (July 1944): 97–105. See also Paul Taylor, "The American Hired Man: His Rise and Decline," *Land Policy Review* 6 (Spring 1943): 3–17. Not enough is known about the history of rural women to establish whether this pattern applied to female farm workers as well. Faye Dudden has demonstrated that in general women's domestic service changed from work that was performed by "helps," equal in social status, on a task basis, to work done by "domestics," of a lower class than the employer, performed on a time basis. This pattern may have prevailed in rural areas as well.

38. H. Huffman, "Plan of a Small House," *AC* 3rd ser. 6 (June 1858): 184.

39. J. J. Thomas, "Gothic Country House," *AC* 3rd ser. 4 (January 1856): 25; "Plans of Houses," *AC* 3rd ser. 9 (November 1861): 345.

40. *Moore's* 10 (May 28, 1859): 173.

41. Dore Hamilton, "Our Housekeepers' Club," *Moore's* 23 (April 1, 1871): 207; Mary

Wager-Fisher, "Concerning the System of Housework," *Moore's* 42 (January 27, 1883): 58; "Grandmother," "Pleasant Sitting-Rooms," *Moore's* 42 (March 31, 1883): 206.

42. E. L. Nye, "Chats with My Neighbors," *MF* 3rd ser. 12 (August 2, 1881): 7.

43. On architectural segregation of servants, see Blaine McKinley, "Strangers in the Gates: Employer Reactions Toward Domestic Servants in America 1825–1875" (Ph.D. diss., Michigan State University, 1969), chapter 6.

44. George Cattell, house plan, *GF* 19 (June 1858): 185; B. Steere, "House of Moderate Cost," *Rural Affairs* 7 (1873–75): 55.

45. McMahon, "Comfortable Subsistence," 210; "Talking at Table," *PF* 47 (July 29, 1876): 243.

46. "Mrs. F.," "My Kitchen Table," *Moore's* 43 (February 9, 1884): 91; Mrs. E. H. Leland, *Farm Homes: Indoors and Out* (New York: Orange Judd, 1881): 22.

47. Boris Emmet, *Catalogues and Counters: A History of Sears Roebuck and Company* (Chicago: University of Chicago Press, 1950).

48. Laura Lyman, "Letters of a Young Housekeeper," *AA* 26 (February 1867): 65.

49. L. D. Snook, "The Convenient Arrangement of a Kitchen," *AA* 35 (April 1876): 144.

50. Mrs. R. W. Springmire, "Economizing Work—Saving Steps," *PF* 57 (April 18, 1885): 251. For other examples, see *PF* 57 (February 21, 1885): 122; *PF* 57 (February 28, 1885): 139; *PF* 58 (February 6, 1886): 91.

51. Mrs. Case, "Only One Pair of Hands," *PF* 57 (May 6, 1885): 299; Snook, "A Peep into the Kitchen," *Moore's* 21 (February 26, 1870): 143.

52. Mary Edwood, "Improving Your Old-Fashioned Kitchen," *Moore's* 43 (June 21, 1884): 406.

53. L. L. Pierce, house plan, *AA* 16 (January 1857): 33.

54. "Want of Cheery Kitchens," *GF* 24 (August 1863): 257; "A Farm Wife," "Larger Yards About the House," *AA* 27 (May 1868): 190; *Moore's* 20 (September 25, 1869): 619.

55. L. D. Snook, "Farmer's Cottage," *Moore's* 20 (August 21, 1869): 533.

56. S. Goss, house plan, *Moore's* 23 (February 19, 1871): 126; "$6,000 Farm House," *Moore's* 21 (March 19, 1870): 185; "Residence of Edgar Sanders," *PF* n.s. 18 (August 18, 1866): 101.

57. L. L. Pierce, house plan, *Moore's* 16 (September 30, 1865): 309; Leland, *Farm Homes*, 19.

58. *Moore's* 26 (February 15, 1873): 105; correspondence with Mr. and Mrs. Robert Geddes and Mrs. R. K. Irvin, Lower Muskingum Historical Society; D. J. Lake, *Atlas of Washington County Ohio* (Philadelphia: Titus, Simmons & Titus, 1875): 12, 13, 86.

59. "Beatrix," "Farmers' Homes," *MF* 3rd ser. 13 (February 21, 1882): 7.

60. Lewis Falley Allen, *Rural Architecture* (New York: Orange Judd, 1860): 79–80. Thomas Hubka, at a conference on "Rural Improvement and Reform," (Bethel, Maine, October 1985) has pointed out that shifts to roadside orientation also were a response to improved heating technology.

61. "Alteration of an Old House," *Rural Affairs* 2 (1858–60): 262.

62. Paul Johnson, *A Shopkeeper's Millenium* (New York: Hill & Wang, 1978), 46, notes that in the city of Rochester, New York, "the custom of providing room and board as part of a workman's wages was alive in 1827. But it certainly was in decay." Johnson associated the conversions of the Finney revival with the economic values of a free-labor economy and classbound society. Revival converts, according to this argument, tended to be small proprietors or master workmen who tended to exclude employees from the home residence. Perhaps the movement in rural areas to provide laborers' cottages was a parallel phenomenon.

FIVE

City Parlor, Country Sitting Room

ALTHOUGH division of home and work began to resemble the urban model, the progressive farmers' culture—and their domestic space—was not uniformly "urbanized." In fact, these families developed distinctive leisure spaces which were ultimately integrated into other American domestic landscapes. Over the course of the century, farm writers and designers rejected the formal parlor, which they associated with urban customs and with conspicuous consumption, for the informal, family-centered sitting room. The story of the rural sitting room illustrates how progressive planners shaped their material culture to suit their own circumstances. In the rural press everywhere, the debate over the parlor produced a body of thought and vernacular design which explored alternatives to both urban and rural versions of this room. These alternatives were consistent with rural social patterns—especially with women's culture and with traditions of informality in social life—but were also highly ambiguous, simultaneously criticizing and imitating urban sophistication. Nonetheless, these experiments with leisure spaces resulted in a fund of experience. By the turn of the century, when most Americans had only begun to abandon the parlor, progressive farmhouse planners had been de-emphasizing, realigning, and eliminating parlors for decades.

The term "parlor" derives from the Old French *parleur,* "room used for conversation." The parlor appeared during medieval times in well-to-do European homes, and by the eighteenth century its repertoire of social uses was extensive. In colonial and early national America, the parlor was well-established as a "best room," used for tea ceremonies, clergymen's calls, weddings, and funerals. It was usually in the front of the house and contained the family's most valued possessions; often the master bedstead was among them. The parlor's heyday came in the nineteenth century, with the growth of cities and an urban culture. In the city, the room took on a new physical appearance and additional functions and meanings—so much so that it may be regarded as an index to middle-class urban culture in the nineteenth century.[1]

A traveler approaching a town, suburban, or city middle-class residence in the nineteenth century had little doubt about where the parlor was located. In a detached single-family dwelling it often faced the street or roadside, extending from the main body of the house (Figure 5–1). Where it did not form a wing, perhaps a bay window or verandah indicated its location. In a city row house (Figure 5–2), the parlor occupied the front part of the house, and was flanked by a hallway ending in an imposing front door.[2]

In plan, the parlor usually did not connect directly with other rooms. The New York City brownstone offers the most dramatic example: parlors and living areas often occupied entirely different floors. In detached houses, the parlor commonly could be entered only from a hall or vestibule, although occasionally it opened into the dining room or library. Bedrooms were rarely connected with the urban parlor; if they did, designers usually took care to disguise them.[3]

According to prescriptive literature, fiction, illustrations, "household art" books, and personal accounts, the parlor's interior (Figure 5–3) represented the best the family could afford. Architectural ornament—panelling, mouldings, and mantelpieces—followed popular styles; other items changed as fashions changed. Books, fancy needlework, pictures, musical instruments, small sculptures, and other "objects of taste" were casually arranged around the room's focus, the center table. Later, decorators recommended more, smaller, dispersed tables. There were books, now more available and more widely read than ever before, including "gift books" (popular illustrated works, usually with a religious message), the Bible, and works of fiction. New methods in lithography enabled most families to own prints such as those produced by Currier and Ives of New York. Musical instruments might include a piano or a parlor organ.[4]

Inventories and personal accounts reinforce the prescriptive outlines of the parlor's appearance. In 1841, young Mary Wood, newly married to merchant Warren Wood, in a small upstate New York community, proudly wrote to her parents about her new home. Her letter describes the parlor of their new house:

> As you enter the door in front you find your self [sic] ushered into the parlor of Mr. and Mrs. Wood's house one moment if you please and take a

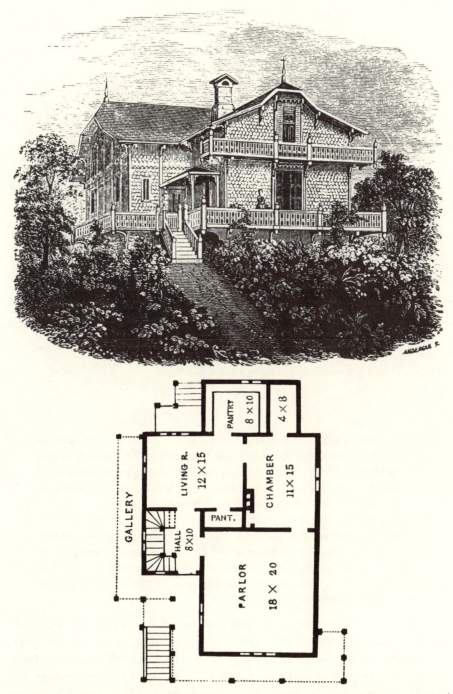

Fig. 5–1. A. J. Downing, design for a "Swiss Cottage" (1850). The parlor projects outward.

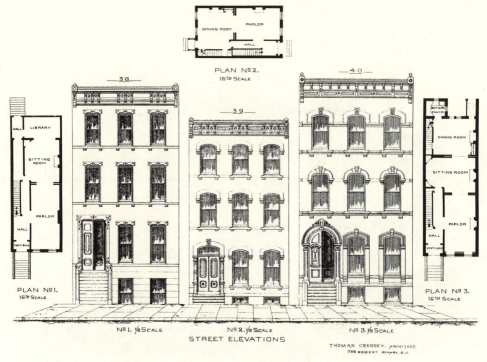

Fig. 5–2. A. J. Bicknell, designs for city row houses (1875).

peek at the appearance of the room. You find it containing four windows which look very neat ornamented with that piece of furnation [sic] calico brought from Ithaca: the floor is carpeted with a very pretty igrane [sic] carpet the furnature [sic] consists of . . . one set of chairs and a rocking chair a stand which groans under its weight of books and a table covered with a green and white spread with several books beside several little ornaments scattered here and there which look rather pretty. We will now pass along towards the next room and observe as we do some pictures hanging against a wall that is covered with very neat paper. We now find ourselves gliding through a set of *folding* doors as white as the snow that now carpets the earth here.[5]

Parlor furnishings were prominent among the factory-made consumer goods being produced in the nation's fast-growing economy (Figure 5–4). Yet fitting out a fashionable parlor could entail considerable expense. Polly Bennett, a general store owner's wife from Bridport, Vermont, kept detailed inventories of several furniture buying trips to New York City in the

1840s. For the parlor, she bought in 1846 a Brussels carpet, stuffed sofa and chairs, side table, stand, work table, pier glass, and marble-top center table at a total cost of $150. Her parlor inventory also noted "some nice Books on Table." As her mother's furniture had been handmade by an uncle, her own trips to the city for ready-made furniture epitomized the significant changes in both production and consumption patterns. Moreover, her inventory shows that she kept up with the fashions suggested by contemporary literature and illustrations.[6]

Women like Polly Bennett and Mary Wood obviously took pride and interest in parlor decorations. According to the "cult of domesticity," the mistress of the home arranged her parlor to express the family's personality to visitors, much as the house's façade indicated the family's status to passersby. She chose from among consumer goods, handmade items (often her own fancy-work), and other articles (for instance, natural history specimens or flowers) to make her statement.[7]

It was believed the parlor also influenced character, according to the "associationist" aesthetic of the day. A. J. Downing, for example, in a chap-

Fig. 5–3. Parlor scene.

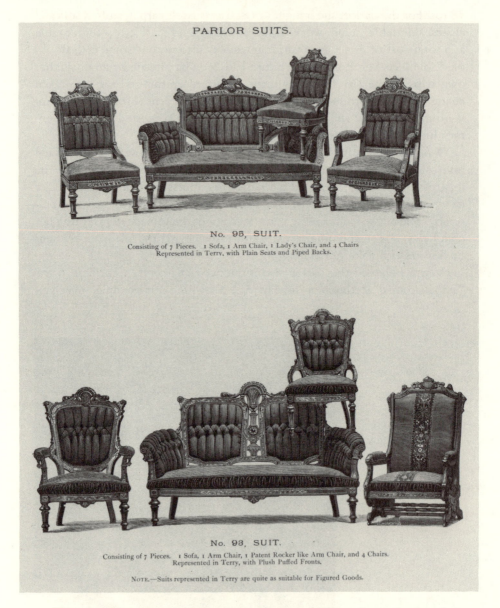

PARLOR SUITS.

No. 95, SUIT.

Consisting of 7 Pieces.   1 Sofa, 1 Arm Chair, 1 Lady's Chair, and 4 Chairs
Represented in Terry, with Plain Seats and Piped Backs.

No. 93, SUIT.

Consisting of 7 Pieces.   1 Sofa, 1 Arm Chair, 1 Patent Rocker like Arm Chair, and 4 Chairs.
Represented in Terry, with Plush Puffed Fronts.

Note.—Suits represented in Terry are quite as suitable for Figured Goods.

Fig. 5–4. Furniture catalog illustrations of "parlor suits" (late nineteenth century).

ter entitled the "Interior Finishing of Country Houses" (*The Architecture of Country Houses,* 1850), suggested "engravings or [plaster] medallion casts" as appropriate decor, explaining that "it is no mean or trifling part of our worship of the Deity to cultivate a daily love for those beautiful forms in art which human genius has revealed and made permanent for us, the study of which will, next to a higher worship, most tend to purify our hearts and lives."[8]

These well-filled settings served two fairly distinct functions, family rituals and social (or semipublic) activities. Private family rituals held in the parlor reinforced ideas of family solidarity, continuity, and patriarchy. The social aspect of the parlor encompassed female hegemony, entertainment of friends, and the display of feminine accomplishments.[9]

Fiction and etiquette guides often portrayed the parlor's role in the middle-class family's emotional and religious life. In the 1835 novel *Home,* Catharine Maria Sedgwick links religious observances to the parlor: "The family Bible is for daily use, and has its proper station in the parlor." Mrs. Sedgwick also portrayed the parlor of a successful city businessman's family as the setting for a family ritual; before her baptism in a public church ceremony, the Barclay's infant daughter is "dedicated" in a private service held in the parlor. The ties binding one generation to the next are reinforced as the child is named for its grandmother, who is herself present at the ceremony. *Godey's* idealized the center table as a device which promoted family solidarity and piety (Figure 5–5); its "Center-Table Gossip" column, with its allusion to that prominent piece of furniture, was intended to encourage an exchange of ideas and information among family members, especially the women.[10]

The private functions of the parlor were undeniably important, but the social rituals stood out most sharply in contemporary accounts. In particular, the parlor's role as a presentation area, around which our twentieth-century stereotypes are shaped, was most prominent. Its very existence established the gentility and class of the house owner. When Downing included a parlor in one of his more modest houses, he felt compelled to explain that "The American cottager is no peasant, but thinks, and thinks correctly, that he can receive his guests with propriety, as well as his wealthiest neighbor" [sic]. A parlor, Downing maintained, expressed the "social ambition" of a family "whose circumstances allow them to entertain." Conversely, cottages for workingmen lacked parlors because such pretensions were inappropriate among the poorer classes.[11]

Fiction and etiquette books elaborated upon the general theme of entertainment. Daytime callers were received according to an elaborate ritual, beginning with calling cards, a kind of social currency. Callers were advised

Fig. 5–5. Parlor scene from *Godey's* (1842).

to leave a card for every person they wanted to see. Once the card was delivered the call could commence. In *Godey's* fiction, a favorite formula involved settings in which a maid would usher visitors into the parlor, where they awaited the matron of the house; after a few moments had elapsed, the hostess quietly appeared. Courting scenes—special instances of calling—were set in the parlor. Evening parties and musical events were also held there, sometimes in elegant double parlors. These events served both to entertain guests and to display the accomplishments of the young women players. Besides fiction, *Godey's* featured an occasional column of "parlor amusements": games, scientific demonstrations, and magic tricks were described.[12]

Nineteenth-century etiquette manuals suggest that people's body attitudes and behavior may have contributed to the creation of a ritual space in the parlor. Readers eager to move in polite circles were told, for example, that gentlemen callers should neither take up the room's principal place, nor sit too far away from the hostess. A gentleman always carried his cane with him, and ladies kept gloves on, to reassure the hostess that they would not stay long. The guides gave instructions on cultivating conversational talent; the bounds of appropriate subjects were as clearly defined as the physical boundaries of parlor space. When the call was over, the hostess was to conduct the departing guests only as far as the parlor door.[13]

While social entertainments were paramount among parlor activities, story writers also chose the parlor as a setting of solitary musing, reading, or sewing, always by female characters. Each character also invariably possessed her own work table. Lest the genteel housewife lack a project for her work table, *Godey's* supplied innumerable patterns and instructions for making pillows, lace cloth, and other parlor accoutrements.[14]

Pattern-book writers, etiquette advisors, and domestic economists all agreed that the semipublic, social functions of the urban parlor were dominated by women (see Figure 5–3). Women controlled access to the parlor, and they directed activity there. Perhaps the parlor can be viewed as a physical manifestation of the "female world of love and ritual"—the network of women's friendships—that historian Carroll Smith-Rosenberg has described. A short piece in the *Atlantic* for 1903, "The Passing of the Parlor," recalled the functions that the parlor had served for the two preceding generations. This anonymous contributor placed the room squarely within the woman's domain: the parlor had "belonged to Mother." It was "that room wherein the heart of the mistress swelled fullest with sense of householdership." The previous "grandmother" generation of house mistresses had also assumed a proprietary attitude toward the parlor:

> The grandmother parlors were never lost, never while the grandmothers lived in the houses that had grown about them, and expressed them as the dress does its wearer. In these parlors were carpets abloom with bouquets of green and vermilion, under the bell glass were the wax flowers wrought when grandmother's fingers were white and soft, and there were the portraits and the slippery haircloth and the antimacassars and the faint mustiness of the straw under the carpet,—all so ugly, and so precious to grandmother![15]

Henry Williams, in *Beautiful Homes* (1877), compared the housewife in her parlor to a "queen-mistress" in her "state-chamber." Any "ambitious" housewife, Williams wrote, would see to it that her parlor was well-ornamented.[16] As a woman's preserve, the parlor subordinated other family members: "Here husband and children do not corrupt, here household cares do not break through." Children especially were out of place in the parlor, literally and psychologically. "It was not a room for children . . . . it had chairs on which one must not sit, and table legs one must not kick, and curios one must not handle; it was not of *our* home at all." The architecture of the room reinforced these patterns by inhibiting traffic from other parts of the house. Downing explicitly excluded children by proposing a partition "intended to serve as the extreme limits of the nursery excursions, on all occasions when decorum in the parlor is the order of the day."[17]

The housewife cherished the parlor because as long as "the parlor is there, the door-bell stirs not her heart-strings."

> Here you may enter, O Stranger, you Polite Impertinence who tirl [sic] our pin and demand that we deliver up to you the privacy of our homes. Here we receive you, here is our best and our tidiest; we are not afraid of you.

Reflectively mourning the parlor's passing, the author concluded by wondering "Must you see our homes and our hearts, o ye Strangers that break through our gates?"[18]

As the literature and house plans suggest, the parlor figured prominently in the ideology of town and city middle-class social activity and family life, imparting identity and stability to these households. It provided a setting for a flourishing middle-class women's culture. As family privacy became more important, the parlor served as a mediating space between the family and the outside world. Easily accessible from the street but insulated from everyday family rooms, it offered an effective resolution of potentially conflicting demands upon the household. On the one hand, it accommodated the social customs which flourished in the "walking city" of mid-century: callers could be appropriately received during times specified by the house mistress. At the same time, by limiting social interaction with outsiders to a well-defined space within the house, it permitted the maintenance of the "home as haven" for family privacy. The parlor allowed the middle-class woman to balance the worlds of family and society.[19]

In rural settings, notions associated with the developing urban parlor culture did not apply. At mid-century, most rural houses in the North contained parlors, used for ceremonial occasions such as funerals and weddings. Like the city parlor, it too usually occupied the front portion of the house, and often stood in isolation from the main part of the house. Although the practice of building parlors in rural houses was well established, their presence dismayed agriculturists. Condemnations of this room appeared sporadically in other types of publications, but the rural press was consistently and unusually negative regarding this room. The arguments were both pragmatic and moral: the conventional parlor was not merely an excrescence, but an unwelcome and insidious symbol of city ways out of place in a rural culture.[20]

The agricultural journals throughout the century agreed that a country family rarely entered its parlors, which, along with the front entrance leading to it, remained closed. Indeed, the image of the unused front door became a cliché describing country living habits. Even today, many country families seldom open their front doors. "Hawk Eye" wrote to the *Country Gentleman* in 1855 that "If you are from the city, your notions of etiquette require you to knock at the front door. What do you hear? Nought but the echo of your own hand. . . . Travel around the corner to the door of a 7 × 9 addition next to the pump and wood-house, and here you find the family happy as larks . . . ready to receive you." Another contributor reflected in the *Rural New Yorker* in 1853 that the parlor was "welcome to its darkness and solitude" while the kitchen served as a cozy family gathering place.[21]

Reminiscences of nineteenth-century farm life corroborate these statements. Anne Gertrude Sneller, for example, recalled that her family homestead in Onondaga County, New York (built in 1868), had boasted two parlors separated by double doors, but "it was only when company came that the big double doors were opened." Neighbors visited in the dining room, but "more impressive and less intimate callers were guided to the back parlor." In Ellen Chapman Rollins's childhood home, the "fore-room or best room was seldom used."[22]

Many people remembered the parlor chiefly as the setting for life's landmark occasions. Harriet Connor Brown was married in her family's "best room." Edward Eastman, who grew up on farms in the late nineteenth-century Northeast, recalled that country dwellers' parlors were "not open to the sunlight" except for "quiltings, weddings, and funerals." As a small boy in the 1880s, Jared Van Wagenen attended a funeral in Schoharie County, New York; he was impressed to see that "the big front room of the old farm house was crowded with friends and neighbors and business associates."[23]

Rural families' infrequent use of their parlors reflected the facts of their everyday lives. One columnist in the *Country Gentleman* noted that while city dwellers might set aside a day for calls, people living in the country had to be ready all the time for unexpected visitors. Visitors in rural areas often came for extended stays, unlike city callers, who would stay only a short while. These visitors were part of the family's everyday life. The farm work went on and more often than not the visitors pitched in; they did not expect to be formally entertained in the parlor. They did, however, frequently sleep in a parlor bedroom. Although city plans almost never showed bedrooms connecting to a parlor, rural house plans often did. When in the 1840s Harriet Connor visited her fiancé's family farm in Ohio, a substantial distance from her own home, she stayed in the bedroom off the "best room."[24]

Rural work patterns also militated against a city-style life. Farm families often labored from morning until evening; they gathered from their various pursuits for a large midday meal, then dispersed again. At busy times, the family worked in the evening, too. Thomas Atkeson, an early leader of the West Virginia Grange, remembered that "in the fall everybody in the house peeled pumpkins at night." Leisure time was concentrated in a single season—winter—rather than spread throughout the year in small daily portions. One women expressed exasperation with city peoples' inability to appreciate farmers' work schedules: "We do not engage," she exclaimed, "in the absurd custom of making calls." Local social visits happened when breaks in work allowed, not by advance appointment. Caroline Kirkland agreed: "There are no fixed 'business hours' or 'visiting hours'." In 1906, an elderly Oneida County resident told sociologist James Mickel Williams that "I used to take the baby in one arm and some knitting in the other and go over to the neighbors' and stay all afternoon to tea. We went back and forth whenever we felt like it without waiting to be asked."[25]

Under such circumstances, rural social entertainments tended to be spontaneous and informal. Even *Godey's* recognized the difference between rural and urban customs. In an 1857 "Editors' Table" vignette on "American Country Life," Mrs. Hale portrays a holiday visit to an aunt in the country: "And now they are beginning to rush into that cozy parlor—loads of friends from a distance—all unexpected they come, and are received— oh, so welcomely! No matter if the nice precision with which that parlor has been arranged is broken up."[26]

This preference for informality influenced rural perceptions of the conventional parlor. Country writers objected to the parlor as "stiff and cold." A contributor to the *American Agriculturist* in 1862 rejected homes he judged "too smart and uncomfortably fine" for farmers. In 1853 the *Ohio Cultivator* carried a feature on "Rooms and their Ornaments." The author compared the parlor to a "prim old lady"; the visitor, he said, "feels like a piece of statuary" there. He cannot see by the "few sickly rays of light," but unmistakably senses the room's physical, and by extension social, rigidity: "every item stands at precise angles and exact distances . . . it would be impossible [for me] to sit on one without moving it." City fashion called for artful informality in furniture arrangement, but some country observers perceived more artfulness than informality.[27]

Rural social entertainments were also more mixed—young and old, men and women—than urban parlor gatherings. Although economic patterns were changing, farm families still operated as units; parents and children worked to sustain the farm, and as families worked together so they socialized together. Arthur C. Hackley, a Bridgewater, New York, farm boy, frequently mentioned in his diary that he and his parents went visiting together. By contrast, urban middle-class families stressed consumption rather than cooperative work, and the social worlds of parents and children diverged. Moreover, children of the new urban middle class were raised with the expectation that they would pursue varied individual careers, and the specialized, individualized domestic spaces of the urban Victorian home may have mirrored this attitude. But agriculturists still clung to the notion that farm youths would follow in their parents' paths, and in fact this old rural tradition, though much weakened, still applied to many families. As late as 1939, twice as many farm children from the previous three generations had followed their parents' occupation than their peers in other occupational categories.[28]

In rural social life gender lines were not established as rigidly as in urban social settings, where women were consistently highlighted and men appeared only as shadowy presences. Apparently, while differences between the sexes were being carried out spatially in other parts of the farmhouse, such distinctions did not extend to the sitting room. This also reflected rural social life: patterns of mixed socializing were part of rural women's "strategies of mutuality" in gender relations. Historian Nancy Grey Osterud has demonstrated how farm women of the Nanticoke Valley, New York, secured "sexually mixed modes of sociability" as a means of "[breaking] down gender-defined separation between husbands and wives," and "[creating] arenas in which women and men were more equal to one another than they were in either conjugal families or the public world."[29]

Most observers concluded that, because country people habitually avoided their parlors, they were an unconscionable waste of farmers' financial resources. A *Cultivator* commentator in 1855 illustrated this objection to the parlor by relating an anecdote of a neighboring "farmer of good means and superior intelligence" who had "reserved one room as a parlor." The story continued:

> But it [the parlor] has been kept shut up as a dead property, and to our certain knowledge, has been used but twice in 15 years, once for a quilting party, and once for a wedding. The owner, to have more room, added in the first place a kitchen to his main building, so as to have a dining or living room and "save" his parlor; next, the kitchen was converted into a dining room, and the wood house was lathed and plastered for a kitchen; and several successive additions have been made—the parlor remaining in solitary loneliness. Now if this room, *kept for show, and never made visible*, with its furniture cost $500, then its use once in seven years, with interest, decay, etc.[,] about *four hundred dollars* for each occasion.

This critique, while undoubtedly hyperbolic, was nevertheless telling. The very fact of the parlor's uselessness jeopardized values crucial to progressive farmers—economy and productive enterprise.[30]

The conspicuous expenditures of the urban middle class on parlor items annoyed rural writers. The *Michigan Farmer* in 1855 marshaled aesthetic, moral, and practical arguments against costly parlor furnishings: "Who, with correct notions, would not prefer a neatly swept domestic carpet, with a few articles of plain, well-kept, old fashioned furniture, to a more expensively-furnished room, where the dust is suffered to accumulate in the veins of the carved mahogany." In the same year, "Hawk Eye" declared that "halls and parlors are luxurious nuisances, only to be indulged in by those living in or near towns. . . . Every thing about the farmer's house should be plain and substantial, and expressive of his everyday life." He urged farmers instead to "furnish the house with every possible contrivance for the easy performance of everyday labors." Hawk Eye's remarks intimated that ostentation was morally wrong. The parlor, filled with consumer goods, violated the progressive farmer's duty to economize by prompting expenditures on little-used articles and by diverting the farm family's resources from household conveniences.[31]

The agrarian critique of conspicuous consumption crystallized around images of women. Throughout the century, rural writers viewed the parlor, symbolic of urban women consumers, as the polar opposite of the kitchen, symbolic of rural women producers. The sharpness and persistence of this image suggests that stereotypes of rural and urban women (and parlors) were culturally potent among progressive farm families. There was some basis in reality for these stereotypes, but that does not fully account for their intensity, especially by the late nineteenth century, when rural women's lives were changing. It is more likely that the two images focused critical thought upon the culture of consumption then developing in America, and stimulated thinking on how to define alternatives or compromises.

Contributors consistently chose the parlor as a setting whenever they wished to describe the antithesis of a good farm wife. They associated parlor culture with idle, unskilled, unproductive females. "Eva" wrote in the *American Agriculturist* in 1849 that "We are frequently pained to see drawing-rooms and parlors filled with young ladies, for hours, together, without any visible employment." "Eva" considered this a "sad perversion of the intellects and bodies." "A plain parlor and a comfortable kitchen," agreed an *Ohio Cultivator* contributor in 1853, "give far more evidence of good sense, than a showy parlor and an inconvenient and poorly arranged kitchen." Some took this logic to its extreme and decided that a well-kept country parlor was a sure sign of a poor farm wife.[32]

Farm writers commonly equated the female habitués of the parlor with the objects that surrounded them there. One women, writing in the *Ohio Cultivator* in 1845, declared that she refused to be identified with "worthless parlor ornaments." Orville Dewey, prominent Unitarian minister and educational reformer, in 1838 wrote to the *Genesee Farmer* to censure the man who sought a wife to "furnish a parlor rather than a kitchen or dining room," and who consequently went "into the world in search of a wife as he would into a cabinet maker's shop." Perhaps Dewey's youth on a western Massachusetts farm influenced his assessment of parlor culture.[33]

A woodcut in *Moore's Rural New Yorker* in 1888 summarized the moral opposition of kitchen and parlor eloquently. Two contrasting scenes are followed by a chain of equally opposite consequences. The first (Figure 5–6) depicts a rural kitchen: here, three women work together; one washes laundry, one peels apples, and the third cooks over a modern range. The background outlines an orderly storage area. Clearly a cooperative, efficient, productive enterprise flourishes here. Four vignettes coupled with this scene (Figure 5–7) illustrate the happy consequences of cooperation. Scenes two and three feature healthful outdoor leisure pursuits, a wagon ride, and a game of croquet. Scene four, an evening scene, shows the daughter reading (from *Moore's*, of course) to her elderly parents. The inevitable consequence of the daughter's hard work and devotion appears in scene five, the wedding; here the cycle begins again.

In vivid contrast, the companion scene (Figure 5–8) portrays a parlor. The daughter, elaborately dressed, plays the piano to display her accomplishments to her dandified suitor. Pictures and stylish furniture adorn the room. The background is a pointed indictment of the daughter's inconsiderate behavior: the mother, old, wrinkled, thin, tired, and harrassed, bends over a steaming washtub in an inadequate kitchen. The stark consequences of the daughter's selfish pursuit of leisure accomplishments, and by implication, of misplaced architectural priorities, appear in the next four vignettes (Figure 5–9). Low-paid labor (scenes two and three), unemployment (scene four), and ultimately (the picture implies) prostitution (scene five) await the prodigal daughter.

The *Moore's* woodcut illustrates what many rural reformers suspected, that parlor culture literally divided families. Mrs. E. H. Leland gave full expression to this idea in *Farm Homes* (1881). In her opinion the parlor should be "least in every genuine home—the home that is made to be used and enjoyed by the family." She related a story about a farm woman who sacrificed the rest of the house in order to furnish her parlor. Because of this woman's misguided choice, her sons left the farm; her husband retreated to the kitchen or porch for fear of dirtying her parlor; even the neigh-

Fig. 5–6, 5–7, 5–8, 5–9. Sequence of engravings (1888) contrasting the virtues of kitchen and sitting room (Figs. 5–6, 5–7) to the vices of parlor accomplishments (Figs. 5–8, 5–9).

bors found no place to visit in her home. Mrs. Leland concluded, maliciously, that this parlor would only be used when the time came for its mistress to lie in state, "all unmindful . . . of the neighbors' feet upon her sacred carpet."[34]

The agricultural press became a forum for the discussion of alternatives to the parlor. Some solutions were directed toward those who were building new homes, but the most popular recommendation concerned the countless parlors in existing farmhouses "lying in state" for once-a-year visitors. Writers proposed that families transform the seldom-used parlor into a cheery family sitting room where all family members would share a common space. This solution was more practical than those predicated on the construction of new houses. At the same time, it was drastic, because it implied a significant transformation.

Descriptions of the 1850s and 1860s consistently prescribed the switch from parlor to sitting room. In 1852 Major Marsena Rudolph Patrick addressed the Jefferson County, New York, Agricultural Society, condemning the "practice, which prevails in some families, of keeping a portion of the dwelling almost wholly closed." Instead, he urged farm families "first to let the *front* part of the house be thrown open, and it selected as the *family room*. Let its doors be ever open, and when the work of the kitchen is completed, let mothers and daughters be found there with their appropriate work. Let it be the room where the family altar is erected, on which the father offers the morning and evening sacrifice. . . ." Patrick suggested that "useful" (not ornamental) periodicals ought to be placed on the center table. In another account, "Anna Hope," a regular *American Agriculturist* contributor, recommended (1857) that farm families "use and enjoy what we have and permit our children to use it" rather than "shut up a part of the house for weddings, parties, and funerals." She suggested that flowers and books, "carelessly" (casually) set out, improved the moral tone of the farm home, and that furniture selected according to individual taste would also contribute to that end. Pictures should grace the walls, furniture should be set at "easy angles," and a table, laden with magazines and flowers, would look out over a spacious window.[35]

By the 1870s and 1880s, some writers went beyond general description, developing a vision of a sitting-room material culture that would reinforce rural values. An article on "Beautifying the Home" in the 1875 *Prairie Farmer* suggested that

> a rag carpet, made up of bits of every color which has distinguished the family garments through the changing seasons, mixes all these varying

tints into a harmonious and indistinguishable web, where red and blue, and green and gray, and parti-color, combine into one warm harmonious color which brings everything in the room into harmony with it.

A rag carpet is a very good type of real honest family life and love, where every shred of character and habit, old and new, agreeable and disagreeable, is worked up into the loom of daily life together, and comes out in breadths of family character.

The "rag carpet" epitomized the sitting room's moral virtues: it was hand-made, it symbolized family harmony, and it literally tied family members and their domestic environment together.[36]

D. G. Mitchell, author of numerous popular books on rural life, pursued this thinking in an 1876 article on the "Farmer's Homestead." Mitchell described the proper trappings for the progressive farmer's sitting room or "living-room," as he called it, mentioning objects as diverse as a "home-wrought rug" and the family's "best china." Botanical specimens, fruits, and stuffed birds would "stamp [it] as a farmer's homestead" (see Figures 5–10, 5–11). He continued:

To a home of such belongings, children coming back from schools of whatever sort will not find their minds starved by contact with bareness, but piqued and gratified and stimulated by its fresh and suggestive aspect. In gone-by times, there were something coarser ways of finding entertainment. There were the husking-bees and apple-parings . . . Well, your daughters now, do not want to take their tournures and trains into a barn. They have come by schooling, reading, lecture-going . . . to a different level. They perceive that the husking business is given over to a different set of fellows, who do it for two or three cents a bushel, and "be jabbers are as good as iver the nixt jintilman."

We cannot declaim against this new aspect of the family. We cannot take our female country population out of their new plane—out of their bustles, and land them in gingham aprons; ask your wives if we can! The old social zest that lay in a pleasant coarseness will not come back; but we can lay the basis of a new and riper social zest.[37]

Mitchell's description is particularly interesting because of the complexity of the furnishings he presents. His "living-room" contains articles representing three worlds. "Found" objects, presumably collected from the farmer's fields and woods, represented the natural world and the farmer's (allegedly) close relation to it (which was growing more distant all the time). Hand-crafted items, like the "home-wrought rug," came from the traditional world of home manufactures and rural self-sufficiency. And the fami-

Fig. 5–10. A rural sitting room scene, titled "The Return Home for the Holidays" (1881).

Fig. 5–11. A rural sitting room scene, titled "The Farmer at Home" (1870).

ly's "best china" represented the new realm of mass-produced consumer goods.

By the 1880s and 1890s, the sitting-room image had become still more elaborate. In 1882, E. C. Gardner, a popular architectural writer, urged the farmer to "keep up with the rest of the world" by opening the parlor to everyday use. He reasoned that "sons and daughters will never be gentlemen and gentlewomen unless they learn to respect what is good and clean and beautiful by daily familiarity with whatever good things the house contains." The previously scorned "accomplishments" also gained limited acceptance; one woman urged that farmers allow the "softening light" of music and art to shine upon the family in the sitting room instead of remaining confined to the parlor's special occasions (see Figures 5–10, 5–11). Another writer envisioned the sitting room for reading, discussion of books, or debate of political issues. "Alice Chittenden," a regular columnist for the *American Agriculturist,* injected these ideas into a homily about a young farm girl (1890). Privileged to have spent a year at boarding school but still committed to country life, "Cicely" returns home to open up and redecorate the old-fashioned parlor. In the process, she interests her younger brother in the home, and also draws her father into the new sitting room to read the issues of the *American Agriculturist* she has procured for him.[38]

All of these images, whether from mid-century or later, prescribed certain standards of cleanliness and dress appropriate for the sitting room. An 1858 *Genesee Farmer* contributor believed that informality should be obtained without compromising refinement:

> In the first place ladies should not consider any part of their house too nice for use, and wherever the ladies [sic] sitting-room is, there the husband, sons, and brothers should be welcome . . . . there is a nicely carpeted, airy sitting room, where the ladies can sit down after their morning work, and read or sew, and where the light knitting work is always convenient. When the dirty men come in, provide them with an inviting place to wash; if there is company for tea, furnish clothes for parlor or table. . . .[39]

These prescriptions suggested that family members literally ought to transform themselves in order to enter the sitting room. Mrs. Leland wrote that when she left the kitchen, she could "lay aside her cares and kitchen apron together." She also recommended that house planners include a vestibule for storing coats; this hall would contain a mirror so that children could "see that they are presentable prior to appearing in the sitting-room or dining-room." By this means children would learn "order and self-control."[40]

The irony of the rural sitting-room ideal is apparent: imaginary accounts of the parlor-turned-sitting room described physical settings which closely resembled urban parlors. The rural formula emphasized tastefully selected furniture, pictures, flowers, books, and other objects, arranged around a center table; these were supposed to elevate the family's taste and moral sensibilities. Later in the century, music and games became acceptable sitting-room activities. The formula also mimicked the urban parlor's role as a center of family devotions; Major Patrick's imagery, for example, recalled the engravings of "Evening Devotions" in *Godey's*. And the rituals of dress and behavior paralleled urban calling customs. To be sure, country sitting-room furnishings were supposed to be simpler, perhaps homemade, less ostentatious, more informal and utilitarian, and they were supposed to emphasize "rural" themes, but the basic forms were the same.

One reason for this ambiguity was the rapid development of a national consumer economy. Consumer goods had been available in rural areas since the early nineteenth century; rural people responded with tremendous enthusiasm to itinerant peddlers of clocks and daguerrotypes. As the scale and productivity of industry expanded, and as the railroads facilitated distribution, mass-produced goods became still more widely available. The Midwestern mail-order houses of Montgomery Ward and Sears, Roebuck were established in the last quarter of the century, catering to rural markets. These changes were reflected in the pages of the agricultural journals: more and more advertising appeared, promoting articles from pocket-watches to melodeons. And ultimately the goods turned up in farmhouses. James Mickel Williams noted that by the 1880s, Oneida County, New York "farmhouse[s] [were] enlarged, repainted and refurnished, like village houses, with piano, bright-colored carpets, white curtains, sideboard, and writing desk." As Williams's comment reveals, at the same time that rural writers were seeking alternatives to parlor culture, the proliferation of consumer goods made it increasingly difficult to define those alternatives in rural terms, and to reconcile agrarian values of production with new values of consumption. Agricultural writers and thinkers who took part in shaping the sitting-room ideal were torn between their desire to "keep up with the rest of the world" and their misgivings about consumer culture, expressed in their praise for home-wrought items and in their continuing critique of conspicuous consumption.[41]

Despite increasing physical similarities, urban parlor and rural sitting-room images still diverged in one crucial way: social composition. The express purpose of the sitting-room ideal was to describe a place where everyone could sit together, and so portrayals invariably included the entire farm family (see Figure 5–12), from the grandparents to the smallest child. Caroline Kirkland's portrayal was typical:

> where could we get another grandmamma for the warm corner? And in the corner next to the window . . . there is mama, with her capacious work-basket before her . . . When papa sits down to his paper, he must have sunshine . . . What cheerful rendezvous this makes for the children when they come from school . . .[42]

The rural sitting room tea table, around which the entire family gathered for an evening meal, expressed a contrast to the urban parlor center table, locus for daytime gossip among women. Moreover, the sitting room's synonyms—"family-room," "living-room,"—also suggested the rural demand for a socially heterogeneous space.

The sitting-room image was soon invoked as a means of ensuring family solidarity not only in the present, but in the future. Even though some farm children would still become farmers, their experience was less typical than that of the rural sons and daughters who migrated to the city. Fred Shannon estimates that between 1860 and 1900, "for every city laborer who took up farming, twenty farmers flocked to the city . . . The farms lacked by 18,000,000 of keeping pace with the ratio of population growth of the whole nation, while the nonfarm areas gained 18,000,000 over the same ratio." In response to this alarming situation, the farmer's sitting room became an important element in proposed solutions to the problem of mass migration; farm journalists hoped to make attractive, family-oriented sitting rooms into a magnet, a haven of leisure and refinement. The *Michigan Farmer,* for example, described "How The Boys Were Reconciled" to staying on the family farm by the introduction of a family sitting room.[43] However, this vain hope ignored the fact that mechanization had vastly reduced the demand for farm labor. Agricultural reformers touted the virtues of country life, consistently showing an inability (or unwillingness) to appreciate the appeal of the city. They placed mass-produced goods in their imaginary country sitting rooms next to homemade furnishings. Moreover, they invested these objects with the power to instill a refinement which would allow rural people to join the urban stream of American cultural life and yet retain a distinctive identity as country people. The rural sitting room, then, was charged with the formidable task of simultaneously preserving and transforming the family farm.

Despite this ambivalence in cultural images and stereotypes, rural house planners mounted a significant challenge to the parlor. They focused on the practical, architectural aspects of the problem—access and proximity of the

Fig. 5–12. Poster, titled "Gift for the Grangers" (1873). Note vignette in upper left.

sitting room in relation to other rooms; placement of entranceways; exterior indications of its position—and they designed and built houses that realized their desire to work out a domestic setting appropriate for the country. Between 1850 and 1900, a significant and increasing number of farmer-planners experimented with alternatives to the conventional parlor. Many kept the parlor but de-emphasized it, either by shifting it to a less prominent location within the house, or by reducing its size in relation to the other rooms. Others reduced the parlor's isolation by expanding links between it and other rooms. Finally, some—a steadily growing percentage, to half by the turn of the century—discarded the parlor altogether.

One version of relocating the parlor was proposed by H. T. Vose of Jackson, Ohio. His octagon plan (1859) moved the room upstairs, "in accordance," he explained, "with rule 4th, Annual Register (of *Rural Affairs*), no. 3., p. 316." This rule had explained that less used rooms ought to be placed in less accessible locations.[44]

Some planners, preoccupied with getting sunlight, reasoned that the most used rooms ought to enjoy the best location within the house. In *Moore's* (1866), "S. W. A." of Cortland, Illinois, contributed "Advice about Building Houses" which urged readers "Above all things . . . to have the room or rooms which you intend most to occupy (as the sitting room or common living room) on the south side, with windows so as to secure a full share of the sun's rays in winter." In 1864, "Lavendar," a contributor to the *Country Gentleman,* advised "those about to build": "on the parlor side, as that room is used but little in the country, make it one large room, and have a room back for say a spare bedroom." Lavendar also urged readers to "arrange the house so the sitting-rooms and rooms most used will be cheerful and pleasant ones, where the sun comes in." Mrs. Leland concurred: "people who come and go can be cheerful for awhile in a north-windowed apartment, but the constant dwellers in a house need its sunniest rooms." These writers all advocated a realignment which would push the parlor into the background.[45]

Actual plans illustrate the effects of these changes upon the arrangement of leisure space. For example, L. D. Snook's 1869 plan of a "Farmer's Cottage" (Figure 5–13) placed the kitchen lengthwise, parallel to the road. The living room shared the kitchen's axis, while the parlor was placed behind the living room, out of sight from the road. Certainly this contradicted the custom of placing the parlor where passersby could judge its location within the house.

The reorientation of the most used rooms could also elevate sitting rooms or living rooms to equal status with the parlor. For example, in a plan published in *Moore's* about 1873, the living room, not the parlor, jutted out

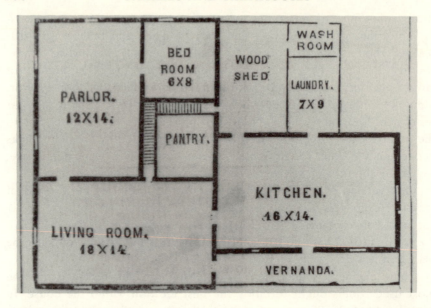

Fig. 5–13. L. D. Snook, plan for a farmhouse in Yates County, New York (1869).

beside the entranceway. *Moore's* "First Class Farm House" of 1870 conformed to its designer's dictum that "The sitting-room should divide prominence with the parlor, with the choice of the sunniest aspect." His sitting
room, with its prominent bay window, actually overshadowed the parlor
(Figures 5–14, 5–15).[46]

These axial shifts often resulted in a subtle change in the visual messages
imparted by the façade design. Solon Robinson, in his handbook, *Facts for
Farmers* (1866), recommended that "the whole house appear to every pas-
ser-by, as though built for use, rather than show. It is a great convenience
that strangers can find some other than the front door entrance." Indeed,
"Amos," designer of a "Sucker Cottage" for pioneers, which appeared in
the *Prairie Farmer* (Figure 5–16), not only placed folding doors between
parlor and sitting room, but also arranged his plan so that the "front door
opens into the dining or common sitting room." Similarly, the "Six Thou-
sand Dollar Farm House" (see Figures 4–14, 4–15) lacked a single, prominent entrance to the parlor. Instead, the visitor was forced to choose among
three entrances: the main entrance (which betrayed no external clue
whether it led to parlor or living room); the subordinate kitchen entrance
(far left); or the nearly hidden parlor entrance around the corner (far right).
The signals which conventionally indicated the parlor's position to an out-
sider were scrambled.[47]

Fig. 5–14. (Above). Anonymous design for a "First-Class" farmhouse (1870). Elevation.

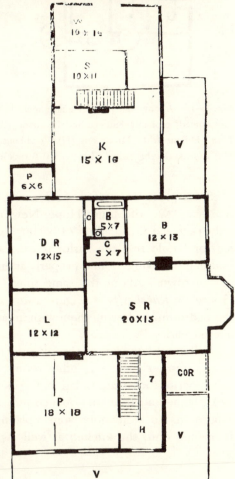

Fig. 5–15. (Right) "First-Class" farmhouse, plan. (B) Bathroom, Bedroom. (C) Closets. (COR) Conservatory. (DR) Dining room. (H) Hall. (K) Kitchen. (L) Library. (P) Pantry, Parlor. (SR) Sitting room. (S) Storeroom. (V) Veranda. (W) Wood room.

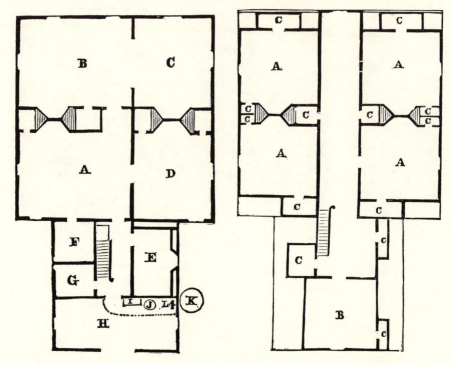

Fig. 5–16. Anonymous plan for a farmhouse in Illinois (1852). (Left) *Ground Floor:* (A, D) Not named; probably Kitchen and Bedroom. (B) Parlor. (C) Sitting or Dining room. (E) Bath. (F) Pantry. (G) Milk room. (H) Wood house. (I) Not named. (J) Well. (K) Cistern. (L) Not named. (Right) *Second Floor:* (A, B) Bedrooms. (C) Closets.

Some planners, instead of relocating the parlor, simply reduced its relative size. "W." of Mount Hope, New York, explained that "the parlor is only 14.2 × 13.9 to admit of having a good-sized bedroom in the rear of it—for I hold that the parlor is generally the most useless room in the house, if the living room is properly attended to . . . for those of us residing out of town." About the same time (1860) the "Alteration of a Farm House" in *Rural Affairs* (Figure 4–23) enlarged both the living room and the bedroom, endowing them with greater prominence relative to the unaltered parlor.[48]

Still another means of changing the parlor's social meaning was to integrate it more closely with other rooms, thus creating an alternative to the urban parlor's inviolate isolation. Cyrus Bryant, for instance (see Figure 2–10), planned a parlor that opened into an entranceway, bedroom, and sitting room. An anonymous woman planner even arranged her parlor so that it opened onto the kitchen as well as to a bedroom (see Figure 3–10).

Others connected the parlor to the dining room. These connections were accomplished by substituting folding doors for narrower, conventional openings. Morris Clinton of Newark Valley, New York (1882) (Figures 5–17, 5–18), employed folding doors between sitting room and parlor, merging the two rooms. The entrance, moreover, opened onto the sitting room, and the bay marked that room instead of the parlor. In another plan (Figure 5–19) in *Moore's* (1874), eight-foot-square folding doors separated dining room and parlor in order to make a "Large saloon [sic], thus greatly adding to the hospitable look of the house, without demanding great unused spaces."[49]

Some people even removed walls in existing houses and replaced them with openings: farm boy Arthur C. Hackley wrote in his diary on January 29, 1861, that "[we] are preparing to make folding doors between dining room and parlor," and the next day he reported that he and his father had "been taking away the partition" so as to accomplish this.[50]

Finally, increasing numbers of farmer-planners eliminated parlors from their designs. In the 1840s, only 5 percent of the owner-designed plans lacked a parlor, but by the 1880s 25 percent of plan contributors dispensed with the parlor, and in the 1890s half discarded the parlor altogether.

Those who omitted the parlor believed, with the journalist reformers, that the parlor was inappropriate for country social life and necessities. One anonymous planner (1856) substituted for the parlor a "family room," which he said "answers all the purposes of a parlor, and to our fancy is much the most friendly and comfortable to visit in. If our friends cannot enjoy themselves there, we prefer them to stay away" (Figure 5–20). The same journal a few years later (1859) advised the farmer who was in the process of building to drop his plans for a parlor because it was the "most useless room of all. If you are as good as your neighbors you will have but few visitors too good to set down in your living-room and enjoy a farmer's luxuries—apples, butternuts, and cider. It is better to build a small house to live in yourself, than a large one to lock up for want of proper furniture, or to open only for visitors." This sentiment remained popular in the agricultural press throughout the century.[51]

An informal home, these remarks implied, presented the farmer's family as it really was, not as a carefully constructed image. Visitors were not screened as in the city, but invited directly into the family living area. A "Maryland Matron," writing in the *Country Gentleman* for 1888, regarded the parlor as a kind of crutch for people lacking in social competence: "People with refined habits," she argued, "do not need to have rooms shut up for the occasional visitor. They respect themselves so far as to suppose that their guests will be pleased to see them amid their usual surroundings,

Fig. 5–17. Morris Clinton, design for a farmhouse in Newark Valley, New York (1882). Elevation. Sitting-room window is on the right.

Fig. 5–18. Morris Clinton house, plan. (A) Parlor. (B) Sitting room. (C) Sleeping or Dining room. (D) Kitchen. (E) Pantry. (F) Washroom. (G) Wood house. (a) Porch. (4) Stove. (c) Sink. (d) Stairs. (e) Sash doors.

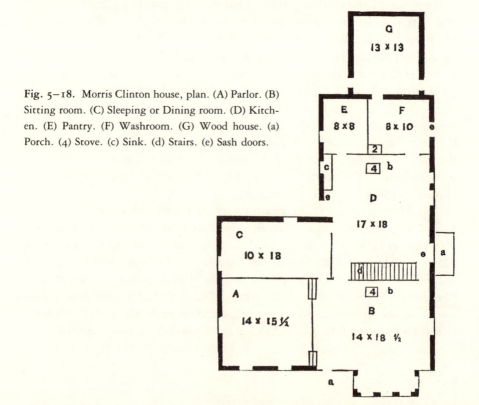

where the home atmosphere serves to make all parties at ease and in-
terested in each other." Her parlorless plan (Figure 5–21) reflected her
conviction.[52]

Mrs. Leland (1881) also added cultural reasons to the economic rationale for eliminating the parlor from farmhouse plans:

> Just here I want to enter my humblest protest against any parlor that
> pinches and stints other rooms in order to exist. First secure the conve-
> nient kitchen, the pleasant dining-room, the well-sunned and well-venti-
> lated bedrooms, the bath-room, the simple pantry and milk-room. Then,
> if space permits, have a parlor by all means—as pretty a parlor as possi-
> ble—and use it. It is bad taste and bad morals to make 'most anything'
> answer for family use day after day, while the best room and the best of
> everything is sacredly reserved for outside people, people who are not
> greatly benefited after all, for when we visit do we not observe that it is
> the simple, easily served meal that we enjoy, and not the stiff atmosphere
> of a seldom used room, the laboriously prepared dishes and the general
> feeling that we are creating an unusual and perhaps troublesome stir in
> the everyday lives of our friends?
>
> Unless a home-keeper can afford to keep help and so find time to
> enjoy her family, it is better to defer such an apartment. A cozy little nook

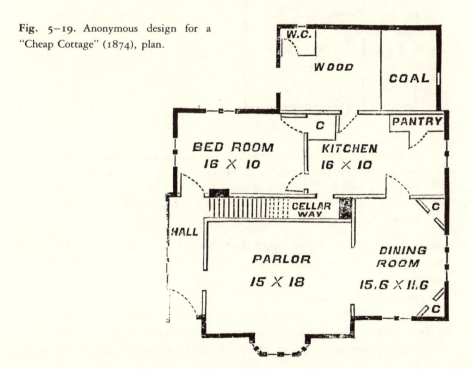

Fig. 5–19. Anonymous design for a
"Cheap Cottage" (1874), plan.

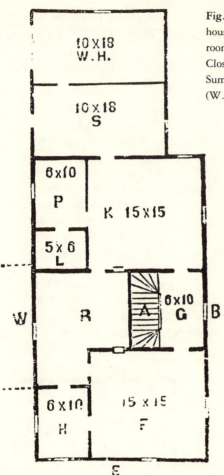

Fig. 5–20. Anonymous plan for a farm-
house (1856), plan. (A) Stairs. (F) Family
room. (G, H) Hall. (K) Kitchen. (L)
Closet. (P) Pantry. (R) Bed recess. (S)
Summer kitchen and Wash house.
(W.H.) Wood house.

off the dining room, separated from it by an arched space, or a little recess
without the arch, but having a pleasant window and an easy chair or two,
are good substitutes. In such a place a visitor can sit and feel that pleasur-
able comfort of being in a 'home' room and giving no one any trouble or
distress.[53]

Leland's explanation rested upon the informal and family-centered social
life of rural culture, and her plans (Figures 5–22, 4–9) reflect those
qualities. Not one has a parlor, but each features a centralized family room
and compact arrangement.

By the end of the century, rural leaders had accumulated several decades of theoretical and actual experience with alternatives to the parlor. By
contrast, a survey of urban pattern-books and mail-order plan books of the

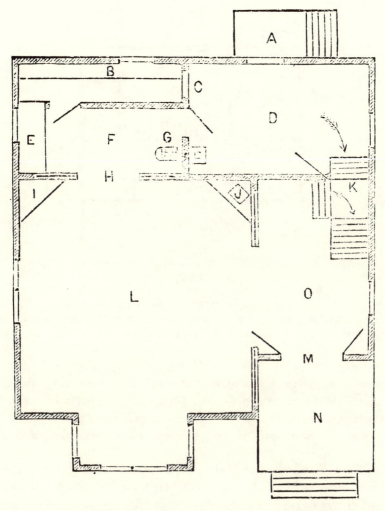

Fig. 5–21. Anonymous plan for a farmhouse in Maryland (1888). (A) Back porch. (B) Shelves. (C) Cellarway. (D) Washroom. (E) Sink. (F) Recess. (G) Cookstove. (H) Sliding doors. (I) China closet. (J) Fireplace. (K) Door. (L) Living room. (M) Front door. (N) Porch. (O) Hall.

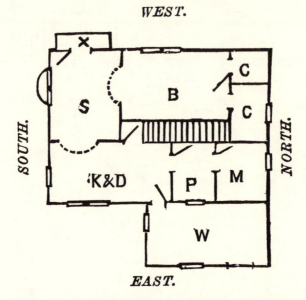

Fig. 5–22. E. H. Leland, woman's plan for a farmhouse (1881). (B) Bedroom. (C) Wardrobe and Bath. (D, K) Dining room and Winter kitchen. (M, P) Milk room and Pantry. (S) Sitting room. (W) Wood house and Summer kitchen. (X) Portico.

time reveals no comparable experimentation by designers and popularizers such as the Pallisers, Shoppells, and Bicknells. The Pallisers' 1887 *New Cottage Homes and Details* did feature some parlorless plans, but (significantly) many of these were "settlers' cottages" for homesteaders in the rural West.

Not until the last quarter of the century did urbanites begin to express numerous misgivings of their own about parlor culture. Reformers and popular writers began to regard informal social life—and consequently informal house plans—more favorably, and the parlor fell into widespread disrepute. Prominent advisors on domestic decor such as Clarence Cook, E. C. Gardner, and Edward Bok called for the abolition of the parlor, writing in such widely circulated periodicals as *Scribner's* and the *Ladies' Home Journal.* They objected to the custom of reserving the best for strangers, to the parlor's formality, to its emphasis on conspicuous display, and to its clutter. Only the last objection, rising from new aesthetic preferences, departed from the longstanding complaints voiced in the farm press. It is perhaps no coincidence that in speaking out against the parlor, these urban writers continually invoked the example of the rural past. When Cook argued against the parlor, for example, he recalled that "in the country one could easily forget the existence of the parlor, and the real life of the family went cheerily on."[54]

Another prominent source of twentieth-century criticism of the parlor came from the emerging home economics movement. This movement had strong ties with the agricultural community; many home economics departments originated in land-grant agricultural colleges, educating farmers' daughters to be home economists. Helen Campbell, early leader of the movement, campaigned against parlors in her influential writings:

> Let the conviction become part of the builder, that if there can be but two good rooms in the house, these rooms should be, not parlor and dining-room, but kitchen and sitting-room. . .[55]

By the 1920s, parlors were the exception rather than the rule in most new middle-class homes. Of course, a number of factors contributed to the parlor's demise, the rise of the auto and the growth of health care and funeral industries among them. However, we should also consider the impact of rural culture on this change. In the late nineteenth century, large numbers of native-born residents had migrated from country to city, carrying with them, perhaps, rural traditions of informal socializing and prejudice against parlor culture—ideas which might influence or reinforce a nationwide campaign against the parlor. The farm designers' architectural experiments also provided some of the only precedents for alternatives to the parlor. While most predominant trends in turn-of-the-century American culture originated in urban environments, perhaps this cultural current flowed in the opposite direction.[56]

Thus, in the era when Vincent Scully detects a "nostalgia for a lost agrarian simplicity" and a "desire for informal living" behind the spatial and aesthetic explorations of pioneer professional architects of the Shingle Style, vernacular planners may have been responding to a similar impulse. And the evidence of a strong rural tradition of alternatives to the nineteenth-century home's most formal space, the parlor, suggests that perhaps the rural past of turn-of-the-century vernacular designers contributed substantive architectural ideas as well as nostalgic memories.[57]

NOTES

1. *The American Heritage Dictionary* (Boston: American Heritage Publishing Co., 1975), 954; Mark Girouard, *Life in the English Country House* (Harmondsworth, U.K.: Penguin Books, 1980), 58, 138, 237–238; Abbott L. Cummings, *The Framed Houses of Massachusetts Bay 1625–1725* (Cambridge: Harvard University Press, 1979), chapter 3; Margaret Schiffer,

Chester County, Pa., Inventories, 1684–1850 (Exton, Pa.: Schiffer Publishing, Ltd., 1974), 210–212; E. H. Arr [Ellen Chapman (Hobbs) Rollins], *New England Bygones* (Philadelphia: Lippincott, 1880), 46–51; Meyric Rogers, *American Interior Design* (New York: Norton, 1947), 72; Fiske Kimball, *Domestic Architecture of the American Colonies* (1922. Reprint, New York: Dover Publications, 1966); Carole Shammas, "The Domestic Environment in Early Modern England and America," *Journal of Social History* 14 (Fall 1980): 1–25; Samuel Backus, "Hints upon Farm Houses," U.S. Patent Office *Report* (1859): 398–399; Edward Cooke, "Domestic Space in the Federal-Period Inventories of Salem Merchants," *Essex Institute Historical Collections* 116 (October 1980): 248–265; Cummings, "Notes on Furnishing a Small New England Farm House," *Old-Time New England* 48 (Fall 1957): 78–80; Rexford Newcomb, *Architecture of the Old Northwest Territory* (Chicago: University of Chicago Press, 1950), 29; Herbert Congdon, *Old Vermont Houses* (1945. Reprint, Peterborough, N.H.: Noone House, 1968).

2. "House-Hiring and Furnishing," *Godey's* 50 (February 1855): 185; Mrs. A. M. F. Buchanan, "The Three-Story House," *Godey's* 19 (October 1839): 185–187.

3. I derive these conclusions from a study of pattern-books and architectural handbooks, among them A. J. Downing, *The Architecture of Country Houses* (1850. Reprint, New York: Dover Publications, 1969), and *Cottage Residences* (1842. Reprint, Watkins Glen, N.Y.: American Life Foundation, 1967); R. W. Shoppell, *Shoppell's Modern Houses* (New York: Cooperative Building Plan Association, 1877); George Woodward, *Woodward's National Architect* (New York: Korff Brothers, 1869); Calvert Vaux, *Villas and Cottages* (1864. Reprint, New York: Dover Publications, 1970); Samuel Sloan, *City and Suburban Architecture* (1852. Reprint, New York: Dover Publications, 1980); Palliser's *Model Homes* (Bridgeport, Conn.: Palliser and Palliser, 1878); Palliser's *New Cottage Homes and Details* (1888. Reprint, Watkins Glen, N.Y.: American Life Foundation, 1978); A. J. Bicknell, *Bicknell's Wooden and Brick Buildings* (New York: A. J. Bicknell, 1875); and John Calvin Stevens, *Examples of American Domestic Architecture* (New York: William Comstock, 1889).

4. Information on the parlor's appearance comes from a variety of sources. Alan Gowans, *Images in American Living: Four Centuries of Architecture and Furniture as Cultural Expression* (Philadelphia and New York: Lippincott, 1964) made one of the first attempts to study furnishings as material culture. Russell H. Kettell, *Early American Rooms* (Portland, Me.: Southworth, Anthoensen Press, 1936) provides views of period rooms accompanied by representative documents from each period. James Maass, *The Victorian Home in America* (New York: Hawthorn Books, 1972) and *The Gingerbread Age* (New York: Rinehart, 1957) are popular histories which defend Victorian aesthetics. Harold Peterson, *Americans at Home: From the Colonists to the Late Victorians* (New York: Charles Scribner's Sons, 1971) collects interior views with the intention of demonstrating their potential as historical documents. Edgar Mayhew and Minor Myers, *A Documentary History of American Interiors* (New York: Scribner's, 1980), Meyric Rogers, *American Interior Design,* and Harriet Bridgeman, *Encyclopedia of Victoriana* (New York: Macmillan, 1975) supply descriptions and illustrations of nineteenth-century decorative arts and furnishings. Russell Lynes, in *The Tastemakers* (New York: Harper, 1954) and *The Domesticated Americans* (New York: Harper & Row, 1963) offers anecdotal accounts of parlor customs. Roger Gilman, "The Romantic Interior," in George Boas, ed., *Romanticism in America* (Baltimore: Johns Hopkins University Press, 1940) analyzes Downing's philosophy of decoration in the context of literary and aesthetic romanticism. Edgar Martin, *The Standard of Living in 1860* (Chicago: University of Chicago Press, 1942), 98–102, gives a general account of representative furnishings in a typical parlor of the period. Margaret Schiffer, *Chester County, Pennsylvania Inventories, 1684–1850,* collects actual room-by-room probate inventories. William Seale, *The Tasteful Interlude,* 2nd ed. (Nashville, Tenn.: Ameri-

can Association for State and Local History, 1981), contains period photographs from the late nineteenth century, many of parlors. See also Harvey Green, *The Light of the Home: An Intimate View of the Lives of Women in Victorian America* (New York: Pantheon, 1983), chapter 4. Finally, for information about specific forms of decoration, see Peter Marzio, *The Democratic Art: Pictures for a Nineteenth Century America* (Boston: David R. Godine, 1979), on chromolithographs; Walton Rawls, *The Great Book of Currier and Ives' America* (New York: Abbeville Press, 1979), on that famous firm; and Kenneth Ames, "Material Culture and Nonverbal Communication," *Journal of American Culture* 3 (Winter 1980): 619–642, on the parlor organ and its symbolism. See also Nancy A. Smith, "Pianoforte Manufacture in Nineteenth-century Boston," *Old-Time New England* 69 (Summer–Fall 1978): 27–48; Gwendolyn Wright, *Building the Dream: A Social History of American Housing* (New York: Pantheon, 1981), chapter 5; Martha McClaugherty, "Household Art: Creating the Artistic Home, 1868–1893," *WP* 18 (Spring 1983): 1–26; Candace Wheeler, ed., *Household Art* (New York: Harper, 1893), 28–30, 185–186; Henry T. Williams and Mrs. S. C. Jones, *Beautiful Homes* (New York: Henry T. Williams, 1877), 11–13, 56, 81, 110–112; Robert Edis, *Decoration and Furniture of Town Houses* (New York: Scribner and Welford, 1881), 192–213.

5. Mitchell-Barnes family papers, Cornell University Archives, letter dated "Hume, December 26, 1841," from Mary Wood to her parents. I thank Neil Schwartzbach for bringing this letter to my attention.

6. On the industrialization of the furniture industry, see Bridgeman, *Encyclopedia,* 14–16; Earle Shettleworth and William Barry, "Walter Corey's Furniture Manufactory in Portland, Maine," *Antiques* 121 (May 1982) 1199–1206; Kenneth Ames, "Grand Rapids Furniture at the Time of the Centennial," *WP* 10 (1975): 24–29. On Polly Bennett, see Pauline Inman, "House Furnishings of a Vermont Family," *Antiques* 96 (August 1969): 228–234. Other accounts of parlor furnishings include "Parlor Furnishing," *Godey's* 50 (April 1855): 381, and "The Manufacture of Parlor Furniture," *Scientific American* n.s. 43 (October 9, 1880): 229.

7. Gwendolyn Wright, *Moralism and the Model Home: Domestic Architecture and Cultural Conflict in Chicago, 1873–1913* (Chicago: University of Chicago Press, 1980), 16–21; Wright, *Building the Dream,* chapter 6; Louise Tuthill, *The Young Lady's Home* (Boston: William J. Reynolds, 1847); Lynn Barber, *The Heyday of Natural History 1820–1870* (Garden City, N.Y.: Doubleday, 1980).

8. A. J. Downing, *Country Houses,* 371. The interaction of character and environment was summarized by Wheeler in the introduction to *Household Art* (p. 14): "a perfectly furnished house is a crystallization of the culture, the habits, and the tastes of the family, and not only expresses but *makes* the family." See also Williams and Jones, *Beautiful Homes,* preface.

9. For analytical purposes, I have drawn a deliberately rigid line between these two categories of activities. There are always exceptions. For example, Lydia Maria Child advised mothers to make the parlor pleasant for children (*The Mother's Book* [Boston: Carter, Hendee, Babcock, 1831], 118) and David Handlin argues that parlor games counteracted the parlor's image as a stiff, formal adult space (*The American Home: Architecture and Society, 1815–1915* [Boston: Little, Brown, 1979], 384).

10. Catharine Maria Sedgwick, *Home* (Boston: James Munroe, 1835), 11, 50; "Center-Table Gossip," *Godey's* 50 (February 1855): 185. On the parlor as a symbol of family solidarity, see also Ames, "Material Culture and Nonverbal Communication."

11. Downing, *Country Houses,* 97, 115. Downing wrote extensively on rural matters; he entitled his book *Country Houses,* and in it he denounced country imitations of city life, including the custom of keeping elaborate parlors (370, 410), but he aimed primarily at an audience of businessmen and professionals who left their "country homes" daily to work in

town, or who used their "country homes" as holiday retreats rather than permanent residences. When Downing spoke of women, it was most often with regard to their role as arbiters of taste, a characteristic of new middle-class women. The parlor's function as a room for public display persisted to Wheeler's day. Wheeler saw parlors as "a kind of homage we pay to friendship . . . the idea of being prepared for observation . . . properly underlies all that goes to make up the parlor." (26)

12. Ann Douglas, *The Feminization of American Culture* (New York: Knopf, 1977); Caroline Garnsey, "Ladies' Magazines to 1850," New York Public Library *Bulletin* 58 (February 1954): 74–89; Lawrence Martin, "The Genesis of Godey's Lady's Book," *New England Quarterly* 1 (January 1928): 41–70; Ellen Rothman, "Sex and Self-Control: Middle-Class Courtship in America, 1770–1870," *Journal of Social History* 15 (Spring 1982): 409–427, n. 8; George Hersey, "Godey's Choice," *JSAH* 18 (October 1959): 104–112. In *Godey's* itself, for calling scenes: "The Orphan," 19 (October 1839): 156; Miss Leslie, "The Beaux" 24 (January 1842): 19; 24 (May 1842): 259; and Alice Neal, "The Furnished House," 51 (December 1855): 520; for parties: "Penn Yan," "Male Coquetry," 19 (August 1839): 70; for family gatherings: Mrs. C. Lee Hentz, "Aunt Mercy," 24 (January 1842): 47. *The Illustrated Manners Book* (New York: Leland, Clay and Co., 1855) described calling customs on pp. 86–90, 123–124. See also Emily Holt, *Encyclopedia of Etiquette* (Garden City, N.Y.: Doubleday, Page, and Co., 1913), chapters 2, 3; and Almon C. Varney, *Our Homes and Their Adornments* (Chicago: People's Publishing Co., 1885), 19–22. Sarah Josepha Hale, in *Manners* (Boston: Lee and Shepard, 1889), 218, predictably defended calling customs.

13. Sarah Josepha Hale, *Manners*, 219; Holt, *Encyclopedia*, 37; *The Illustrated Manners Book*, 123; Louisa Tuthill, *The Young Lady's Home*, 155. A. M. Schlesinger, *Learning How to Behave* (New York: Macmillan, 1947) discusses etiquette advice literature. Karen Halttunen, *Confidence Men and Painted Women: A Study of Middle-Class Culture in America, 1830–1870* (New Haven: Yale University Press, 1982), explores the dynamic of middle-class parlor etiquette in chapter 4.

14. For scenes of working or solitary musing in *Godey's:* "Lady of Maryland," "My Aunt's Story," 24 (April 1842): 192; Ezra Holden, "Mary Lloyd," 19 (August 1839): 60; "S. D. A.," "Emma Emlin," 19 (September 1839): 136; "The Votary of Fashion," 24 (February 1842): 86.

15. Carroll Smith-Rosenberg, "The Female World of Love and Ritual," *Signs* 1 (Autumn 1975): 1–29. "Passing of the Parlor," *Atlantic Monthly* 91 (May 1903): 712–714. For other examples in which adult women dominate parlor scenes, see *Godey's* 61 (September 1860): 220; 60 (May 1860): 424; 70 (January 1865): 33; 70 (April 1865): 321. Household Art proponents invariably maintained that the parlor or drawing room was a woman's domain. See Edis, *Decoration and Furniture*, 192. Mrs. Hale contended that married women ought to control social life (*Manners*, 92). See also Holt, *Encyclopedia*, 37.

16. Williams and Jones, *Beautiful Homes*, 13, 111.

17. "The Passing of the Parlor," 713; Downing, *Country Houses*, 121; *Illustrated Book of Manners*, 158. See also William Dean Howells, *A Boy's Town* (New York: Harper, 1890), 75–76; Clarence Cook, "Some Chapters on House-Furnishing," *Scribner's* 10 (June 1875): 172.

18. "The Passing of the Parlor," 714.

19. Sam Bass Warner, *Streetcar Suburbs: The Process of Growth in Boston, 1870–1900* 2nd ed. (Cambridge: Harvard University Press, 1978). See Stephen Kern, "Explosive Intimacy: Psychodynamics and the Victorian Family," *History of Childhood Quarterly* 1 (Winter 1974): 437–463. The interpretation given here of parlor culture draws upon current historians' emerging understanding of the new urban middle class in the antebellum period. Mary Ryan, in *Cradle of the Middle Class: The Family in Oneida County, New York, 1790–1865* (New York:

Cambridge University Press, 1981), for example, suggests that the growing class of families headed by business and professional men responded to the experience of industrialization and urbanization by fashioning a domestic ideology which emphasized family privacy, the role of the mother as guardian of moral virtue, and a shift of women's duty from production to consumption. New prescriptions for social behavior and new standards for cultural accomplishment followed. Parlors might provide what Ryan calls "moral collateral" in the marketplace.

20. For an example of an unusual criticism of the parlor in *Godey's,* see 60 (February 1860): 136.

21. "Hawk Eye," "Our Farmers' Farm Houses," *CG* 5 (March 29, 1855): 205; "The Kitchen," *Moore's* 4 (May 21, 1853): 169; Solon Cooley, "Farm Houses in Michigan," *GF* 18 (April 1857): 115.

22. Anne Gertrude Sneller, *A Vanished World* (Syracuse, N.Y.: Syracuse University Press, 1964), 42, 46; Ellen Chapman Rollins, *New England Bygones,* 94, 203.

23. Harriet Connor Brown, *Grandmother Brown's Hundred Years* (Boston: Little, Brown, 1929), 77; Edward Eastman, *Journey to Day Before Yesterday* (Englewood Cliffs, N.J.: Prentice-Hall, 1963), 168–169; Jared Van Wagenen, *Days of My Years* (Cooperstown: New York State Historical Association, 1962), 20.

24. Brown, *Grandmother Brown.* 743. Etiquette manuals often recognized this difference between country visiting and city calling. For example, Caroline Kirkland, *The Evening Book* (New York: Scribner's, 1852), 40–42, viewed city customs as promoting a superficial social life. See also the *Illustrated Manners Book,* 124, 154; *CG* 40 (February 11, 1875): 94; *Godey's* 20 (February 1860): 121; Jane Pederson, "The Country Visitor: Patterns of Hospitality in Rural Wisconsin, 1880–1925," *Ag. History* 58 (July 1984): 347–365.

25. Thomas Atkeson and Mary Meek Atkeson, *Pioneering in Agriculture* (New York: Orange Judd, 1937), 35–36; "Education of Farmers' Daughters," *OC* 2 (November 1, 1846): 165; Kirkland, *The Evening Book,* 137; Williams, *An American Town,* 42; Lillian Krueger, "Social Life in Wisconsin, Pre-Territory Through the Mid-Sixties," *Wisconsin Magazine of History* 22 (December 1938): 156–171; 22 (March 1939): 312–329; 22 (June 1939): 396–427.

26. *Godey's* 54 (January 1857): 80.

27. *AA* 21 (March 1862): 182–184; "Rooms and Their Ornaments," *OC* 9 (April 1, 1853): 109. See also "Michigan Homes," *MF* n.s. 1 (February 12, 1859): 54; "The Joys of Beautiful and Ornamental Housekeeping," *MF* 3rd ser. 17 (March 16, 1886): 7.

28. Arthur C. Hackley diary, New York State Historical Association, Cooperstown. W. A. Anderson, "Transmission of Farming as an Occupation," *Rural Sociology* 4 (December 1939): 433–448.

29. Nancy Grey Osterud, "Strategies of Mutuality: Relations Among Women and Men in an Agricultural Community," (Ph.D. diss., Brown University, 1984), 512.

30. "Farm House," *AC* 3rd ser. 3 (September 1855): 268–270.

31. *MF* 13 (September 1855): 276; "Hawk Eye," "Our Farmers' Farm Houses."

32. "Eva," "Female Amusements of the Present Day," *AA* 8 (January 1849): 34; "Mrs. B.," "The Kitchen and Its Accessories," *OC* 9 (May 15, 1853): 156; May Maple, "Two Homes Contrasted," *Moore's* 31 (May 15, 1875): 323; "L.R.," "To The Young Ladies of Michigan," *MF* 1 (November 15, 1843): 147; "Fanny," "An Attempt at Housekeeping," *MF* 7 (January 1, 1849): 14.

33. "Elizabeth," "Letter from a Farmer's Wife," *OC* 1 (February 1, 1845): 21. Orville Dewey, "Female Industry," *GF* 8 (January 27, 1838): 30; *DAB* 5:272.

34. E. H. Leland, *Farm Homes* (New York: Orange Judd, 1881), 71–72.

35. Major Patrick, "Two Pictures of a Farmer's Home," *Moore's* 3 (January 15, 1852): 18; "Anna Hope," "Selecting Furniture, Arranging Rooms, etc.," *AA* 16 (November 1857): 265; "Parlors and Parlor Ornaments," *AA* 22 (November 1863): 342; "Beatrix," "That House Plan," *MF* 3rd ser. 13 (July 11, 1882): 7.

36. "Beautifying the Home," *PF* 44 (July 10, 1875): 219.

37. D. G. Mitchell, "The Farmer's Homestead, and its Relation to Farm Thrift," *Annual Report,* Massachusetts Board of Agriculture 24 (1876): 131–141.

38. E. C. Gardner, "Farm Architecture," *American Architect and Building News* 12 (August 19, 1882): 84–85; Lucern Elliott, "Farmers' Homes and Wives," *PF* 43 (May 4, 1872): 139; "Alice Chittenden," "Improvements for Cicely's Parlor," *AA* 49 (February 1890): 76.

39. "A.M.," "Personal Habits at Home," *GF* 19 (March 1858): 94.

40. Leland, *Farm Homes,* 24; "Why The Boys Were Discontented," *MF* n.s. 1 (April 9, 1859): 118; "To The Man in Search of a Wife," *MF* 11 (June 1853): 188.

41. Daniel Walker Horowitz, *The Morality of Spending: Attitudes Toward the Consumer Society in America, 1875–1940* (Baltimore: Johns Hopkins University Press, 1985), 130–136; David Jaffee, "One of the Primitive Sort: Portrait Makers of the Rural North, 1760–1860," in Steven Hahn and Jonathan Prude, eds., *The Countryside in the Age of Capitalist Transformation: Essays in the Social History of Rural America* (Chapel Hill and London: University of North Carolina Press, 1985), 103–141; Daniel Boorstin, *The Americans: The Democratic Experience,* Vintage Books ed. (New York: Vintage Books, 1974), 130–136, 147–157; Boris Emmet, *Catalogs and Counters: A History of Sears, Roebuck and Company* (Chicago: University of Chicago Press, 1950); Williams, *An American Town,* 119–120; "Selecting Carpets," *MF* 3rd ser. 12 (January 18, 1881): 7. Angel Kwollek-Folland, "Domesticity and Moveable Culture in the United States, 1870–1900," *American Studies* 25 (Fall 1984): 21–37; Mrs. Howard, "Woman's Rural Life," *PF* 46 (April 10, 1875): 115; "Beatrix," "The Parlor," *MF* 3rd ser. 13 (March 14, 1882): 7; "A Hint or Two About That Parlor," *MF* 3rd ser. 12 (March 22, 1881): 7; "The New Parlor Furniture," *PF* 47 (October 14, 1876): 331; "Household Taste," *PF* 47 (April 22, 1876): 133.

42. Kirkland, *The Evening Book,* 14; *GF* 6 (July 30, 1836): 245; "Arozina," letter, *MF* 1 (December 1, 1843): 155; Rollins, *New England Bygones,* 147, 196, 203; *PF* 44 (January 25, 1873): 27; Williams, *An American Town,* 35; *PF* n.s. 3 (January 1859): 10.

43. Fred Shannon, *The Farmer's Last Frontier* (New York: Farrar and Rinehart, 1955), 357. For more information on the impact of migration, see Harold Wilson, *The Hill Country of New England* (New York: Columbia University Press, 1936); Robert J. Mitchell, "Tradition and Change in Rural New England," *Maine Historical Society Quarterly* 18 (Fall 1978): 78–107; Rebecca Shepherd, "Restless Americans: The Geographical Mobility of Farm Laborers in the Old Midwest 1850–1870," *Ohio History* 89 (Winter 1980): 25–46. "How the Boys Were Reconciled," *MF* n.s. 1 (April 16, 1859): 126; "The Boys and the Parlor," *AA* 48 (May 1889): 248; A. L. Jack, "What to Do in the Evenings," *Moore's* 42 (June 30, 1883): 414; "Grandmother," "Pleasant Sitting-Rooms," *Moore's* 42 (March 31, 1883): 206; "Lavendar," "Hints to Those About to Build," *CG* 23 (March 10, 1864): 154; D. G. Mitchell, "The Farmer's Homestead," 139–140.

44. H. T. Vose, "Octagon House," *AC* 3rd ser. 7 (July 1859): 214; *Rural Affairs* 2 (1858–60): 316. [Vose was incorrect in citing the volume number.]

45. "S. W. A.," "Advice about Building Houses," *Moore's* 17 (April 7, 1866): 110; "Lavendar," "Hints to those About to Build"; Mrs. Leland, *Farm Homes,* 16. See also, "B," "On The Situation and Construction of Farm Buildings," *MF* 13 (July 1855): 195–199.

46. "First-Class Farm House," *Moore's* 22 (August 20, 1870): 121.

47. Solon Robinson, *Facts for Farmers* (New York: A. J. Johnson; Cleveland: F. G. & A. C. Rowe, 1866), 282; "Amos," "Sucker Cottage," *PF* 12 (January 1852): 20.

48. "W," "Plan of a Farm House," *AA* 22 (September 1863): 265; anon., "Alteration of an Old House," *Rural Affairs* 2 (1858–60): 262.

49. Morris Clinton, "A Convenient and Cheap Farm House," *Moore's* 41 (December 16, 1882): 849; "A Cheap Cottage," *Moore's* 30 (December 5, 1874): 361.

50. Arthur C. Hackley diary, New York State Historical Association, Cooperstown.

51. "P.," "Farm Houses," *Moore's* 7 (February 16, 1856): 53; "House-Building-#1," *Moore's* 10 (April 30, 1859): 141; Lillian Mayne, "Using the Parlor," 654.

52. "Maryland Matron," "A Simple But Convenient House," *CG* 55 (January 5, 1888): 17.

53. Leland, *Farm Homes,* 19–20. That so many farmer-designers omitted the parlor altogether is somewhat surprising, because, though few people wrote to praise its positive qualities, the parlor continued to fulfill an important purpose. Crucial rites of passage were often observed in the home parlor. Some otherwise pragmatic, economical farmers must have felt compelled to retain this room: its symbolic importance, its association with ancestors and with solemn commitments, outweighed its everyday impracticality. An understanding of the demise of the parlor as a sacred space must await a more extensive study of rural social practices that can be undertaken here. I would offer a conjecture. Arthur Cole has associated the demise of private customs of childbirth, weddings, funerals—"rites of passage"—with the price system: commercial services such as hospitals and funeral homes replaced the traditional home ceremonies. Progressive farm families, more extensively committed to the "price system" than other rural residents, may have switched to extra-domestic services sooner than others (Arthur H. Cole, "The Price System and the Rites of Passage," *AQ* 14 [Winter 1962]: 527–545).

54. John Higham, "The Reorientation of American Culture in the 1890s," in *Writing American History: Essays on Modern Scholarship* (Bloomington: Indiana University Press, 1970), 16–86, detects a "revolt against rigidity" and a turn to informality in the 1890s. Specific criticisms of the parlor by Cook and Bok may be found in Clarence Cook, "Some Chapters on House-Furnishings," *Scribner's* 10 (June 1875): 169–181; Edward Bok, "Is It Worth While?" *Ladies Home Journal* 17 (November 1900): 18. In his autobiography, Bok claimed to have reformed Americans' tastes and to have singlehandedly influenced Americans to abandon their parlors (*The Americanization of Edward Bok* [New York: Scribner's, 1920], 241–243). But the public received mixed signals from Bok's journal, because most of the house plans he featured and many of the columns he carried still supported parlor culture. See for example Mrs. Hamilton Mott, "Giving an Afternoon Tea," *Ladies Home Journal* 10 (March 1893): 4, or Mrs. Burton Harrison, "The Small Courtesies of Social Life," *Ladies Home Journal* 12 (March 1895): 10. For other late nineteenth-century attacks on the parlor, see "Best Parlors," *Scribner's* 2 (October 1871): 658–659; "Mrs. Nipper's Best Room," in William Thayer, *Womanhood: Hints and Helps for Women* (New York: Thomas Whittaker, 1895), 107–113; "The Sacrificial Parlor," *Scribner's* 9 (March 1875): 762. Williams, *Beautiful Homes,* 13, 111, 138, advocated that families have both a sitting room and parlor.

55. Helen Campbell, "A Comfortable Home," *Cosmopolitan* 3 (1887): 195–197.

56. Folke T. Kihlstedt, "The Automobile and the Transformation of the American House," *Michigan Quarterly Review* 4 (Fall 1980/Winter 1981): 555–570, convincingly demonstrates how the auto contributed to the parlor's fall. For an account of the development of the funeral home industry and profession, see James J. Farrell, *Inventing the American Way of Death, 1830–1920* (Philadelphia: Temple University Press, 1980).

57. Vincent Scully, *The Shingle Style and the Stick Style: Architectural Theory and Practice from Downing to the Origins of Wright,* rev. ed. (New Haven: Yale University Press, 1971), 88. Scully argues that open planning was associated with the domestic architecture of the Shingle Style in the 1870s and 1880s. Most of the plans Scully discusses derived their "openness" from a spacious "living hall." The hall, formerly planned as a circulation space, expanded to occupy a much larger area. Some architects experimented with vertical space; large fireplaces and staircases provided visual focus. Scully attributes these developments to an "insistent suburban evocation of a lost agrarian simplicity" (because many of these monuments were designed in the Colonial Revival style) and to a desire for "informal living." The plans and monuments described by Scully derive mostly from "high-style" architecture designed by professionals for affluent clients. While the plans in his book unquestionably illustrate original spatial experimentation, it is significant to note that experimentation is limited to halls and verandas. Parlors (which appear in nearly every plan, even to the twentieth century), dining rooms, and kitchens usually retain their spatial specialization. Thus in a sense the hall was the ultimate in "waste space." Scully himself acknowledged this when he wrote that plans for smaller houses could not successfully incorporate both (73). Consequently it was in vernacular, middle-class homes, not in high-style monuments, that spatial informality was realized most fully.

SIX

Supervision to Self-Culture: Children's Spaces on the Progressive Farmstead

IN DESIGNING work and leisure spaces, progressive farmhouse designers had acted as cultural mediators, selectively combining ideas from the wider society with their own sense of what a distinctively rural culture demanded. But in attempting to accommodate changing concepts of childhood and adolescence with ideals that were specifically rural in planning nurseries, playrooms, and children's bedrooms, progressive farmer-designers met with frustration. The age-segregated farmhouse was an ambiguous response to a complex web of social changes ranging from falling birth rates to anxiety over the future of agriculture. More than any other aspect of domestic planning, the design of children's space presented intractable difficulties for farmhouse planners, forcing them to confront a major implication of agricultural change: fewer and fewer farmers' children would grow up to live on farms themselves. Children's spaces designed to facilitate the reproduction of farming families were unrealistic by the end of the century, and farmhouse planners had to grapple with deep tension between their own commitment to rural life and their realization that farm children were as likely to become clerks and milliners as farmers and farm wives. The children's spaces in their designs reflected this dilemma. Over the course of the century, they became more independent of other spaces and more differentiated by age and by gender. Designers justified these rooms for children on the grounds that they were necessary to keep children on the farm, but separate rooms for children lent themselves equally well to separate, individual pursuits.

Fifty-seven of the farmhouse plans sent by subscribers between 1832 and 1900 included at least one room designated for children. Until about 1860, these rooms usually took the form of nurseries or "family bedrooms," and their occupants were infants and young children. The nursery was in a cluster of ground-floor family rooms including the kitchen, sitting room or dining room, bath, and bedrooms. Older children received little special consideration, which mirrored their variable status in the wider society. In the two decades after 1860, removal of the nursery from the kitchen's vicinity not only increased the latter room's isolation but also emphasized the growing importance of child nurture. Moreover, older children's spaces assumed more prominence: the "playroom" appeared, along with appropriate furniture to fill it. After 1870, discussions in the farm literature expanded to include a range of special rooms and outdoor play areas for children and adolescents, sometimes designated for a particular age or for boys or girls only. By the last decades of the century, an intense preoccupation with a "room of one's own" heralded a shift from strict

Fig. 6–1. Anonymous plan for a farmhouse in Buffalo, New York (1848). (A) Hall. (B) Parlor. (C) Family room. (D) Kitchen. (E) Bedrooms. (F) Family bedroom. (G) Young children's bedroom. (H) Storeroom. (I) Pantry or Milk room. (K) Wood house. (c) China closet. (o) Clothes presses. (s) Stairs.

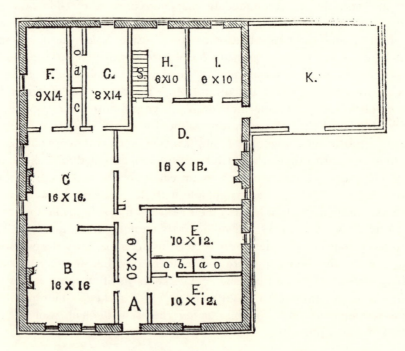

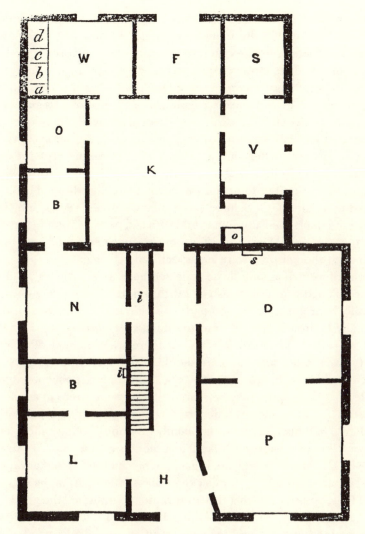

Fig. 6–2. Anonymous plan for a farmhouse, probably in Illinois or Wisconsin (1847). (B) Bedrooms. (D) Dining room. (F) Wood house. (H) Hall. (K) Kitchen. (L) Library. (N) Nursery. (O) Bath. (P) Parlor. (S) Storeroom. (V) Veranda. (W) Washroom. (a) Boiler. (b) Water tank. (c) Pump. (d) Wash form. (i) Closets. (o) China closet. (s) Sliding door.

supervision of children within the home to more independence. Children's rooms were still within the home's compass, but now had more privacy.

During the antebellum decades, the nursery, child's bedroom, and "family bedroom" were the most conspicuous children's spaces in farmer-designers' plans. The nursery was for young children or for the sick. The term "family bedroom" usually meant sleeping accommodations for parents plus one or more young children. Children's bedrooms, when mentioned, were also intended for babies and toddlers. Planning of spaces for small children took on a consistent pattern in this period: all nurseries were on the ground floor; the nursery or young child's bedroom was placed near the kitchen, dining room, or family room; and the nursery usually adjoined a bedroom occupied by adults. J. O. Schultz (1850), Lewis Allen (1848), and George Rand (1859) all planned adjoining children's and parents' rooms (Figures 2–29, 6–3, 6–4, 6–5). Many other bedroom arrangements followed the same pattern even though they were not specifically labeled.

The earliest plan among those collected here, Lewis Allen's 1832 farmhouse, contained two rooms designed with children in mind. Plan No. I had two family bedrooms, a common parlor and kitchen (Figure 2–26). In Plan II, a family bedroom opened onto the kitchen (Figure 2–26). Lucy Ellis's 1847 plan reflected her opinion that "if there are a number of small children, it is very important that there should be a nursery upon the first floor, connected with a bathing-room, and as near the dining room and kitchen as possible, that the mother may be spared all *unnecessary* steps in attending to her duties in these several departments" (Figure 3–7). Similarly, in "H.A.P.'s" 1848 plan, family room, family bedroom, young children's bedroom, and kitchen were all linked together in an intimate arrangement (Figure 6–1). "H.A.P." explained that "young children should always sleep near their parents, on account of sickness and sudden calls in the night." He echoed Ellis, pointing out that this arrangement permitted "the good housewife . . . [to] oversee the affairs of her family and kitchen without taking too many unnecessary steps." A contemporaneous plan from the *Prairie Farmer* also linked kitchen, nursery, bedroom, and bathing room (Figure 6–2).[1]

The existence of nurseries and young children's bedrooms implied more consideration for small children (and perhaps also more rigid sexual mores) than in the eighteenth-century days of the trundle-bed; these spaces are strong evidence that children were regarded as individuals. However, the clustering of family-oriented and work rooms with children's rooms suggests that individual rooms did not necessarily bring increased autonomy for children. Where adult supervision was facilitated by direct communication with kitchen, dining room, living room, or family bedroom, the cre-

Fig. 6–3. (Right) J. O. Schultz, plan for a farmhouse in Sloatsburg, New York (1850). (A) Parlor. (B) Sitting room. (C) Kitchen. (D) Bedroom. (E) Children's bedroom or Library. (F) Wash house. (G) Wood house. (H) Hall. (P) Piazza.

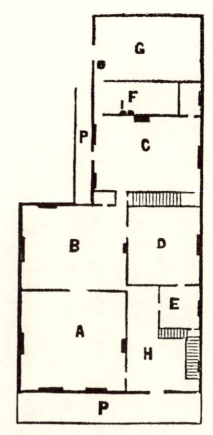

Fig. 6–4. (Below) George B. Rand, design for a farmhouse in St. Johnsville, Vermont (1859). Elevation.

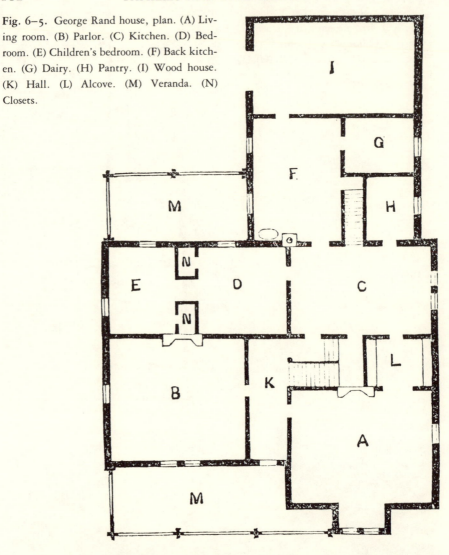

Fig. 6–5. George Rand house, plan. (A) Living room. (B) Parlor. (C) Kitchen. (D) Bedroom. (E) Children's bedroom. (F) Back kitchen. (G) Dairy. (H) Pantry. (I) Wood house. (K) Hall. (L) Alcove. (M) Veranda. (N) Closets.

ation of a specific space for young children suggests confinement to a well-defined, and therefore potentially restrictive, spatial environment. Farmer-planners often described the nurseries as their own possessions rather than the child's; an example is the "Working Woman" who referred to "her nursery" in the *Genesee Farmer*.[2]

These room arrangements may have expressed in spatial terms new concepts of child rearing. During the early years of the century, religious liberalism (specifically the decline of the theology of innate depravity), Lockean psychology, and the political ideology of republicanism all led to a reassessment of the nature of the child. Beginning about 1830, a flood of prescriptive literature on child rearing poured out of American publishing houses—literature which revealed changing concepts if not actual practice. One important new idea was the "unequivocal affirmation of the mother's predominance," sealing the previous generation's idealization of "republican motherhood." Concepts of discipline also gradually changed (although there was little agreement on this question): subtle manipulation of the child's affections and concerns with the development of the child's character replaced direct punishment. Education of the small child also passed from the "world of words and ideas, to the world of things." Precocity became a quality feared rather than encouraged, and childhood was sentimentalized. Under a regime of gradual, monitored unfolding of the child's capacities, the mother appeared "in the role of constant attendant." Some historians relate these developments in child nurture to the necessity in a capitalist economy for steadiness, character, and a good name in business. Progressive farmers, as good capitalists, also valued these qualities. The agricultural journals at mid-century frequently published articles addressed to parents (especially to mothers) that stressed the importance of developing a child's conscience, of wielding moral influence upon families, and of cultivating children's cheerful obedience. For the children themselves, the mid-century journals featured short stories which unequivocally illustrated cardinal virtues—honesty, discipline, punctuality—and their rewards.[3]

Historian Joseph Kett has written that the mid-nineteenth century growth of interest in gradually inculcating moral restraints (as opposed to the sometimes vain hope of a child's spontaneous religious "conversion") led to "planned, engineered environments" to facilitate the steady, maternally controlled formation of the child's character. Kett speaks of an "environment" broader than architecture alone, but his terminology is suggestive for domestic spaces. Within the home the nursery—conducive to the constant administering of moral precepts, religious instruction, and intellectual concepts—was likely to be the center of moral discipline.[4]

The farmhouse nursery expressed this concern spatially, and also perhaps represented a growing sentimental awareness of children. Still, the nursery on the progressive farmstead was as much a provision for the farm wife as for the child. By contrast, designers addressing nonagricultural audiences often removed the nursery to the second floor, perhaps because the non-farm wife's work was more exclusively domestic and did not require continually moving in and out of doors, and also because some child-care duties would be performed by "domestics." In planning farmhouse nurseries, farmer-designers again adjusted plans to their own needs.[5]

Where rooms for older children (ages 5 and upward) were concerned,

few rural writers or planners in the antebellum years had much to say. This
may have been because in antebellum America, particularly on the farm,
children assumed their place quite early in the family labor force. Boys
helped their fathers plow, sow, and harvest; girls worked with their mothers
in orchard, dairy, poultry yard, and kitchen. As with their elders, not all
children's tasks were rigidly defined by gender: Ellen Chapman Rollins
remembered that in mid-century New England, "the driving of cows to
pasture passed by rotation from one child to another" and that both boys
and girls worked "among the sheaves" in the fields. The agricultural periodicals frequently mentioned instances where mother, boys, and girls
shared the cultivation and the profits of the kitchen garden.[6]

The scanty evidence available indicates that boys' and girls' bedrooms
usually were separate, but neither the function nor appearance of these
rooms were deemed important enough for special comment. Lewis Falley
Allen was the only rural architectural writer to deal with special rooms for
older children in the pre-Civil War period, justifying his interest on the
grounds that farm children deserved fair compensation for their work. In
Rural Architecture, he argued, "If any people are to be well lodged, why not
those who toil for it?" Allen also thought individual rooms for girls would
encourage preparation for housekeeping: "there are other rooms for the
daughters Sally, and Nancy, and Fanny, and possibly Mary and Elizabeth—
who want their own chamber, which they keep so clean and tidy, with
closets full of nice bedclothes, and table linens . . . for certain events not
yet whispered of, but quite sure to come round."[7]

Certain rooms of the house, such as the sitting room, were used by
everyone in the family. Another type of room designated for common use
that appeared in several progressive farmers' plans was a natural history
room, housing collections of minerals, plants, etc. The agricultural press
encouraged farm children to regard the outdoors as a vast laboratory, full of
lessons in botany, geology, and natural history. Early boys' and girls' columns featured rather dense explanations of such topics as "Lime" or "the
Care of Cows." J. J. Thomas's 1844 plan (Figure 6–6) and Cyrus Bryant's
plan (Figure 2–10) show a separate room for this; in George Rand's 1859
plan (Figure 6–5) the collection was kept in a family room. Rand believed
that this "tasteful home" would "keep the children beneath the home roof,
and make their associations of home pleasant, and their enjoyments
pure . . . [and] prove a source of serenest joy to sweeten the declining
years of the parents." The fact that these specimen collections were in a
room used by all suggests that parents and children alike enjoyed and used
them, and were perhaps a part of the children's instruction.[8]

Domestic space for children was for the most part undifferentiated

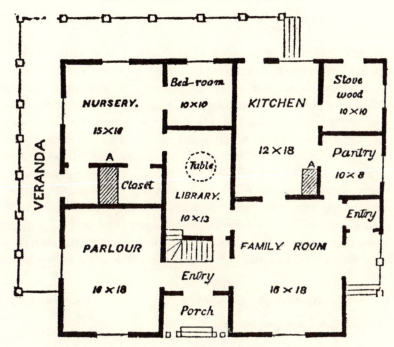

Fig. 6–6. J. J. Thomas, plan for a farmhouse (1844).

because few defining categories could be applied to youth. Young people moved irregularly between the ranks of the dependent and the semidependent. A rural boy might attend school part of the year, usually in winter, and spend the rest of the year working on his family farm or on a neighbor's farm. Farm girls helped with the household chores and the younger children; some might work at neighboring farms as "helps." Farm diaries and children's letters to the journals show that farm children attended school irregularly; if they were needed at home, they stayed home and worked. Young people were not rigidly classed by age in school or in other groups such as lyceums, clubs, and voluntary associations; neither were they set apart in the domestic setting.[9]

Between 1860 and 1880, children's spaces in the progressive farm home began to change from previous patterns. For young children, the practice persisted of planning rooms opening onto rooms occupied by adults. But the nursery now rarely adjoined the kitchen; instead it was moved closer to the dining room, sitting room, or family room. At the same time, for children beyond the nursery years, playrooms began to appear, signaling a shift in concepts of childhood. For older boys and girls, discussions about bedrooms introduced themes which would develop more fully in the 1880s and 1890s.

An early indication of the shift of the nursery away from the kitchen came in S. H. Mann's 1858 octagon plan, which he submitted to the *Country Gentleman* in response to another contributor's octagon plan. Mann criticized the latter plan, explaining that he did not believe a family room ought to open directly onto the kitchen. His own plan showed the nursery opening onto the drawing room (which Mann explained was used constantly by the family), library, bath, and hallway (Figure 6–7). The following year, H. T. Vose planned a nursery which, even though it shared a wall with the kitchen, was not connected to the kitchen by any doorways. This style was followed during the 1860s and 1870s, as illustrated in C. W. Spalding's 1861 plan, another in the *Country Gentleman* for 1872, and B. W. Steere's 1873 plan (Figures 4–7, 6–8, 6–9). Although the nursery had moved away from the kitchen, it was still connected to or near adult rooms to make

Fig. 6–7. S. H. Mann, plan for an octagon house in Beloit, Wisconsin (1858).

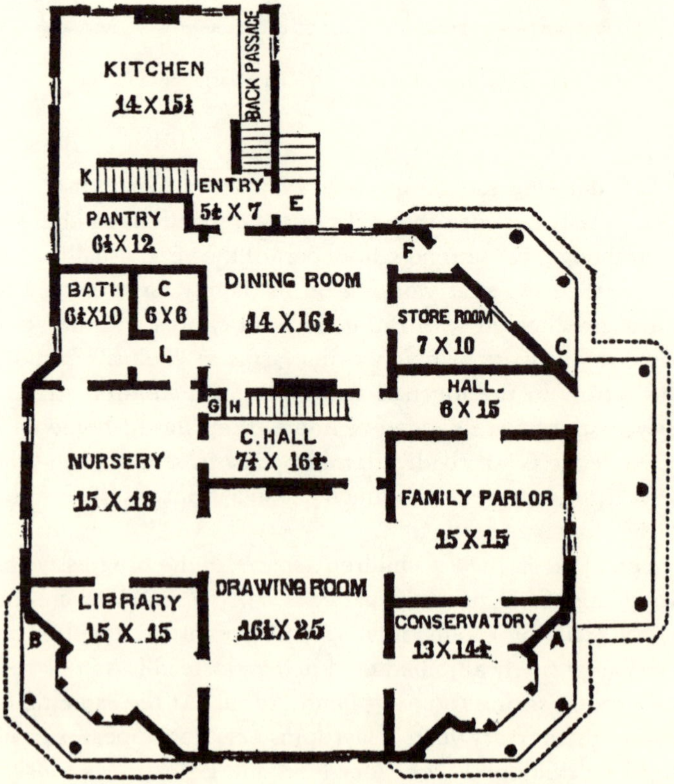

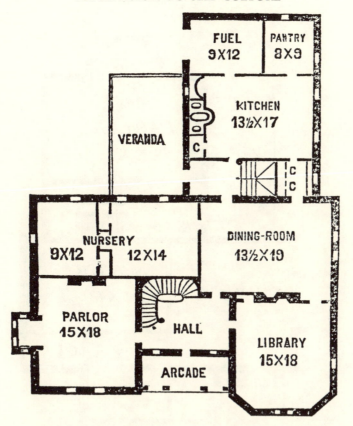

Fig. 6–8. Anonymous plan for a "country house" (1872).

supervision easier. The idea of monitoring children—at least the younger ones—had remained intact.

At the same time, farm wives began to discover drudgery. One critique of drudgery was the belief that excessive farm work prevented farm women from adequately filling the "sacred office" of motherhood. Disillusioned farm wives began to concentrate, in ideology at least if not in practice, on child nurture.

For young children new, more clearly defined spatial arrangements began to appear in the 1860s and 1870s. In particular, progressive farm children began to work for "themselves," in their own designated spaces. By the 1870s the farm press was encouraging farmers to give their children—especially sons—their own plot of land or livestock, and allow them to keep all the money they made. The purpose was education and to instill in the children an interest in agriculture. By this means farmers hoped to "attach

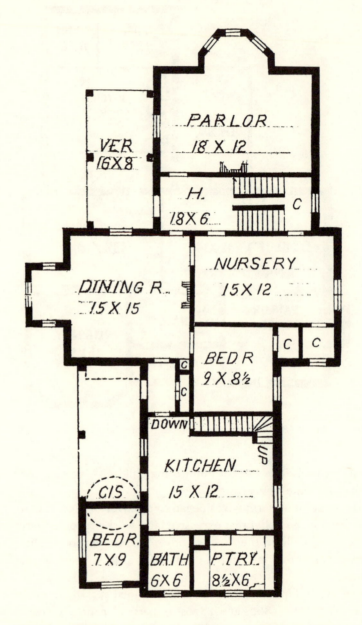

Fig. 6–9. B. W. Steere, plan for a farmhouse in Michigan (1873).

[the child's] heart to the soil" and ensure continuance of the family farm. For the children, the chief attraction was the spending money. Some progressive farm families, apparently, accepted the idea. In agricultural journals' "Girls' and Boys' Letter Boxes," young people wrote about their own farm projects. By the 1880s, Hoosier farm boy Ottis Bland had written, "I have a pig. It was the smallest of the lot. I fed him milk and now he is the largest." "Percy" from Illinois received from his mother "5 hens and a rooster for taking care of the chickens last summer." Amton Trenkle (12, DeWitt County, Illinois) reported that "My popcorn yielded 4½ bushels from five rows, 3 bushels I sold for $1 per bushel, and the rest I kept." "Julia ABP" of Lanesboro, Pennsylvania, was given a lamb to raise, and got one-tenth of the potato crop to sell for keeping bugs off the plants. "May L. L.," an Iowa farm girl, earned spending money by raising and selling pigs and a calf. Children also mentioned receiving wages for work they performed on the farm: "Papa pays me the same as he does the rest of the [berry] pickers," reported Carrie Ritter, Syracuse, in 1882. Writing in his diary in 1861, Arthur C. Hackley, a 10-year-old farm boy in upstate New York, noted: "I have been spading some ground that father gave me." By 1863 he was harvesting strawberries from his patch and selling them at 12½¢ a quart. In the back of the diary, the boy kept his accounts, recording, among other things, his purchase of *Fullers Strawberry Culturist*.[10]

These testimonies from farm children themselves help to build a picture of the changing use of space on the farmstead. Part of the farm, however small, had been set aside for their use, and this established a differentiation within the farmstead according to age. In the 1840s and 1850s, writers spoke of gardens as shared by mothers and children, but by the 1870s, the children had plots of their own.

Children's play and work was also becoming more differentiated within the farmhouse. Eva Collins, in her prize essay "The Playroom Made Over" (*American Agriculturist* 1867), introduced the first extended discussion of a playroom to the agricultural literature. She wrote:

> The play-room is six feet by nine, or would be of those dimensions, only that a chimney occupies a third of one end of the room, protruding eighteen inches into the apartment, which makes it appear even smaller than it is in reality. It was originally a large closet, but had been from time immemorial, so far as I am concerned, given up to the little girls for a play-room . . .

She continued, describing the furnishings in elaborate detail. The little girl, Jennie, helps with the renovation. The girls are given a workbasket on condition that "no work can be undertaken before the article under way is completed, except by permission. Jennie, and I believe children generally, likes the plan of being obliged to decide for herself, and then of being held to her own decision." Miss Collins concluded by praising the playroom:

> Mothers! Do not hastily wrest the play-room from the children. It has a mission to fulfill. It teaches them by constant practice how to make the most of every thing . . . The lessons learned in the play-room, more than anywhere else, are industry, patience, gentleness, economy, and accuracy, while the taste is cultivated, and the affection sacredly cherished . . . The child may be taught, but the lessons can be learned only by itself.

Miss Collins's portrayal revealed new attitudes regarding places in the home for children. First, the playroom was for older children, not denizens of the nursery. Apparently it was on the second floor, away from immediate maternal supervision. There, a little girl imagined that "it [would] seem like keeping house in earnest." Adult supervision still played an important role, for example in regulating and assigning workbasket tasks. But the emphasis now was on having the young learn for themselves, and not simply passively receiving instructions. The children also helped in decorating their own space, and they were expected to develop self-discipline there.[11]

By 1870 a playroom had appeared in a farmhouse plan. This small room (PR, Figure 6–10) opened off the top of the stairs on the second story. It was not entirely self-contained, for even though it occupied a corner of the house, it had no doorway; instead, it opened onto a large, irregularly shaped upstairs hall. The play area probably spilled over into this space, allowing some adult oversight. Still it was a separate space, away from the downstairs. Like Eva Collins's playroom, it combined adult supervision with a measure of children's autonomy. Moreover, while the nursery promoted a variety of social contacts among very small children, the playroom encouraged contacts between older children, reinforcing the trend toward age segregation.

The appearance of playrooms implied acceptance of the idea that play makes a positive contribution to a child's development. Just where this room fits in the history of ideas about children's play is unclear, for a comprehensive history of play has yet to be written. One historian argues that until the early nineteenth century play was seen as an "antidote to idleness and disorder," provided that it fulfilled the Protestant-inspired purposes of "inculcat[ing] good habits, preserv[ing] health, and help[ing] to develop self-control." Concepts of play changed beginning in the eighteenth century. The "no-toy" culture of the eighteenth century (in which children and adults played together in rooms used by the family in common) gave way in the nineteenth century to controlled, didactic, individual play within a domestic setting, and children's toys took a prominent role.

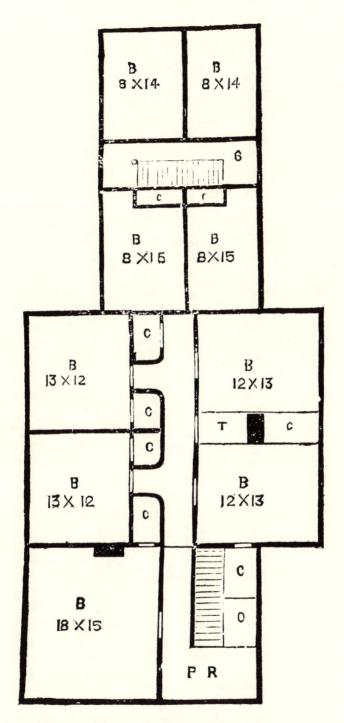

Fig. 6–10. Anonymous plan for a "first-class" farmhouse (1870). *Second Floor Plan:* (B) Bedrooms. (C) Closets. (PR) Playroom. (T) Tank.

After mid-century, the influence of Friedrich Froebel's philosophy spread. Froebel complemented a romantic ideal of childhood with a liberal concept of play which emphasized the discovery of the environment, self-development, and socialization, all carefully directed. Not surprisingly, the farm press publicized his ideas as early as the 1870s, for example in a column in the *American Agriculturist*. Seen from this broad historical perspective, the transitional nature of the playroom is evident: children's activities there were viewed as didactic and individualized, in the tradition of the earlier generation, but the child's own self-development was also emphasized.[12]

Private bedrooms, especially for girls, began to emerge in this period. Young people's letters to the agricultural papers in the early 1870s show that girl correspondents delighted in decorating their bedrooms. In 1870 the "Youth's Corner" in *Moore's* greatly expanded as the farm press recognized children as a distinct constituency. One of the first letters came from a 14-year-old girl who wanted to correspond with other girls "about the way they adorn their rooms. She [her friend] has just the coziest room, Mr. Editor! It is the sweetest place two girls ever sat down to chat, read, and sew." She went on to describe the room, its plants, furniture, and decorations. There were "photographs, and engravings that Annie has made herself out of twigs, straw, thread, paper, and gilt." This letter initiated a correspondence in the column which ranged from descriptions of rooms to a discussion of the health benefits of keeping houseplants in a bedroom.[13]

Two detailed letters give an especially good idea of what these rooms actually looked like, and show how deeply involved their young inhabitants were in adorning and using their own rooms. Mabel Grahame, 16, wrote in August of 1870:

> There are two windows, one south the other west. The room is furnished with light colored furniture. Under the west window I have a small lounge the cover of which I worked myself in worsted; and I have two stools worked after the same pattern. The paper is a spray of "lily of the valley" on lavender-colored paper. In the west window are my two canary birds. I think a great deal of them, they were a present from my brother.
>
> The south window is almost an oriole [oriel] window, it opens down to the floor so that I can sit out on the little porch outside. In the window I have a quantity of Southern plants and Northern ones. My uncle lives South and sends me a great many rare plants; there are three hanging baskets, also.
>
> On the walls, colored pictures of all the family; also cork pictures and oil paintings, water colors, and drawings by myself . . .
>
> Opening off the north side is a room nearly the size of this room with one window facing the west; this room is my sitting-room and is separated

from my sleeping room by glass doors . . . A lounge and an easy chair are almost the only furniture in the room which is filled with flowers and plants of all descriptions and kinds . . . In one corner is my piano—a present from my parents. Over the piano is my bookcase . . .[14]

In another number of the "Young People's Corner," Mattie Martin, 13, wrote:

I have a room with an east window and a little low chair beside it, an ottoman before it, and a little desk at one side. The walls are adorned with photographs of several Presidents and Vice-Presidents, engravings and paintings. I have no brother to make vases for me, so I have to do without them. But what I like best in the whole room is a little library that was given to me, which contains over one hundred volumes. How I do love to go up to my room on Saturday and read![15]

These remarkable letters described little self-contained worlds fashioned by adolescent farm girls. The girls packed their rooms with objects: the young decorators seemed to have the Victorian horror of voids. Some of the objects (pianos, furniture) indicated that consumer goods were coming to the farm, but the girls also placed high value on symbolic things. Hand-worked lounge covers, pictures, even bookcases signified investments of the maker's time and skill, and placed her individual stamp on this private environment. Also prominent were objects associated with the family—even in their physical isolation, these girls were surrounded by reminders of parents, brothers, uncles, aunts, and cousins.

By contrast, no descriptions of boys' rooms—by the boys or by anyone else—appeared in the 1870s or 1880s. The only discussion of domestic space for boys came in the form of prescriptive advice, mostly from adults. Writers of the post-Civil War period repeatedly charged that farmers thought "any room was good enough for the boys," even as they furnished attractive chambers for the girls. In Edmund Morris's 1868 novel, *Farming for Boys:*

the three boys slept in a great garret room, a rough, unfurnished apartment, hung round with cobwebs, and open enough to permit the wasps to enter and build long rows of nests. There was nothing to educate the eye, no neatness or order,—no curtains to the windows, no carpet on the floor, no looking-glass or washstand,—nothing, in short, to give a cheerful aspect to the place in summer, or make it comfortable in the winter. Any room seemed good enough for the boys.

In contrast, Morris pointed to the girls' room, "one of the best chambers, carpeted and furnished, with a dressing-bureau, chairs, and tables, with curtains . . . and a variety of other accessories." The girls had been given the "essentials," and their "native taste" had contributed the rest. In the end, of course, Morris's boys get their rooms, and become virtuous farmers because of it.[16]

Solutions to the perceived problem of domestic space for boys varied. In the 1860s and 1870s, the agricultural journals recommended that boys be given special space in sitting rooms or in jointly occupied bedrooms, or even in the kitchen. Most thought in terms of areas for the boys together, rather than for each one individually. The main idea was that attractive surroundings would prevent boys from drifting cityward.[17]

Between 1880 and 1900, the trend toward age segregation in the progressive farmhouse increased. Children's spaces became more sharply defined, more varied in type, and keyed to particular age groups—from babies' playpens to special corners for children to private bedrooms for adolescent boys and girls.

Beginning about 1880, a new type of structure, the forerunner of the modern playpen, appeared in the columns of the agricultural papers. In 1879 Mr. "H. W. T." of Worcester, Massachusetts, sent to the *American Agriculturist* "drawings of a Baby's Play-House that he [had] constructed" (Figure 6–11). "A corner of the room is penned off by means of a light portable fence, to form an inclosure where the child can not get into mischief, and can amuse itself at will." The subscriber himself explained that:

> Baby is ready for the play-house as soon as he can creep, and for a year and a half afterwards, or until able to climb over the fence, the child will occupy the house very contentedly many hours in the day, and the mother can feel certain that it will not . . . receive injury while she goes to another room or elsewhere. After he gets used to the situation he enjoys it. He can have his playthings here, and they will not get scattered. He can look out of the window, peep through the slats, or climb up and learn to walk by their aid.[18]

This concept became more popular during the 1890s. In 1891, the *American Agriculturist* described "Baby's Corner Lot," a house for the baby made by rearranging sitting-room furniture. The article praised the arrangement for its airiness, light, and safety. She continued, "What if the sitting-room does look a little cluttered? The baby comes first and last."[19]

Such attitudes marked a significant change from the old days of the nursery as a place for discipline and moral instruction. The child now had the power to cause the rearrangement of furniture in a space once symbolic of strict family order. "H.W.T." described his playpen as much in terms of

Fig. 6–11. Engraving titled "View of Baby's Play-House" (1879).

the child's perspective as of the mother's, intimating that while the child was confined it was not constantly supervised.

New conceptions of the nursery itself reinforced this trend. In the 1893 *Agriculturist,* "Palmetta Montclair" declared that "even among [families with no formal nursery] there is one room inhabited by a baby to the exclusion of most of the others; a room where he is at liberty to crawl about, where he takes his nap and makes the most of his infant existence." She recommended that the baby have his own, child-scaled furniture. The nursery now is seen as a space built expressly for the baby and dominated by him. References to discipline or instruction were noticeably less common.[20]

The anonymous author of an 1888 article in the *American Agriculturist* addressed the problem of household clutter created by children's toys, clothing, and other objects. Her solution was to provide a corner with shelves and drawers where each child could keep personal treasures. This specialized furniture was intended to promote orderliness, as in the playroom, but now children had absolute control over it. "The child," she wrote, "is monarch of all he surveys." The supervision apparent in Eva

Collins's playroom of 1867 yielded here to the child. Moreover, a toy chest replaced the workbasket for the child of 1867. The arrangement implied that children now actually owned objects; apparently capitalist values of ownership and acquisition were appearing among progressive farm children. The provision of special spaces and furniture for children had begun to create a separate world for children within the home, and the progressive farmhouse was increasingly incorporating the concept of childhood as a distinctive and creative stage of life.[21]

Perhaps the most significant new architectural expression for young people was the interest in a "room of one's own" for adolescents. Girls had cherished their own rooms since the 1870s. "Every young girl likes a pretty room, a place to keep her treasures, her letters, her photographs," declared the *American Agriculturist* in 1889. Earlier discussions of children's bedrooms had focused only upon girls' rooms, but beginning in the 1880s the idea for all adolescents became more and more popular among progressive farm writers. Boys' rooms in particular were given more attention. One account in *Moore's* (1880) describing "Boys and their Home Surroundings," argued that boys' rooms were not attended to on the grounds that the boys were not often there. The author claimed that the boys (like their sisters) would spend more time in their bedrooms if only the rooms were made more attractive, and urged readers to provide a separate room for each boy. "[L]et the boy's room be just as warm, bright, and cheerful as motherly love and sisterly ingenuity can make it." This would bring several benefits. The boy would develop his own sense of taste, and would have a place for wholesome social activity: "If the room is often full of merry boy companions drawn there because of its attractiveness, don't fret; be thankful that you have succeeded in making 'home the best place' to the boys." A story in *Moore's* (1887) explained "Why Jack Staid at Home." Jack's friends at the corner grocery receive an invitation to visit his "own special den." They accept reluctantly; when they arrive at Jack's home, "anticipating their shyness if he took them in the family-room among his bright-eyed sisters, he ushered them at once upstairs." The visitors marvel at the attractive room, admiring its bed "as white as the spare beds at the[ir own] homes," pictures, a sofa, bookshelves, and games. An advice columnist in the *American Agriculturist* for 1890 counseled parents not to "keep any room shut up as a spare room while your boy sleeps with his younger brother." Rather, give him a separate room and "let him feel that it is his, and that you respect its privacy and sanctity." A studious boy, this writer declared, could learn more in his own room than he could with "the family about him." This room would ensure "one of the sweetest and firmest of home ties to a youth."[22]

Occasionally the "boy" himself (or a columnist) joined the chorus. An article from "One of the Boys" (1888) pleaded with farm parents to "Give the Boys a Chance." "How about their room?" it asked. "Do you let the boys 'bunk' all together in the garret? Or, possibly, do you let them sleep two in a room? If so, do you not notice that they quarrel considerably?" The author went so far as to attribute boys' "gloomy and morbid nature" and even their tendency to drink to overcrowded bedrooms. His solution was to "separate them by giving each a room for himself." This enterprising youth described his own bedroom, which he decorated and furnished by himself. Any boy who did likewise, he believed, would acquire "energy, life, and an ambition to work for larger things, as he has worked for his room."[23]

Columnists went beyond simply separating boys from one another: by the mid-1890s they categorized boys' rooms according to age. The column by Palmetta Montclair in the *American Agriculturist* on "How Some Boys are Housed" set out these distinctions. She first made the familiar contrast between the bare garret, where four boys slept two to a bed, with an ideal home where boys were properly housed. In the latter, the women, instead of "reading trashy literature and working crocheted tidies for the parlor," made rugs for the floor of the boys' rooms; the "boys themselves stained and oiled" the floor. In this particular home the "small boy's room" contained furniture scaled to his size, including a toilet stand, toy chest, and bookshelves (Figure 6–12). The writer noted that "picture cards, discarded birds' and bees' nests, little cabinets filled with beetles, butterflies, and minerals, formed an interesting jungle." Besides all of this, the room had a "Robinson Crusoe Corner" (a cavelike affair for imaginary adventures) and an area for whittling. The boy's "Pocket money depended upon keeping his room neat." The older boy's room was "altogether . . . more different and dignified." It contained a writing desk (in place of the toy box), pictures, sports equipment, nature specimens, a hammock, and chairs "for friends."[24]

The notion of a "room of one's own" emerged along with the newly developing concept of adolescence (first fully articulated by G. Stanley Hall in his landmark study of *Adolescence,* 1904), which stressed biological changes in sexual maturation and associated them with psychological changes. Adolescence was no longer viewed as a time of rising physical power, but as a time when much body energy goes into physical growth, and as a period of emotionalism and idealism.[25]

Young people, it was thought, needed privacy at this difficult stage, and parents increasingly regarded separate rooms as fulfilling this need. The boys in the story of "Jack" were portrayed as being shy with girls, and writers continually cited the need to isolate boys from vaguely defined evil

Fig. 6–12. Engraving titled "A Variety of Rooms for Boys" (1894).

influences which presumably included sexual allurements. Other writers portrayed the private room as a retreat for the "poor, shy school girl, with big hands and big feet . . . the awkward, overgrown daughter."[26]

Privacy for adolescents (especially boys), however, was not viewed in an entirely positive light by fin-de-siècle child-rearing advisers. The fear existed that too much privacy would encourage excessive "self-abuse," or masturbation. The *American Agriculturist* writer who attributed boys' "gloomy and morbid nature" to sharing rooms likely shared this apprehension, for "morbid" was a code-word with sexual allusions. The idea of self-culture associated with private bedrooms for children clearly had limits.[27]

As a leisure space, the "room of one's own" represented farm writers' coming to terms with another element in the changing conception of adolescence—the idea that adolescents were not as physically mature and capable as adults. In the mid-century decades, farm boys worked along with the farmer and his hands; Lewis Allen wanted to house boys decently because they worked for it. In the 1868 novel *Farming for Boys,* the author endorsed relief from unremitting toil, but still ascribed to the boys a large capacity for work. By the last decades of the century, the farm papers not only questioned the farmers' unstinting demand for work, but also reevaluated boys' and girls' capacities. One farmer wrote to the *American Agriculturist* in 1897 that boys of twelve to fifteen were incapable of doing a man's work. By 1913, William McKeever, author of *Farm Boys and Girls,* advised farmers to assign boys work and to "see that the work is for the boy's sake," not for the farm's. McKeever warned the farm father "from [age] 13–15, watch the boy for the beginning of adolescence and be unusually careful not to overwork him. Most of his bodily strength must go into making bone and muscle," and he needed a room of his own where he could relax.[28]

Even children's collecting had changed in location and in purpose, at least from adults' point of view. Stories of the 1890s implied that boys and girls now collected as much for personal expression and ownership as for educational reasons. One writer on the child-study movement, E. A. Kirkpatrick (1903), associated the "collecting instinct" with the "play instinct." "[E]mulation, imitation, pleasure of ownership, and of classifying or arranging" were the reasons for collecting, he wrote. "The educational value is not so much in what is collected as in the physical, mental, and volitional activity called forth." Placing of the collection in the child's own room reinforced its personal meaning, in contrast to the family-centered collection of the antebellum period.[29]

In the period 1860–1900, then, people on the farm began to be "filtered" into different spaces according to age. At first the nursery was still linked to adult rooms, but it was no longer strictly associated with work space, indicating, perhaps, that it was regarded more as a children's space. With time, the nursery became more and more independent. The playroom made its first appearance in the 1860s, signifying a willingness on planners' part to think in terms of space exclusively for children. Adolescent girls' and boys' chambers developed into isolated, self-contained worlds; girls' rooms appeared first, boys' rooms later in the century. Outdoors, separate garden plots and farm projects further set young people apart.

The emergence of well-defined children's spaces on progressive farmsteads was a response to complex social changes during the nineteenth century, especially in its final decades. Demographic change, new concepts of childhood and adolescence, increasing age segregation, and a perception of crisis in rural America all influenced progressive farmhouse designers' domestic reorganization.

The ideal of separate rooms became possible as the fertility rate of white women dropped by 50 percent over the course of the century. Rural fertility rates were higher than urban rates, but dropped more quickly. The number of boarders in rural households also dropped. At the same time, the number of bedrooms in progressive farmers' homes had changed very little: from 1840 to 1900, the number of bedrooms per plan averaged 4.4. So as family size dropped, each family member could claim more private space.[30]

As various stages of childhood were being defined, specialization of rooms in the farm homes according to age was occurring. The child-study movement, influenced by psychology and Darwinism, advocated systematic, scientific, empirical study of child development. One by-product of the movement was a set of normative standards of the capacities and activities that could be expected at specific ages. As childhood stages became intellectually compartmentalized, they also became spatially divided.[31] Finally, the segregation of children within the farm house reflected their changing position in society. Boys and girls now attended graded public schools. In rural areas, district school systems were established beginning in the 1890s, and vocational education for agriculture became the domain of the land-grant colleges; the antebellum farm mother's role in education had now been supplanted by public institutions. Separate study in school was followed by separate study at home. The *American Agriculturist* columnist's remark that a studious boy could not learn "with the family all around" would probably have been regarded with puzzlement a generation earlier, when the schools were filled with students of all ages, all audibly learning their lessons at once. By 1904, the Cornell agriculture college's extension booklets depicted a secluded "Boy's Corner" in the farmhouse lined with books. Boys and girls also joined Sunday schools, clubs, and in rural areas the Juvenile Grange, a forerunner of the 4-H movement. James Mickel Williams, in his classic study, *An American Town* (Waterville, New York), noted that rural youths even began to socialize among themselves, in town, by the latter part of the century, favoring friends of their own age over the more mixed gatherings of an earlier day.[32]

The growing importance of the consumer economy must also figure in the popularity of separate children's farm projects and wages. Consumer goods were numerous, varied, and geared to specific markets. By the 1870s, page after page in the agricultural journals advertised enticing bargains for everything from pocket watches to children's magazines; in 1880, *Moore's* published a story titled "The Children's Acre" in which farm children used the proceeds from their vegetable garden to purchase an organ. Farm boy Oscar Chapman expressed a common viewpoint in *Moore's* "Young People's Corner" (1882). "I like to have the proceeds of my garden to spend as I please, and when I work all the time I would like to have my Saturday's wages for my own use. Boys don't like to ask their parents for every penny."[33]

Another architectural development was the conversion of the spare bedroom into a room for family members, not guests. This recalled the idea that the parlor, as a "company room," ought to yield to family areas. The farm house was becoming more private and insular, excluding outsiders to accommodate family members.

The growing age segregation of the progressive farmstead—manifested in the appearance of playrooms, children's gardens, and later, in adolescents' bedrooms—indicated a fundamental change in the way progressive farm parents regarded their children. It seems likely that in prosperous farm families, despite declining family size, children's work became less crucial as the century went on. Mechanization and the availability of hired hands reduced this need, and by the 1870s there were other reasons for having children work—to educate them, to secure their commitment to farming, and to allow them to earn spending money. The appearance of playrooms perhaps indicates that progressive farmers (along with their urban middle-class counterparts) increasingly sentimentalized childhood, elevating children's emotional value and deemphasizing their purely economic worth. Adolescents' private bedrooms likewise functioned as havens, not rewards for work.

Girls' work on the farm showed signs of diminishing earlier than did boys' work; this was in keeping with the "de-feminization" of agriculture after the Civil War. Many of the girl correspondents of the "Boys and Girls Clubs" omitted all mention of farm work, instead concentrating on discussions of school, houseplants, or music lessons. Within their rooms, cut off physically if not psychically from the rest of the house, farm girls were reading, sewing, visiting, and playing music—all activities which suggested self-culture and required leisure time. Ironically, in the same era when progressive farm mothers were discovering unprecedented drudgery, their daughters apparently were finding time to devote to leisure pursuits. Given the preoccupation with toil so pervasive among progressive farm wives in the same period, it is tempting to dismiss the possibility that farm daughters' experience diverged so sharply from their mothers' lives. But the farm literature suggests that these girls and young women may have been moving in new directions. Contributors complained that farmers' daughters no longer were able to perform traditional farm tasks. Elaine Goodale in 1881 defined the "farmer's daughter" not as "that sturdy, red-cheeked maid-of-all-work, who kneads bread and picks up potatoes," but rather as "one who stands a little aside from the engrossing toil and every-day interests of the farm, with a realizing sense of its value as art, as life . . ." A piece in the *Prairie Farmer* in 1878, titled "Farmers' Daughters as They Were and Are," summarized the trend: a generation ago the farmer's daughter "grew to woman's estate with few advantages; her education neglected, all her more delicate taste smothered and forced to a life of toil that cultivated the muscles and numbed the brain." In the 1870s, though, "the organ and piano have supplanted the buzzing wheel and the great clattering loom"; the daughter finished her work by afternoon, and had time to read and visit.

Others worried about the implications of this trend, even if they welcomed increased opportunities for girls' education. In 1873, a Vermont farmer's wife wrote that "What to Do With Our Girls" was "in many households a subject of serious anxiety. . . . There was a time," she continued, "when girls could milk cows, feed pigs, work in the garden, make butter and cheese, do housework, and turn a deft hand to all kinds of housework. . . . But now they are not needed at home." Yet girls could not afford to be idle, because "it does cost a fortune to keep up with the times!"[34] Girls' rooms, then, expressed their ambiguous status in the household; they foreshadowed a life of domesticity, albeit domesticity of a different kind than their mothers had learned.

Not only was the need for farm children's labor diminishing, but it was increasingly clear by the century's end that farm boys and girls could not count on—and often did not want—a future in agriculture. The United States's farm population was about 60 percent of the total in 1860; by 1900, only about one-third of the population lived on farms. Progressive farm families began to acknowledge that there were fewer opportunities for young people at home; as agricultural modernization continued, it became more difficult to acquire land, and agricultural depression forced more people to migrate. Also, many young people were attracted to the cities by the superior wages and easier work of nonagricultural jobs. Certainly many rural young people found careers in agriculture through education in the expanding land-grant college system, but those who abandoned the country attracted more attention. By the 1890s, social scientists were "discovering" what they perceived to be moribund rural communities, and their publications added to the perception of crisis in rural America.[35]

Again, it was young women whose futures were most likely to be affected. Agricultural writers accepted the need (and the desirability) for young women to learn nonagricultural trades, pointing out that "the girl who can make a dress, set type, teach French . . . keep books, or do anything useful, has a deposit upon the bank of Practical Utility." Columns described the new opportunities for women in the cities: this was the era when the female-dominated fields of clerical work, librarianship, and sales expanded. One young woman acknowledged the attractions of city jobs with a withering comment: she "couldn't imagine why girls should prefer the disagreeable work of teaching and dress-making, to the pleasant little task of cooking when the thermometer is 110° in the shade . . . of watering the flowers or vegetables with their perspiration while working in the hot sun . . . or of being patted by a sentimental cow with the hind legs during the pleasant pastime of milking."[36]

For farm boys as well, the agricultural press reluctantly recognized the need for nonagricultural jobs. To be sure, the call was still to keep the boys on the farm, but more and more recommended training that would match a young man's individual interests and capacities. One writer pointed out that no one worried when ministers' or bankers' sons did not succeed their fathers, and asked why farmers followed a different logic. In 1874 a Madison, Wisconsin, correspondent answered the question of "How Shall the Boys be Kept on the Farm?" by recommending that farm parents not try in the first place; it was "unalterable circumstances," he said, that caused the migration, and parents would do well to adjust rather than choose the path of futile resistance. However, the persistence of the agrarian ideal—the tradition of passing on the family farm and the occupation of farming itself—made it very difficult for progressive agriculturists to face the reality of migration. They had devoted their lives to proving the superiority of rural life, yet they had also helped to stimulate the cityward trend they so deplored.[37]

Progressive farm writers hoped that a "room of one's own" would keep farm boys and girls from fleeing to the cities. Countless pieces repeated the message of an 1888 "Plea for the Boys' Room" linking an attractive room with an "awaken[ing] in the growing mind of many a boy a love for home" and ultimately a commitment to maintain the family farm. But the "room of one's own" could represent an equally strong countervailing force. Because it permitted and even encouraged individual activity, personality, and character, the separate room prepared the child to pursue his or her own interests. By the 1890s, some farm writers were explicitly associating separate rooms with education for nonagricultural occupations. Thus age-segregation both reflected and encouraged the accelerating trend from a predominantly rural, agrarian society to an urban one.[38]

In reshaping children's space, then, progressive farmers were mediating between rural and urban cultures, past and future, but not with the same conviction that they had shown for the introduction of farm technology or capitalist agriculture. In the problem of children's arrangements, they were forced to contemplate the future of the rural society they had helped to create—a future that contained fewer and fewer farmers. The contradictory function of the age-segregated farmhouse reflected their ambivalence.

NOTES

1. *GF* 2 (November 3, 1832): 348–350; *AA* 6 (June 1847): 183–186; *AC* n.s. 5 (January 1848): 29; *PF* 7 (May 1847): 151–153.

2. "Working Woman's Cottage," *AC* n.s. 6 (January 1849): 25; Abbott Lowell Cummings, "Notes on Furnishing a Small New England Farmhouse," *Old-Time New England* 48 (Fall 1957): 79–80.

3. Anne Louise Kuhn, *The Mother's Role in Childhood Education: New England Concepts, 1830–1860* (New Haven: Yale University Press, 1947), 27, 101, 105; Nancy Cott, "Notes Toward an Interpretation of Antebellum Child-rearing," *Psychohistory Review* 6 (Spring 1978): 4, 8, 11; Mary Ryan, *Cradle of the Middle Class: The Family in Oneida County, New York, 1790–1865* (New York: Cambridge University Press, 1981); Joseph Kett, *Rites of Passage: Adolescence in America, 1790 to the Present* (New York: Basic Books, 1977). Daniel Blake Smith, "Autonomy and Affection: Parents and Children in Chesapeake Families," in Michael Gordon, ed., *The American Family in Social-Historical Perspective,* 3rd ed. (New York: St. Martin's Press, 1983), 209–229, argues that in the "child-centered" Chesapeake family, children enjoyed considerable autonomy.

Several bibliographical essays discuss the directions of current scholarship on childhood: Ross Beales, "In Search of the Historical Child: Miniature Adulthood and Youth in Colonial New England," *AQ* 27 (October 1975): 379–398; Miles Shore, "The Child and Historiography," *JIH* 6 (Winter 1975): 495–505; and N. Ray Hiner, "The Child in American Historiography: Accomplishments and Prospects," *Psychohistory Review* 7 (Summer 1978): 13–23. Robert Sunley, "Early Nineteenth Century American Literature on Child Rearing," in Margaret Mead and Martha Wolfenstein, eds., *Childhood in Contemporary Culture* (Chicago: University of Chicago Press, 1955), 150–167, contains a useful bibliography of primary sources. Two attempts to use pictorial materials to analyze the historical experience of childhood occur in Stephen Brobeck, "Images of the Family: Portrait Painting as Indices of American Family Structure, Culture, and Behavior 1730–1860," *Journal of Psychohistory* 5 (Summer 1977): 67–80; and Anita Schorsch, *Images of Childhood: An Illustrated Social History* (New York: Mayflower Books, 1979). See also Mary Cable, *The Little Darlings: A History of Child Rearing in America,* 2nd ed. (New York: Charles Scribner's Sons, 1975); Viviana Zelizer, *Pricing the Priceless Child: The Changing Social Value of Children* (New York: Basic Books, 1985); "Column for Children," *CG* 5 (January 4, 1855): 14; *CG* 5 (May 3, 1855): 286; *CG* 5 (May 10, 1855): 302.

4. Kett, *Rites,* 112; Clifford Clark, "Domestic Architecture as an Index to Social History," *JIH* 7 (Summer 1976): 33–56; William Bridges, "Family Patterns and Social Values in America, 1825–1875," *AQ* 17 (Spring 1965): 3–11.

5. For example, all nurseries in Calvert Vaux's *Villas and Cottages* (1864. Reprint, New York: Dover Publications, 1970) were on the second floor; six of nine nurseries in A. J. Downing's *The Architecture of Country Houses* (1850. Reprint, New York: Dover Publications, 1969) and *Cottage Residences* (1842. Reprint, Watkins Glen, N.Y.: American Life Foundation, 1967) were located on the second floor. Even Catharine Beecher, in the *Treatise on Domestic Economy* (Boston: Marsh, Capen, Lyon, & Webb, 1848), 267, placed a "nursery" and a "room for young children" upstairs. (See Fig. 3–11.)

6. Joan Jensen, *Loosening the Bonds: Mid-Atlantic Farm Women, 1750–1850* (New Haven: Yale University Press, 1986), chapters 3 and 8; E. H. Arr [Ellen Chapman (Hobbs) Rollins], *New England Bygones* (Philadelphia: J. B. Lippincott, 1880), 29, 191–192; "Keeping the

Track," *MF* n.s. 1 (March 12, 1859): 85; *MF* n.s. 2 (July 28, 1860): 238; *PF* 8 (August 1848): 235; *PF* 9 (September 1849): 290; *PF* 12 (December 1852): 537; David Schob, *Hired Hands and Plowboys: Farm Labor in the Midwest, 1815–1860* (Urbana: University of Illinois Press, 1975).

7. Lewis Falley Allen, *Rural Architecture* (New York: Orange Judd, 1852), 108, 109.

8. For early boys' and girls' columns, see *AA* 4 (May 1845): 65; *PF* n.s. 2 (December 9, 1858): 375; *PF* n.s. 7 (February 7, 1861): 96; Lynn Barber, *The Heyday of Natural History, 1820–1870* (Garden City, N.Y.: Doubleday, 1980). Cyrus Bryant's niece remembered that the "cabinet of carefully labelled minerals . . . filled our minds with wonder at the erudition of the uncle whose treasures these were" (*Bryant Association Reunion of 1897*, p. 73).

9. Kett, *Rites;* Kett, "Adolescence and Youth in Nineteenth-Century America," *JIH* 2 (Autumn 1971): 296; Faye Dudden, *Serving Women: Household Service in Nineteenth Century America* (Middletown, Conn.: Wesleyan University Press, 1982); Nancy Cott, *The Bonds of Womanhood: "Woman's Sphere" in New England, 1780–1835* (New Haven: Yale University Press, 1977); *PF* n.s. 3 (March 3, 1859): 138.

10. "Children and Chickens," *CG* 5 (June 7, 1855): 363; *CG* 40 (December 9, 1875): 733; *CG* 40 (July 8, 1875): 430; *Moore's* 29 (April 17, 1874): 259; "Encourage the Child," *PF* 44 (September 20, 1873): 297; S. O. Johnson, "Education for Farmers' Boys," *CG* 35 (January 13, 1870): 88; S. P. P., "Encourage the Boys," *CG* 35 (March 17, 1870): 169; Daisy Eyebright, "Shall Our Boys Stay On the Farm?" *CG* 38 (July 24, 1873): 478; Ulysses P. Hedrick, *The Land of the Crooked Tree* (New York: Oxford University Press, 1948); *Moore's* 31 (April 17, 1874): 259; *PF* 58 (February 6, 1886): 93; *Moore's* 42 (May 5, 1883): 290; *Moore's* 42 (May 12, 1883): 306; *Moore's* 41 (September 9, 1882): 630. Arthur C. Hackley diary, May 25, 1861; July 3, 1863. New York State Historical Association, Cooperstown.

11. Miss Eva Collins, "The Play-Room Made Over," *AA* 26 (September 1867): 331.

12. "Faith Rochester" publicized Froebel's work in the early 1870s. See *AA* 30 (May 1871): 186; see also *PF* 57 (April 14, 1885): 169. On toys, see Bernard Mergen, *Play and Playthings* (Westport, Conn.: Greenwood, 1982), 5, 12; John Brewer, "Childhood Revisited: The Genesis of the Modern Toy," and Evelyn Weber, "Play Materials in the Curriculum of Early Childhood," in Karen Hewitt and Louise Roomet, eds., *Educational Toys in America* (Burlington, Vt: Fleming Museum, 1979), 3–11 and 25–37, respectively. Mergen places the appearance of the playroom in the twentieth century. He asks, "Does the shift from nursery to playroom to family room in house plans reflect shifts in attitudes toward play or changes in play behavior, or both, or neither?" (81). His question does not apply to this work, since I describe not a shift from nursery to playroom but the addition of playroom to the nursery. Moreover, mention of playrooms begins earlier than the twentieth century. As Mergen points out, no uniform methodology for investigating play space (or play itself) has been worked out by scholars. Mergen suggests three possible models for thinking about children's play space: "Control of the exotic" (as in a zoo), "administration of the savage" (as in an Indian reservation) [sic], or "uneasy resignation" (as with an invading army) (81). Amusing and provocative as these conceptualizations may be, they seem to reflect late twentieth-century ways of thinking about children more than they apply to the Victorian playroom described by Miss Collins.

13. "A Girl's Letter," *Moore's* 22 (June 18, 1870): 402.

14. *Moore's* 22 (August 13, 1870): 114.

15. *Moore's* 22 (July 30, 1870): 88.

16. Edmund Morris, *Farming For Boys* (Boston: Ticknor and Fields, 1868), 54–55.

17. See for example, "A Word To The Girls," *PF* 43 (March 2, 1872): 70; "Farmer Boys,"

MF n.s. 1 (September 30, 1859): 294; "Why the Boys were Discontented," *MF* n.s. 1 (April 9, 1859): 118; "Our Boys," *PF* n.s. 19 (November 30, 1867): 346–348; Ellen Baxter, "Leaves From a Home Journal, Number II," *PF* 45 (March 21, 1874): 95.

18. "Baby's Play-House—Fencing in the Baby," *AA* 38 (April 1879): 147.

19. Mrs. Edna Donnell, "Baby's Corner Lot," *AA* 50 (July 1891): 398.

20. Palmetta Montclair, "Suggestions for the Nursery," *AA* 52 (October 1893): 566. On children's furniture, see Karin Calvert, "Cradle to Crib: The Revolution in Nineteenth-Century Children's Furniture" in Mary L. S. Heininger et al., *A Century of Childhood 1820–1920* (Rochester, N.Y.: Margaret Woodbury Strong Museum, 1984), 33–63.

21. "Children's Corners," *AA* 47 (June 1888): 250; *PF* 59 (May 12, 1888): 312; "Room and Rooms for the Young People," *CG* 46 (February 3, 1881): 78. Several perceptive discussions of the role of toys in American cultural life can be found in: Bernard Mergen, "Toys in American Culture: Objects as Hypotheses," *Journal of American Culture* 3 (Winter 1980): 743–751; by the same author, "The Discovery of Children's Play," *AQ* 27 (October 1975): 399–421; and John Brewer, "Childhood Revisited: The Genesis of the Modern Toy," in Hewitt and Roomet, eds., *Educational Toys in America, 3–11.*

22. "A Dainty Room," *AA* 48 (January 1889): 22–23; "Girls and Their Bedrooms," *CG* 52 (February 10, 1887): 117; "A Girl's Room for $15," *AA* 55 (March 1895): 242; "Room and Rooms for Young People," *CG* 46 (February 3, 1881): 78; Virginia Franklin, "Boys and Their Home Surroundings," *Moore's* 39 (October 23, 1880): 709; Selma Claire, "Why Jack Staid at Home," *Moore's* 46 (May 23, 1887): 358; "A Boy's Own Room," *AA* 49 (May 1890): 270.

23. "One of the Boys," "Give the Boys a Chance," *Moore's* 47 (August 18, 1888): 548.

24. Palmetta Montclair, "How Some Boys are Housed," *AA* 53 (January 1894): 24.

25. Kett, *Rites;* G. Stanley Hall, *Adolescence* (New York: Appleton, 1904); William Byron Forbush, *The Boy Problem,* 6th ed. (Boston and Chicago: The Pilgrim Press, 1901–1907).

26. *CG* 50 (July 23, 1885): 614; Kett, *Rites,* 133.

27. Stephen Nissenbaum, *Sex, Diet and Debility in Jacksonian America: Sylvester Graham and Health Reform* (Westport, Conn.: Greenwood, 1980); James Whorton, *Crusaders for Fitness: The History of American Health Reformers, 1830–1920* (Princeton, N.J.: Princeton University Press, 1982).

28. L. V. Hopkins, "Fathers and Sons on the Farm," *AA* 59 (March 13, 1897): 347; William McKeever, *Farm Boys and Girls* (New York: Macmillan, 1913), 171, 181.

29. E. A. Kirkpatrick, *Fundamentals of Child Study* (New York: Macmillan, 1903), 206–207.

30. Carl Degler, *At Odds: Women and the Family in America From the Revolution to the Present* (New York: Oxford University Press, 1980): 181; Susan Bloomberg et al., "A Census Probe of Southern Michigan 1850–1880," *Journal of Social History* 5 (Fall 1971): 26–45; Wendell Bash, "Changing Birth Rates in New York State, 1840–1870," *Milbank Memorial Fund Quarterly* 41 (April 1963): 161–183; Richard Easterlin, "Factors in the Decline of Farm Fertility," [sic] in Michael Gordon, ed., *The American Family in Social-Historical Perspective* 2nd ed. (New York: St. Martin's, 1978).

31. Ernest Belden, "A History of the Child Study Movement in the United States, 1870–1920," Ph.D. diss., University of California-Berkeley, 1965; Bernard Wishy, *The Child and the Republic: The Dawn of Modern American Child Nurture* (Philadelphia: University of Pennsylvania Press, 1968), 94; Kett, *Rites,* 228. See also Karen Feinstein, "Kindergartens, Feminism, and the Professionalization of Motherhood," *International Journal of Women's Studies* 3 (January–February 1980): 28–39.

32. Lee Soltow and Edward Stevens, "Economic Aspects of School Participation in the

Mid Nineteenth Century United States," *JIH* 8 (Autumn 1977): 221–243; Isaac Roberts, *Autobiography of a Farm Boy* (Albany, N.Y.: J. B. Lyon, 1916), 60; Kett, *Rites,* 122, 150; Lawrence Cremin, *The Transformation of the School: Progressivism in American Education, 1876–1957* (New York: Knopf, 1961), 42–48, 75–80; Wayne Fuller, *The Old Country School: The Story of Rural Education in the Midwest* (Chicago: University of Chicago Press, 1982), 147–151, 228; Anne M. Keppel, "The Myth of Agrarianism in Rural Educational Reform, 1890–1914," *History of Education Quarterly* 2 (June 1962): 100–113; *CG* 55 (September 18, 1890): 748; *CG* 55 (September 4, 1890): 708; *Moore's* 33 (April 15, 1876): 255; *Moore's* 32 (December 4, 1875): 371; *Moore's* 29 (April 3, 1874): 225; and *Moore's* 44 (September 26, 1885): 656; Clayton Ellsworth, "The Coming of Rural Consolidated Schools to the Ohio Valley 1892–1912," *Ag. History* 30 (July 1956): 119–128. On 4-H, see Dick Crosby, "Boys' Agricultural Clubs," USDA *Yearbook* (1904), 489–496, and Theodore Erickson, *My 60 Years with Rural Youth* (Minneapolis: University of Minnesota Press, 1956). For an example of a periodical aimed at rural children, see the *Junior Naturalist Monthly,* first published in 1899 at Cornell University. James Mickel Williams, *An American Town* (New York: The James Kempster Printing Co., 1906), 69; Cornell University, *Farmers' Wives Reading Course,* ser. 2 (January 1904): 144.

33. "The Children's Acre," *Moore's* 39 (June 19, 1880): 402; *Moore's* 41 (January 21, 1882): 50.

34. Mrs. C. A. Stephens, "Our Daughters and Their Work," *PF* 45 (December 19, 1874): 403; Elaine Goodale [Elaine Goodale Eastman], *Journal of a Farmer's Daughter* (New York: G. P. Putnam's Sons, 1881), 1–2; "Farmers' Daughters as They Were and Are," *PF* 49 (June 22, 1878): 198; "What To Do with Our Girls," *CG* 38 (April 10, 1873): 235. A similar process had taken place in the late eighteenth and early nineteenth centuries: rural daughters were displaced by economic changes as textile making industrialized. They became, among other things, the first factory labor force. See Nancy Cott, "Young Women in the Second Great Awakening in New England," *Feminist Studies* 3 (Fall 1975): 15–29.

35. Fred Shannon, *The Farmer's Last Frontier: Agriculture, 1860–1897* (New York: Farrar and Rinehart, 1945), 351; Wilbur Zelinsky, "Changes in the Geographic Patterns of Rural Population in the United States 1790–1960," *Geographical Review* 52 (1962): 492–524; Donald Adams, "The Standard of Living During American Industrialization," *Journal of Economic History* 42 (December 1982): 903–917. David B. Danbom, *The Resisted Revolution: Urban America and the Industrialization of Agriculture, 1900–1930* (Ames: Iowa State University Press, 1979); James H. Madison, "Reformers and the Rural Church, 1900–1950," *JAH* 73 (December 1986): 645–668; Lura Beam, *A Maine Hamlet* (New York: Wilfred Funk, 1957), 208.

36. "What Shall We Do with the Girls?" *MF* 3rd ser. 13 (February 14, 1882): 7; "What to Do with Our Girls," *CG* 38 (May 22, 1873): 334. Defenders of rural life agreed that something had to be found for country girls to do, but insisted that young women could find remunerative pursuits in the country if only they exercised their ingenuity, perhaps by keeping poultry, bees, or dairy cows. The problem with these recommendations was that many of these skills were disappearing from women's repertoire because the small-scale operator was less and less competitive in an era of agricultural specialization.

37. "How Shall the Boys Be Kept on the Farm?" *PF* 45 (April 18, 1874): 121; Williams, *An American Town,* 220.

38. "Plea for the Boys' Rooms," *PF* 40 (May 12, 1888): 312; Alice Chittenden, "A Word for Our Boys," *CG* 55 (August 29, 1890): 688. Charles Martin, *Hollybush: Folk Building and Social Change in an Appalachian Community* (Knoxville: University of Tennessee Press, 1984),

found that individualized spaces appeared when families began to realize that in a society governed by the cash nexus, individual initiative was more often rewarded than was collective action. David Potter, in his provocative *People of Plenty: Economic Abundance and the American Character* (Chicago: University of Chicago Press, 1954) tried to link the phenomenon of American abundance to character formation as accomplished within the private family. He believed that abundance encouraged individuality by a variety of means: bottle feeding reinforced the infant's autonomy; home heating eliminated the need for restrictive clothing; and in the room of one's own, "the household space provided by the economy of abundance has been used to emphasize the separateness, the apartness, if not the isolation, of the American child." (197)

SEVEN

From Production to Consumption: Progressive Farmhouse Design at the Turn of the Century

By 1900, the domestic landscape of the progressive farm home was quite different from that of the 1830s. At first planners had organized their designs primarily around farm production, but by the turn of the century, family life had become their main basis for spatial organization. The twentieth-century farmhouse now accommodated fewer functions. On their way out, for example, were the feeding and housing of farm hands, and ritual social occasions (weddings, funerals). Preparing and serving food, family activities, informal visiting, and sleeping quarters assumed greater prominence, and were given a new spatial order. The progressive farmhouse now contained but a few basic rooms: kitchen, dining room, living room, bedrooms. The kitchen was small, specialized, and isolated—no longer the spatially integrated kitchen/dairy/buttery/meal room/child care area of the 1830s. The dining room usually was directly connected to a sitting room, living room, family room, or sometimes to a parlor, creating large, relatively open spaces. Parlors were being replaced by informal, family-oriented spaces. Finally, sleeping rooms were more private and more important. Ground-floor bedrooms were still common, but they no longer opened onto other rooms; instead, hallways or passages provided social buffers. Bedrooms were also more age-segregated, and rooms for children in particular had become especially prominent.

Mrs. Mary A. G. Buell's prize-winning plan in the *American Agriculturist* for 1895 illustrates these trends (Figure 7–1). Kitchen, dining room, hall, and living room are the principal ground-floor spaces. The Buells also had a milk room because they kept a "small dairy" besides their main crops of fruit and garden vegetables. Mrs. Buell thought an advantage of her plan was that "the kitchen may be reached from any part of the house without going through another room," and that the "dining room can also be reached from both front and rear without going through the kitchen." She decided upon a living room, because "we do not care for the conventional parlor, believing that the hall, dining room and living room afford all the necessary rooms for practical use." Upstairs, the four bed chambers were separated by passageways, and a bathroom (fed from a tank in the attic) marked the arrival of indoor plumbing to this up-to-date farmhouse.[1]

By 1900, however, the owner-designed house plan was a disappearing phenomenon. Fewer and fewer appeared in the agricultural journals, even though circulation was rising. Contributors tended to write about installing plumbing or new additions,[2] instead of submitting complete plans. The newest generation of progressive farmers were becoming consumers of domestic architecture, buying plans and materials for their new houses. The peak of progressive agriculturists' design activity had passed along with the old century.

There were several basic reasons for this decline. Inexpensive standardized building materials were available nationwide; it no longer made economic sense to dig stone or make brick on one's own property. Architectural design was becoming the province of professional architects and, more important for progressive agriculturists, of home economists and agricultural extension agents. Finally, changes in progressive farming families' way of life probably contributed to their acceptance of standard designs. During the nineteenth century, farmhouse designers had deliberately altered professional designs they deemed inappropriate for agricultural use, but by 1900 many agricultural dependencies were gone. The progressive farm family was becoming more fully integrated into the national economy and culture as the "island communities" of the old century disappeared.[3]

In the late nineteenth century an extraordinary variety of steam-powered tools industrialized woodworking, and steam-powered manufacture of bricks, hardware, ornamental trim, glass, interior lath, and plaster became speedier and more centralized. So marked was the transformation that construction sites were no longer strewn with shavings. The builder's job now was to assemble, not to fabricate. In large cities like Chicago, the building-supply business became concentrated in relatively few hands, and the contracting system, in which a single contractor (usually a local resident) coordinated the supplies and activities of various workers, was established.

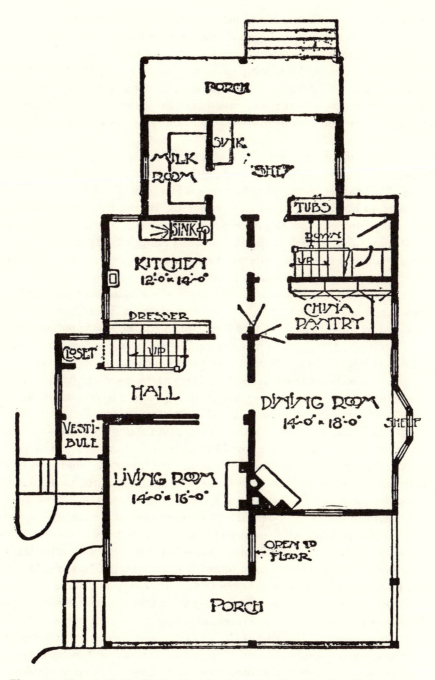

Fig. 7–1. Mary A. G. Buell, plan for a farmhouse near Syracuse, New York (1895).

Apparently the centralization of materials sources threatened some aspects of independent amateur design. Because mass-produced materials were inexpensive, farmer-designers were less inclined to extract materials from their own grounds. Moreover, ordering building supplies from distant sources could be difficult to coordinate. Most important, more and more design elements—dimensions, ornament, the nature of interior plaster work, window and sash forms—were determined away from the construction site.[4]

One way to take advantage of mass production and to avoid the inconvenience of coordinating the flow of materials was to order an entire house by mail. The mail-order housing business was a logical outgrowth from the capacity to mass produce building materials. By the late 1800s, the agricultural periodicals had begun to publish plans sold by the large and successful mail-order firms of the Pallisers and Shoppells. By the early twentieth century at least four different mail-order companies were advertising entire precut homes in the farm press. These were conventional stick-built (balloon-frame) homes designed from professional plans, with precut pieces numbered and shipped by rail to their destination. There they were assembled by the purchaser or by a local contractor. To a farm public already well acquainted with the pleasures of buying from catalogs, mail-order houses (Figures 7–2, 7–3) must have had considerable appeal. The possibility of selecting a house (complete down to the doorbell) from a catalog dramatically demonstrated the shift from production to consumption.[5]

Yet the mass production of building materials alone did not spell the end of the independent design tradition. From about 1870 architects had begun to define, regulate, and establish their profession. In the same years, builders' journals, architectural magazines, pattern-books, and mail-order plan books proliferated. Most of these publications featured professionally designed plans, and the agricultural journals, which had always carried plans from pattern-books, followed the new trend. The *American Agriculturist* and the *Rural New Yorker* published plans from architects in New York, New Jersey, Illinois, and California. These journals were still recording the experiences of owner-designers, but with a new message. In 1915, Mrs. W. S. Middleton reported to the *American Agriculturist* that of all the "mistakes we made in building," the "first was not employing an architect."[6] Her remark contrasted sharply with previous generations' criticism of the architectural profession. The rise of the powerful and prestigious architectural profession had contributed to the eclipse of amateur farmer-designers.

Why were progressive farmers now more likely to listen to architects? One reason was that the land-grant system, dedicated to capital-intensive, scientific agriculture, encouraged farmers to rely upon experts in every

Fig. 7–2. Advertisement for the Gordon-Van Tine Co. Building Materials Catalog (1914).

Fig. 7–3. Advertisement for the Aladdin Co. ready-cut houses (1914).

facet of farming, from crops and stock to buildings. As the institutional realization of progressive farming, the system enjoyed substantial credibility among progressive agriculturists.[7]

Among the experts who laid claim to special knowledge in domestic design were home economists. The early work of home economists shows how they appropriated themes that had been discussed among agricultural journal readers for years. The career of Martha Van Rensselaer at Cornell University was characteristic.[8]

Van Rensselaer (1864–1932) grew up in rural Randolph, New York, the daughter of a prosperous local agriculturist and merchant. She was educated at a local female seminary and through the Chautauqua summer session. After teaching and serving as a county school superintendent, Van Rensselaer accepted agriculture college professor Liberty Hyde Bailey's invitation (1900) to establish extension work among farmers' wives through Cornell's college of agriculture. She began with a Farmers' Wives' Reading Course, which combined new techniques with well-established means of agricultural education. The idea of a correspondence course itself dated to the 1870s and the Protestant evangelical women's missionary efforts. Later, the Chautauqua system of independent education adopted the idea. Other aspects of the Reading Course were still older. In the third bulletin (1903), several farm wives described their kitchens in minute detail, following in the pattern of the farm journals. The material in these bulletins, however, was more tightly organized than the earlier, unstructured exchanges. Each Reading Course bulletin contained questions for study and discussion. Some questions solicited information from farm wives, but others depended upon the text for answers.[9]

The first Farmers' Wives' Reading Course bulletin was entitled, significantly, *Saving Steps*. Van Rensselaer repeated formulas which had been discussed for years in the agricultural press: the partnership of farm women in the farm enterprise, the contrast of household drudgery with mechanized field work, the need for labor-saving house design, and the possibility of using time saved for self-culture. She opened on a familiar strain: "many steps . . . result from lack of plan and forethought. . . . Did you ever know the woman who takes five steps going and coming to a cupboard when she might only move the cupboard where it would demand only four steps? Further, some of this lack of planning pertains to the arrangement of the house." Van Rensselaer recommended that in order to save labor, farmers should design small kitchens, pipe in water, install drains, rearrange furniture, and purchase modern utensils. "Labor on the farm," she observed, "has been much reduced by the application of inventive skill which has supplied labor-saving machinery. A large gain has occurred in this respect in the last 25 years. Less of modern invention has been applied to lighten the burdens of the housewife." The technological gap between farmhouse and field, first noticed a generation earlier, had persisted. Martha Van Rensselaer suggested that time saved could be used in "many pleasant and entertaining ways, perhaps in reading, perhaps in stopping now and then to catch a glimpse of the sunset or to admire the beauty of the outlying fields." There was a newer concern with professionalism, however. "Did you ever have occasion to follow the making of a set of plans by a professional architect for a dwelling house? Were you not impressed with the great amount of thought that was given to every little detail of the building . . . ? And do you think that farmers give equal attention to all these little items when building a house?"[10]

In 1903–04, Van Rensselaer initiated the on-campus home economics curriculum at Cornell. The first three courses offered were "The Homestead," a course on farm architecture taught by faculty from the architecture, horticulture, and civil engineering departments; "Woman's Work and Home Economics"; and "The Home Life and Home Literature." All of the topics covered followed faithfully the well-established conventions of the agricultural press.[11]

By 1912, among the junior-year requirements of the Department of Home Economics was a course on "Rational House Planning," taught by Cornell-trained architect Helen Young. Planning, siting, materials, and costs were included, and "special attention to the kitchen" was given. The course was not intended to train design professionals, but to enable future homemakers to consult intelligently with architectural professionals. Young in fact attached a disclaimer to this effect in her Reading Course bulletin on the "Farm Home" (1913). The endorsement by Van Rensselaer and Young of architectural professionalism shows how the ideology of women's participation in domestic design was changing. Where farm women had once collaborated with their husbands in designing house plans, home economics students—many doubtless from progressive farm families—were now being advised to consult architects.[12]

By 1915, home economists, in conjunction with architects, published farm house plans in textbooks and reading-course bulletins. Helen Young's comments on some of these plans in a 1919 text succinctly summarized how progressive farmhouse planning had changed. She divided the farmhouse into living, working, and sleeping areas, explaining that "spaciousness must be expressed in the living area, compactness in the working area, and privacy in the sleeping area." Her categories further articulated the divisions which had developed in plans of the later nineteenth century.[13]

Young applied her principles to specific plans (Figure 7–4).

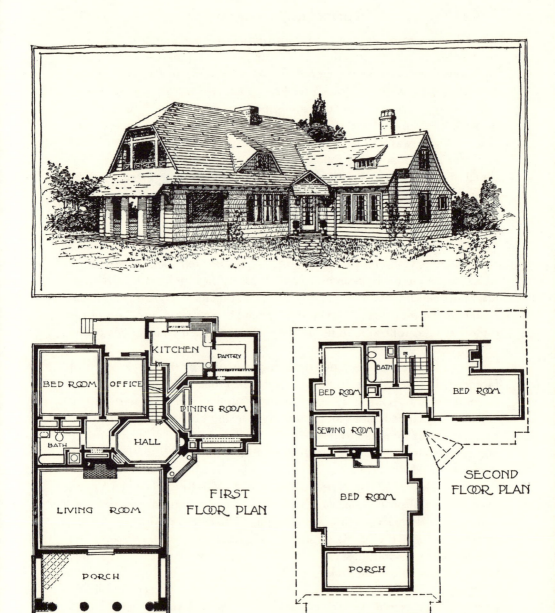

Labels within the floor plans:

KITCHEN
PANTRY
BED ROOM · OFFICE
DINING ROOM
BATH
HALL
LIVING ROOM
PORCH

FIRST
FLOOR PLAN

BATH
BED ROOM · BED ROOM
SEWING ROOM
BED ROOM
PORCH

SECOND
FLOOR PLAN

Fig. 7–4. Helen Young, design for a farmhouse (1919). (Above) Elevation. (Left) First floor plan. (Right) Second floor plan.

A living-room now combines the underused parlor and the overused sitting-room for general family life; an office where the farmer's business is transacted is provided in a place convenient to roadway and barn, but outside the path of housework travel; the kitchen arrangement is compact and well-organized; the downstairs bedrooms open, not from other rooms, but from a hall, thus insuring quiet and privacy; a bathroom is provided on either the first or second floor . . . and the whole plan is arranged so that the rooms lived in most are the sunniest.

In another plan a "Man's Room" for a hired laborer was provided "at the extreme end of the plan, away from the family," and a third plan explicitly labeled the "Boys' Room" and the "Girls' Room"[14] (Figure 7–5).

In these plans, the conflict between sitting room and parlor was resolved through the introduction of a hybrid type, the living room. Privacy for bedrooms was more rigorously enforced than in previous generations. In keeping with the separation of work and family, the farmer's office (now more common) was separated from the woman's portion of the house. (Earlier, the office had been near the pathway leading to the kitchen; Figure 4–2.) Similarly, the "Man's Room" continued the segregation of the family from the hired hands first articulated years earlier. Other ideas were also carried over—orienting rooms to the sun and the interest in well-defined children's rooms are examples. A new element, however, was indoor plumbing, made possible by declining prices and encouraged by changing attitudes to sanitation.[15]

Professional architects and home economists, then, had begun to co-opt the territory of independent farmhouse designers. In an age of increasing reliance upon experts from agronomists to zoologists, progressive farm families could add architectural designers to the list.

Where content was concerned, progressive farm families had fewer special requirements for design than earlier in the century. In the nineteenth century, farmer-designers had regarded plans for nonagricultural audiences as inappropriate for their needs. Pattern-book houses lacked special facilities for dairying, soap-making, poultry raising, swine feeding, and other functions; they contained more ceremonial space and decorative detail than most farmers wanted. But by 1900 the number of farmhouse subsidiary occupations was dwindling, as farm families stopped home manufacture of some items, such as soap. At the same time, urban and suburban single-family houses were becoming more informal. New popular types at the turn of the century were the "bungalow" and "colonial" house, both examples of what architectural historian Gwendolyn Wright has labeled the "minimal" house. Their ground-floor plans typically contained three basic rooms—kitchen, dining room, and living room; the kitchen was usually small and

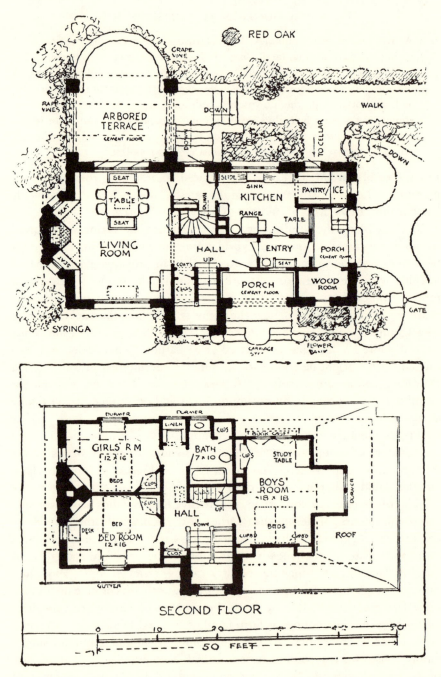

Fig. 7–5. Helen Young, design for a farmhouse (1919). (Above) First floor plan. (Below) Second floor plan.

private, but the rest of the plan was open, compensating for the house's small size and also allowing informality. In short, the gap between rural and nonrural types was narrowing, and it became more feasible for farm families to adapt standard plans to their circumstances. Certainly rural families' needs still differed from those of urban or suburban dwellers, but perhaps not to the extent that an entirely different design was required.[16]

The turn-of-the-century progressive farmhouse may have shared some key qualities with the "minimal" house, but they were the product of a very different process. The later farmhouse could be seen as an attempt to come to terms with urbanization, industrialization, and capitalist farming. A smaller private kitchen may have given farm wives more control over their workplace, but it also exacerbated the differentiation of men's and women's work and reduced farm women's importance in the primary processes of farm production. Informal family space represented a tenuous balance between the agrarian "producer's" contempt for conspicuous display, and aspirations for material comforts and refinement. Finally, a "room of one's own" offered opportunities for personal development and privacy, but conflict could occur when individual rooms usurped functions formerly associated with collective space.[17]

The shift from owner-designed to professional plans also involved trade-offs. Just as the land-grant system absorbed some risks of agricultural experimentation but also made farmers more dependent on the advice of others, the shift from production to consumption in house design implied more pragmatically built houses, but with the increased price came increased dependence. Consumers now had a simpler task than their predecessors; they could have a satisfactory, technologically sophisticated house without possessing design or building skills. But they also had less latitude for choice.[18] Thus as the twentieth century opened, progressive farm families had exchanged one set of problems and opportunities for another in their domestic design and in their lives.

NOTES

1. "First-Prize Farmhouse," *AA* 55 (February 23, 1895): 193.

2. R. V. Blasingame, "Running Water in Every Farm Home," *Farm Journal* 45 (January 1921): 16; *Moore's* 64 (April 22, 1905): 346, published winning plans in a contest for bathroom design.

3. Robert Wiebe, *The Search For Order 1877–1920* (New York: Hill and Wang, 1967).

4. Gwendolyn Wright, *Moralism and the Model Home* (Chicago: University of Chicago Press, 1980), 82–96; Carl Condit, *American Building: Materials and Techniques From the First*

Colonial Settlement to the Present, 2nd ed. (Chicago: University of Chicago Press, 1982); James Marston Fitch, *American Building: The Historical Forces That Shaped It,* 2nd ed. (New York: Schocken Books, 1973); Michael J. Doucet and John C. Weaver, "Material Culture and the North American House: The Era of the Common Man, 1870–1920," *JAH* 72 (December 1985): 560–588; Sam Bass Warner, *Streetcar Suburbs: The Process of Growth in Boston 1870–1900,* 2nd ed. (Cambridge: Harvard University Press, 1978), 126–132.

This assessment is, unfortunately, largely conjectural; it follows the pattern outlined by general histories of building that have been written to date. But surprisingly little scholarly work exists to explain precisely how the process of building was organized, and how industrialization changed that process. Dell Upton and John Vlach note this gap in their bibliographical addition to *Common Places: Readings in American Vernacular Architecture* (Athens: University of Georgia Press, 1986), 514. Carl Lounsbury, "From Craft to Industry: The Building Process in North Carolina in the Nineteenth Century," Ph.D. diss., George Washington University, 1983, is one exception.

5. James L. Garvin, "Mail-Order Plans and American Victorian Architecture," *WP* 16 (Winter 1981): 309–334; Wayne E. Fuller, *RFD: The Changing Face of Rural America* (Bloomington: Indiana University Press, 1964), 249–255; Daniel Boorstin, *The Americans: The Democratic Experience,* Vintage Books ed. (New York: Vintage, 1974), 118–130; Boris Emmet, *Catalogues and Counters: A History of Sears, Roebuck and Company* (Chicago: University of Chicago Press, 1950); Kay Halpin, "Sears, Roebuck's Best-Kept Secret," *Historic Preservation* 33 (September/October 1981): 25–29; Katherine Cole Stevenson and H. Ward Jandl, *Houses by Mail* (Washington, D.C.: Preservation Press, 1986).

6. Dell Upton, "Pattern-Books and Professionalism: Aspects of the Transformation of Domestic Architecture in America, 1800–1860," *WP* 19 (Summer/Autumn 1984): 107–151; Spiro Kostof, ed., *The Architect: Chapters in the History of the Profession* (New York: Oxford University Press, 1977); Wright, *Moralism,* chapters 1 and 2; Richard M. Levy, "The Professionalization of American Architects and Civil Engineers, 1865–1917," Ph.D. diss., University of California-Berkeley, 1980; Michael Tomlan, "Popular and Professional American Architectural Literature in the Late Nineteenth Century," Ph.D. diss., Cornell University, 1983; Mrs. W. S. Middleton, "Mistakes We Made in Building," *AA* 96 (October 31, 1915): 21.

7. Fred Shannon, *The Farmer's Last Frontier: Agriculture, 1860–1897* (1945. Reprint, White Plains, N.Y.: M. E. Sharpe, 1973), chapter 12; Gould Colman, *Education and Agriculture, A History of the New York State College of Agriculture at Cornell University* (Ithaca: Cornell University Press, 1963); Margaret Rossiter, *The Emergence of Agricultural Science* (New Haven: Yale University Press, 1975); Rossiter, "The Organization of the Agricultural Sciences," in A. Oleson and John Voss, eds., *The Organization of Knowledge in America* (Baltimore: Johns Hopkins University Press, 1979), 211–219; Charles E. Rosenberg, "Rationalization and Reality in the Shaping of American Agricultural Research, 1875–1914," *Social Studies of Science* 7 (1977): 401–422; Rosenberg, *No Other Gods, On Science and American Social Thought* (Baltimore: Johns Hopkins University Press, 1976).

8. Margaret W. Rossiter, *Women Scientists in America, Struggles and Strategies to 1940* (Baltimore: Johns Hopkins University Press, 1982); Wright, *Moralism,* chapter 5; Linda Fritschner, "The Rise and Fall of Home Economics," Ph.D. diss., University of California-Davis, 1973; Keturah Baldwin, *The AHEA Saga* (Washington, D.C.: American Home Economics Association, 1949); Marjorie East, *Home Economics* (Boston: Allyn and Bacon, 1980); Anne McCleary, "Domesticity and the Farm Woman: A Case Study of Women in Augusta County, Virginia, 1850–1940," in Camille Wells, ed., *Perspectives in Vernacular Architecture* (Annapolis, Md.: Vernacular Architecture Forum, 1982), 25–30; Susan Strasser, *Never Done:*

A *History of American Housework* (New York: Pantheon, 1982), chapter 11; Caroline M. Percival, *Martha Van Rensselaer* (Ithaca: Cornell University Press, 1957); Flora Rose, *A Page of Modern Education: Forty Years of Home Economics at Cornell* (Ithaca: New York State College of Home Economics, 1940); Ruby Green Smith, *The People's Colleges* (Ithaca: Cornell University Press, 1949).

9. Joan Brumberg, "Zenanas and Girlless Villages: The Ethnography of American Evangelical Women," *JAH* 69 (September 1982): 347–372; Theodore Morrison, *Chautauqua: A Center for Religion, Education, and the Arts in America* (Chicago: University of Chicago Press, 1974).

10. Martha Van Rensselaer, "Housekeeping," *Farmers' Wives Reading Course* Series 1 (January 1903): 47–48; Van Rensselaer, "Saving Steps," *Farmers' Wives Reading Course* Series 1 (November 1902), 1–2, 9–10. Wright, *Moralism,* chapter 5, sees early twentieth-century home economists' preoccupation with science and efficiency as a break with the rural past, but the integration of scientific agriculture with domestic economy in the progressive farmers' culture suggests continuity.

11. Cornell University *Announcements,* 1903–04: 319; 1904–05: 63.

12. Cornell University *Announcements,* 1912: 43; Helen Binkerd Young, "The Modern Home," *Farmers' Reading Course Bulletin # 369* (1913), introduction. Mary Meek Atkeson, *The Woman on the Farm* (New York and London: The Century Co., 1924), 26, agreed that "it is unwise for the farmer to depend upon his own ideas of building."

13. These plans date at least to 1906. They appeared in Clarence Martin, "The Plan of a Farm Home," *Cornell University Reading Course for Farmers* 6 (January 1906): 540–548. (Martin was a faculty member in Cornell's College of Architecture.) They appeared again in Young's *Bulletin* (1913), and again in Martha Van Rensselaer et al., *A Manual of Homemaking* (New York: Macmillan, 1919), chapters 1, 11.

14. Helen Binkerd Young, "The Modern Home," in Van Rensselaer et al., *Manual,* 19.

15. For other, similar approaches to the farm home in the twentieth century, see Isabel Bevier, *The House* (Chicago: American School of Home Economics, 1907), 74–90; "A Good Farmhouse for $3500," *Ladies Home Journal* 17 (October 1900): 21; Isaac Phillips Roberts, *The Farmstead* (New York: Macmillan, 1900); Helen Dodd, *The Healthful Farmhouse,* 2nd ed. (Boston: Whitcomb and Barrows, 1911). See also May N. Stone, "The Plumbing Paradox," *WP* 14 (Autumn 1979): 283–311.

16. Wright, *Moralism,* chapter 8.

17. Charles E. Martin, *Hollybush: Folk Building and Social Change in an Appalachian Community* (Knoxville: University of Tennessee Press, 1984), 83–89. For another provocative assessment of broad social change and vernacular architecture, see Henry Glassie, "Vernacular Architecture and Society," *Material Culture* 16 (Spring 1984): 5–25.

18. Wright, *Moralism,* chapter 9, finds a loss of control over design features for early twentieth-century Chicago suburbanites. Margaret Marsh, "The Suburban House: The Social Implications of Environmental Choice," paper presented at the 1986 meeting of the Organization of American Historians, also discusses the social space of suburban homes.

EPILOGUE

IN THE NINETEENTH CENTURY, a flourishing rural culture took shape in the vernacular landscape as progressive farmers helped create new communities, and experimented with new architectural forms, field arrangements, machinery, crop strains, and agricultural specialties. Contemporary agricultural landscapes, with their struggling rural towns, high-technology silos, computerized milking parlors, extensive irrigation systems, and aluminum barns, are lineal descendants of the nineteenth-century landscape of progressive agriculture. In fact, it can be argued that from being a minority element in the nineteenth-century rural landscape, progressive agriculture has emerged as the dominant force, as rural residents unable or unwilling to deal with agricultural competition are surrendering the field. Of course, progressive agriculture has not been the only factor in the landscape's transformation; the auto, for one, has also had a tremendous impact. But modernization in agriculture has unarguably been a powerful force for change.

Nineteenth-century progressive farmers could not foresee the unsettling implications of their zealous improving activity. They sought improvement not only in production but in their own standard of living; they would probably be as ambivalent about the problems and successes of American agriculture as are Americans today, who enjoy an abundant, varied supply of inexpensive food even as they contemplate a deepening farm crisis. Ironically, progressive farmers' very success in manipulating space, technology, and money contributed to chronic overproduction, to intermittent agricultural crisis, and ultimately to massive urbanization. Today less than 3 percent of all Americans live on farms; among these farms, a small number receive the lion's share of agricultural income. Many of the large-scale producers are corporations rather than family farms. Farmers' reliance upon pesticides, chemical fertilizers, and energy-intensive equipment has created serious environmental problems. The problems persist in part because the radical disjunction that separates producer from consumer in the American food system has impeded public discussion of agricultural issues.

A new generation of reforming agriculturists is beginning to appear, however, made up of people who challenge the present structure and practice of agriculture. Their aims are to reduce use of pesticides and chemical fertilizers, to practice soil conservation, to make intelligent use of genetic engineering, to conserve energy, and to find ways of reducing production without losing income. These people, too, are part of the legacy of progressive agriculture; they too are drawing upon the reform impulse that provided the original impetus for progressive farming. Many contemporary reformers' programs bear little resemblance to the ideas of earlier generations, but others are common to past and present. Soil erosion, for example, has always been a major concern of progressive agriculture, and the social consequences of dwindling farm populations have worried progressive farmers past and present. Finally, like their nineteenth-century predecessors, modern progressive agriculturists are creating a new agricultural landscape and as before, new domestic forms will be key elements of that landscape. For example, experiments in energy-efficient housing, especially with solar power, are consistent with the search for a less energy-intensive agriculture. These buildings will look quite different from progressive farm homes of a century ago, but both forms share a common lineage and a common inspiration; both represent a process of change, as rural families adjust to new circumstances and influence the shape of things to come.

BIBLIOGRAPHY

Primary Sources

PERIODICALS

American Agriculturist. 1841–1900.
American Farmer. 1819–1826.
Cornell University *Announcements.* 1899–1912.
Country Gentleman. 1853–1900.
Cultivator (Albany). 1834–1897.
Genesee Farmer. 1831–1839; *(New) Genesee Farmer.* 1840–1865.
Godey's Lady's Book. 1839–1870.
Junior Naturalist Monthly. 1899–1902.
Ladies' Home Journal. 1893–1905.
Michigan Farmer. 1843–1861, 1881–1886.
Moore's Rural New Yorker. 1850–1900.
New England Farmer. 1822–1846.
Ohio Cultivator. 1845–1854.
Ohio Farmer. 1858–1860.
Prairie Farmer. 1841–1895.
Rural Affairs. 1855–1882.
Transactions, New York State Agricultural Society. 1841–1851.

BOOKS

Allen, Horace L. *The American Farm and Home Cyclopedia.* Indianapolis: Davis and Curtis, 1881.
Allen, Lewis Falley. *American Short-Horn Herd Book.* Buffalo: Jewett, Thomas, & Co., 1846.
————. *The History of the Short-Horn Cattle.* Buffalo: by the author, 1872.
————. *Rural Architecture.* New York: Orange Judd, 1852.
The American Farmer's Hand-Book: an Improved and Complete Guide. 2nd ed. Worcester, Mass.: Edward Livermore, 1851.
Arr, E. H. [Ellen Chapman (Hobbs) Rollins]. *New England Bygones.* Philadelphia: J. B. Lippincott, 1880.
Atkeson, Mary Meek. *The Woman on the Farm.* New York and London: The Century Co., 1924.
Atkeson, Thomas C., and Mary Meek Atkeson. *Pioneering in Agriculture.* New York: Orange Judd, 1937.
Bailey, Liberty Hyde. *The Country Life Movement.* New York: Macmillan, 1911.

Bailey, Liberty Hyde, ed. *Cyclopedia of American Agriculture*. New York: Macmillan, 1907–1909.

Beam, Lura. *A Maine Hamlet*. New York: Wilfred Funk, 1957.

Beecher, Catharine E. *The American Woman's Home*. New York: J. B. Ford & Co., 1869.

———. *Treatise on Domestic Economy*. Boston: Marsh, Capen, Lyon, & Webb, 1848.

Bevier, Isabel. *The House*. Chicago: American School of Home Economics, 1907.

Bicknell, Amos J. *Wooden and Brick Buildings with Details*. 2 volumes. New York: A. J. Bicknell, 1875.

Blake, John Lauris. *The Farmer's Every-day Book*. Auburn, N.Y.: Derby, Miller, & Co., 1851.

Bok, Edward. *The Americanization of Edward Bok*. New York: Scribner, 1920.

Bordley, John Beale. *Essays and Notes on Husbandry and Rural Affairs*. Philadelphia: Thomas Dobson, 1799.

———. *Country Habitations*. Philadelphia: Charles Cist, 1798.

Brown, Harriet Connor. *Grandmother Brown's Hundred Years*. Boston: Little, Brown, 1929.

Buel, Jesse. *The Farmer's Companion*. Boston: Marsh, Capen, Lyon, & Webb, 1839.

Child, Lydia Maria. *The Mother's Book*. Boston: Carter, Hendee, & Babcock, 1831.

Cleaveland, Henry. *Village and Farm Cottages*. New York: Appleton, 1856.

Copeland, Robert Morris. *Country Life*. 5th ed. Boston: Dinsmoor & Co., 1866.

Crow, Martha Foote. *The American Country Girl*. New York: Frederick A. Stokes, 1915.

Dodd, Helen. *The Healthful Farmhouse*. 2nd ed. Boston: Whitcomb and Barrows, 1911.

Downing, Andrew Jackson. *The Architecture of Country Houses*. 1850. Reprint, New York: Dover Publications, 1969.

———. *Cottage Residences*. 1842. Reprint, Watkins Glen, N.Y.: American Life Foundation, 1967.

———. *Hints to Persons About Building in the Country*. New York: John Wiley, 1851.

———. *Rural Essays*. New York: G. P. Putnam, 1853.

———. *Treatise on the Theory and Practice of Landscape Gardening*. 4th ed. New York: G. P. Putnam, 1849.

Eastman, Edward R. *Journey to Day Before Yesterday*. Englewood Cliffs, N.J.: Prentice-Hall, 1963.

Edis, Robert. *Decoration and Furniture of Town Houses*. New York: Scribner and Welford, 1881.

Erickson, Theodore. *My 60 Years With Rural Youth*. Minneapolis: University of Minnesota Press, 1956.

Forbush, William Byron. *The Boy Problem*. 6th ed. Boston and Chicago: Pilgrim Press, 1901–1907.

Fowler, Orson Squires. *A Home for All, or, the Gravel Wall and Octagon Mode of Mode of Building*. 1848. Reprint, New York: Dover Publications, 1973.

Gardner, E. C. *Homes and How to Make Them*. Boston: J. R. Osgood, 1874.

———. *The House that Jill Built*. Springfield, Mass.: W. F. Adams, 1896.

———. *Illustrated Homes*. Boston: J. R. Osgood, 1875.

A Girl's Room. Boston: D. Lothrop & Co., 1886.

Goodale, Elaine. [Elaine Goodale Eastman]. *Journal of a Farmer's Daughter*. New York: G. P. Putnam's Sons, 1881.

Goodholme, Todd. *Domestic Cyclopedia of Practical Information*. New York: Henry Holt, 1882.

Greenough, Horatio. *Form and Function*. Edited by Harold Small. Berkeley: University of California Press, 1947.

Hale, Sarah Josepha. *Manners*. Boston: Lee and Shepard, 1889.

Hall, G. Stanley. *Adolescence*. New York: Appleton, 1904.

Hedrick, U. P. *The Land of the Crooked Tree*. New York: Oxford University Press, 1948.

Holt, Emily. *Encyclopedia of Etiquette*. Garden City, N.Y.: Doubleday, Page, and Co., 1913.

Home Cottage Seminary, Clinton, New York. Catalog. 1856.

Howells, William Dean. *A Boy's Town*. New York: Harper, 1890.

The Illustrated Manners Book. New York: Leland, Clay & Co., 1855.

Kirkland, Caroline. *The Evening Book*. New York: Scribner, 1852.

Kirkpatrick, Edwin A. *Fundamentals of Child Study*. New York: Macmillan, 1903.

Larcom, Lucy. *A New England Girlhood*. Boston: Houghton-Mifflin, 1889.

Leland, E. H. *Farm Homes: In-Doors and Out-Doors*. New York: Orange Judd, 1881.

Leslie, Eliza. *The House Book*. Philadelphia: Carey and Hart, 1841.

Lincolnshire Farmer. *The Complete Grazier*. 4th ed. London: Baldwin, Cradock, & Joy, 1816.

Lyman, Laura, and Joseph Bardwell Lyman. *The Household Guide and Philosophy of Housekeeping*. 14th ed. Hartford, Conn.: James Betts, 1869.

McKeever, William A. *Farm Boys and Girls*. New York: Macmillan, 1913.

Mitchell, Donald Grant. *My Farm of Edgewood*. New York: Charles Scribner, 1863.

Morris, Edmund. *Farming for Boys*. Boston: Ticknor & Fields, 1868.

Nash, John Adams. *The Progressive Farmer*. New York: A. O. Moore, 1857.

Palliser, Palliser, and Co. *Palliser's Model Homes*. Bridgeport, Conn.: Palliser & Palliser, 1878.

Palliser's New Cottage Homes and Details. 1888. Reprint, Watkins Glen, N.Y.: American Life Foundation, 1978.

Roberts, Isaac Phillips. *Autobiography of a Farm Boy*. Albany: J. B. Lyon, 1916.

————. *The Farmstead*. New York: Macmillan, 1900.

Robinson, Solon, ed. *Facts for Farmers*. New York: A. J. Johnson; Cleveland: F. G. and A. C. Rowe, 1866.

Savery, Lillie. (pseudonym, Solon Robinson.) *Home Comforts*. New York: Bunce and Brothers, 1855.

Sedgwick, Catharine Maria. *Home*. Boston: James Munroe, 1835.

Shoppell, Robert W. *Modern Houses*. New York: Cooperative Building Plan Association, 1887.

Sloan, Samuel. *City and Suburban Architecture*. 1852. Reprint, New York: Dover Publications, 1980.

Sneller, Ann Gertrude. *A Vanished World*. Syracuse, N.Y.: Syracuse University Press, 1964.

Stephens, Henry. *The Book of the Farm*. 2 volumes. New York: Greeley & McElrath, 1847.

Stevens, John Calvin, and Albert W. Cobb. *Examples of American Domestic Architecture*. New York: William Comstock, 1889.

Storke, E. G., ed. *The Family Farm and Gardens and the Domestic Animals*. Auburn, N.Y.: Auburn Publishing Co., 1859.

Thayer, William. *Womanhood: Helps and Hints for Women*. New York: Thomas Whittaker, 1895.

Todd, Sereno Edwards. *Todd's Country Home and How to Save Money*. Hartford, Conn.: Hartford Publishing Co., 1870.

Tuthill, Louisa C. *The Nursery Book*. New York: G. P. Putnam, 1849.

————. *The Young Lady's Home*. Boston: William J. Reynolds, 1847.

Underwood, Francis. *Quabbin: The Story of a New England Town*. Boston: Lee & Shepard, 1893.

Van Rensselaer, Martha, et al. *A Manual of Homemaking*. New York: Macmillan, 1919.

Van Wagenen, Jared, Jr. *Days of My Years*. Cooperstown: New York State Historical Association, 1962.

Varney, Almon C. *Our Homes and Their Adornments.* Chicago: People's Publishing Co., 1885.

Vaux, Calvert. *Villas and Cottages.* 1864. Reprint, New York: Dover Publications, 1970.

Wheeler, Candace, ed. *Household Art.* New York: Harper, 1893.

Wheeler, Gervase. *Homes for the People.* rev. ed. New York: The American News Co., 1867.

Williams, Henry T., and Mrs. S. C. Jones. *Beautiful Homes.* New York: Henry T. Williams, 1877.

Williams, James Mickel. *An American Town.* New York: The James Kempster Printing Co., 1906.

Woodward, George. *Woodward's National Architect.* New York: Korff Brothers, 1869.

ARTICLES

Allerton, Mrs. E. P. "Dairy Factory System—A Blessing to the Farmer's Wife." Wisconsin Dairymen's Association *Annual Report* 3 (1875): 17–20.

Backus, Samuel D. "Hints Upon Farm Houses." United States Patent Office *Report* (1859): 397–441.

Beecher, Catharine E. "How to Redeem Woman's Profession from Dishonor." *Harper's New Monthly Magazine* 31 (October 1865): 710–714.

"Best Parlors." *Scribner's* 2 (October 1871): 658–659.

Blasingame, R. V. "Running Water in Every Farm House." *Farm Journal* 45 (January 1921): 16.

Bok, Edward. "Is It Worth While?" *Ladies Home Journal* 17 (November 1900): 18.

Campbell, Helen. "A Comfortable Home." *Cosmopolitan* 3 (1887): 195–197.

Comstock, Samuel. "The Comparative Advantages of the Old and New Systems of Cheese Manufacturing." *Annual Report,* New York State Cheese Manufacturer's Association 2 (1864): 63–69.

Cook, Clarence. "Some Chapters on House-Furnishing." *Scribner's* 10 (June 1875): 169–181.

Crosby, Dick J. "Boys' Agricultural Clubs." United States Department of Agriculture *Yearbook* (1904): 489–496.

"Dates and Events in the History of the Home Economics Movement." *Journal of Home Economics* 3 (October 1911): 336–341.

Gardner, E. C. "Farm Architecture." *American Architect and Building News* 12 (August 19, 1882): 84–85.

Halsted, Mrs. H. B. "Essay on Woman's Influence on Agriculture." *Transactions,* Illinois State Agricultural Society 6 (1865–66): 269–278.

Holland, N. G. "Farming Life in New England." *Atlantic* 2 (August 1858): 334–341.

Hood, Thomas. "The Song of the Shirt." In Miriam Schneir, ed., *Feminism: The Essential Historical Writings.* New York: Vintage Books, 1972.

Johns, Mrs. H. C. "The Farmer's Home." *Transactions,* Illinois State Agricultural Society 6 (1865–66): 292–299.

"The Manufacture of Parlor Furniture." *Scientific American* n.s. 43 (October 9, 1880): 229.

Martin, Clarence A. "The Plan of the Farm House." Cornell University *Reading Course for Farmers* 6 (January 1906): 540–548.

Matthews, Albert. "Hired Man and Help." Colonial Society of Massachusetts, *Publications* 5 (March 1898): 225–254.

Mitchell, Donald Grant. "The Farmer's Homestead, and its Relation to Farm Thrift." *Report,* Massachusetts Board of Agriculture 24 (1876): 131–141.

"Passing of the Parlor." *Atlantic* 9 (May 1903): 712–714.

"The Sacrificial Parlor." *Scribner's* 9 (March 1875): 762.

Trowbridge, Mrs. J. L. "Relations of Women to the Labor and Duties of Agriculture." Wisconsin Dairymen's Association *Annual Report* 3 (1875–76): 38–40.

Van Rensselaer, Martha. "Housekeeping." Cornell University *Farmers' Wives Reading Course* 1 (January 1903): 46–49.

————. "Saving Steps." Cornell University *Farmers' Wives Reading Course* 1 (November 1902): 1–20.

Willard, X. A. Report on the factory system of cheese production. Reprinted in the New York State Cheese Manufacturers' Association *Report* 1 (1863–64): 39–47.

Wing, Joseph E. "A House for $4061 That Really Satisfied." *Country Life* 11 (March 1907): LXXXIII–XCI.

Wood, Eugene. "The Parlor Back Home." *McClure's* 33 (September 1909): 475–481.

Young, Helen Binkerd. "The Farmhouse." Cornell University *Farmer's Reading Course Bulletin* II (May 1, 1913): 153–184.

Secondary Sources

BOOKS

Atack, Jeremy, and Fred Bateman. *To Their Own Soil: Agriculture in the Antebellum North.* Ames: Iowa State University Press, 1987.

Baldwin, Keturah. *The AHEA Saga.* Washington, D.C.: American Home Economics Association, 1949.

Barber, Lynn. *The Heyday of Natural History, 1820–1870.* Garden City, N.Y.: Doubleday, 1980.

Bardolph, Richard. *Agricultural Literature and the Early Illinois Farmer.* Urbana: University of Illinois Press, 1948.

Barron, Hal S. *Those Who Stayed Behind.* Cambridge: Cambridge University Press, 1984.

Belden, Ernest. "A History of the Child Study Movement in the United States, 1870–1920." Ph.D. diss., University of California-Berkeley, 1965.

Berger, Michael. *The Devil Wagon in God's Country: The Automobile and Social Change in Rural America, 1893–1929.* Hamden, Conn.: Archon Books, 1979.

Bidwell, Percy Wells, and John Falconer. *A History of Agriculture in the Northern States, 1620–1860.* 1925. Reprint, New York: Peter Smith, 1941.

Bogue, Allan. *From Prairie to Corn Belt: Farming in the Illinois and Iowa Prairies in the Nineteenth Century.* Chicago: University of Chicago Press, 1963.

Boorstin, Daniel. *The Americans: The Democratic Experience.* Vintage Books ed. New York: Vintage Books, 1974.

Bowers, William L. *The Country Life Movement in America 1900–1920.* Port Washington, N.Y.: Kennikat Press, 1974.

Bridgeman, Harriet. *Encyclopedia of Victoriana.* New York: Macmillan, 1975.

Brumberg, Joan Jacobs. *Mission For Life.* New York: Free Press, 1980.

Brunger, Eric. "Changes in the New York State Dairying Industry 1850–1900." Ph.D. diss., Syracuse University, 1954.

Buck, Solon J. *The Granger Movement.* Cambridge: Harvard University Press, 1913.

Cable, Mary. *The Little Darlings, A History of Child Rearing in America.* 2nd ed. New York: Charles Scribner's Sons, 1975.

Carman, Harry J. *Jesse Buel*. New York: Columbia University Press, 1947.

Clark, Christopher, "Household, Market, and Capital: The Process of Economic Change in the Connecticut Valley of Massachusetts, 1800–1860." Ph.D. diss., Harvard University, 1982.

Colman, Gould. *Education and Agriculture: A History of the New York State College of Agriculture at Cornell University*. (Ithaca: Cornell University Press, 1963).

Condit, Carl. *American Building: Materials and Techniques From the First Colonial Settlements to the Present*. 2nd ed. Chicago: University of Chicago Press, 1982.

Congdon, Herbert. *Old Vermont Houses*. 1945. Reprint, Petersborough, N.H.: Noone House, 1960.

Conover, Jewel Helen. *Nineteenth-Century Houses in Western New York*. Albany: State University of New York Press, 1966.

Conzen, Michael. *Frontier Farming in an Urban Shadow*. Madison: State Historical Society of Wisconsin, 1971.

Cooper, Grace Rogers. *The Sewing Machine: Its Invention and Development*. Washington, D.C.: Smithsonian Institution, 1976.

Cott, Nancy. *The Bonds of Womanhood: "Woman's Sphere" in New England, 1780–1835*. New Haven: Yale University Press, 1977.

Cowan, Ruth Schwartz. *More Work for Mother: The Ironies of Household Technology From the Open Hearth to the Microwave*. New York: Basic Books, 1983.

Cremin, Lawrence. *The Transformation of the School: Progressivism in American Education, 1876–1957*. New York: Alfred A. Knopf, 1961.

Cummings, Abbott Lowell. *The Framed Houses of Massachusetts Bay, 1625–1725*. Cambridge: Harvard University Press, 1979.

Danbom, David B. *The Resisted Revolution: Urban America and the Industrialization of Agriculture, 1900–1930*. Ames: Iowa State University Press, 1979.

Danhof, Clarence. *Change in Agriculture: The Northern United States, 1820–1870*. Cambridge: Harvard University Press, 1969.

Deetz, James. *In Small Things Forgotten*. Garden City, N.Y.: Doubleday, 1977.

Degler, Carl. *At Odds: Women and the Family in America From the Revolution to the Present*. New York: Oxford University Press, 1980.

Demaree, Albert L. *The American Agricultural Press, 1819–1860*. New York: Columbia University Press, 1940.

Dick, Everett. *The Sod House Frontier*. Lincoln, Nebr.: Johnsen Publishing Co., 1954.

Dilliard, Maud E. *Old Dutch Houses of Brooklyn*. New York: Richard R. Smith, 1945.

Douglas, Ann. *The Feminization of American Culture*. New York: Alfred A. Knopf, 1977.

Dublin, Thomas. *Women at Work, The Transformation of Work and Community in Lowell, Massachusetts, 1826–1860*. New York: Columbia University Press, 1979.

————, ed. *Farm to Factory, Women's Letters, 1830–1860*. New York: Columbia University Press, 1981.

Dudden, Faye E. *Serving Women: Household Service in Nineteenth Century America*. Middletown, Conn.: Wesleyan University Press, 1983.

East, Marjorie. *Home Economics*. Boston: Allyn & Bacon, 1980.

Ellis, David Maldwyn, et al. *A History of New York State*. Ithaca: Cornell University Press, 1967.

————. *Landlords and Farmers in the Hudson-Mohawk Region, 1790–1850*. New York: Octagon Books, 1967.

Emmet, Boris. *Catalogues and Counters, A History of Sears, Roebuck and Company*. Chicago: University of Chicago Press, 1950.

Faragher, John Mack. *Sugar Creek: Life on the Illinois Prairie*. New Haven: Yale University Press, 1986.

————. *Women and Men on the Overland Trail*. New Haven: Yale University Press, 1979.

Farrell, James J. *Inventing the American Way of Death, 1830–1920*. Philadelphia: Temple University Press, 1980.

Fishwick, Marshall, ed. *American Studies in Transition*. Philadelphia: University of Pennsylvania Press, 1964.

Fitch, James Marston. *American Building: The Historical Forces That Shaped It*. 2nd ed. New York: Schocken Books, 1973.

Fite, Gilbert. *The Farmers' Frontier, 1865–1900*. New York: Holt, Rinehart, and Winston, 1966.

Flaherty, David. *Privacy in Colonial New England*. Charlottesville: University of Virginia Press, 1967.

Fletcher, Stevenson W. *Pennsylvania Agriculture and Country Life, 1840–1940*. 2 vols. Harrisburg: Pennsylvania Historic and Museum Commission, 1955.

Frary, Ihna T. *Early Homes of Ohio*. Richmond, Va.: Garrett & Massie, 1936.

Fritschner, Linda M. "The Rise and Fall of Home Economics," Ph.D. diss., University of California-Davis, 1973.

Fuller, Wayne E. *The Old Country School: The Story of Rural Education in the Middle West*. Chicago: University of Chicago Press, 1982.

————. *RFD: The Changing Face of Rural America*. Bloomington: Indiana University Press, 1964.

Gates, Paul Wallace. *Agriculture and the Civil War*. New York: Alfred A. Knopf, 1965.

————. *The Farmer's Age: Agriculture, 1815–1860*. New York: Holt, Rinehart, and Winston, 1960.

Geib, Susan. "Changing Works: Agriculture and Society in Brookfield, Massachusetts, 1785–1820." Ph.D. diss., Boston University, 1981.

Giedion, Siegfried. *Mechanization Takes Command*. New York: Oxford University Press, 1947.

————. *Space, Time and Architecture*. 5th ed. Cambridge: Harvard University Press, 1967.

Girouard, Mark. *Life in the English Country House*. Harmondsworth, U.K.: Penguin, 1980.

Glassie, Henry. *Pattern in the Material Folk Culture of the Eastern United States*. Philadelphia: University of Pennsylvania Press, 1968.

————. *Folk Housing in Middle Virginia*. Knoxville: University of Tennessee Press, 1975.

Goody, Jack, ed. *The Developmental Cycle in Domestic Groups*. London: Cambridge University Press, 1958.

Gordon, Michael, ed. *The American Family in Social-Historical Perspective*. 2nd ed. New York: St. Martin's Press, 1978.

————. *The American Family in Social-Historical Perspective*. 3rd ed. New York: St. Martin's Press, 1983.

Gowans, Alan. *Images of American Living: Four Centuries of Architecture and Furniture as Cultural Expression*. Philadelphia and New York: Lippincott, 1964.

Green, Harvey. *The Light of the Home: An Intimate View of the Lives of Women in Victorian America*. New York: Pantheon, 1983.

Hahn, Steven, and Jonathan Prude, eds. *The Countryside in the Age of Capitalist Transforma-*

tion: Essays in the Social History of Rural America. Chapel Hill and London: University of North Carolina Press, 1985.

Hall, Edward T. *The Hidden Dimension*. Garden City, N.Y.: Anchor Books, 1969.

Halttunen, Karen. *Confidence Men and Painted Women: A Study of Middle-Class Culture in America, 1830–1870*. New Haven: Yale University Press, 1982.

Hamlin, Talbot. *Greek Revival Architecture in America*. 1944. Reprint, New York: Dover Publications, 1964.

Hammond, Charles. "Where the Arts and Virtues Unite: Country Life Near Boston, 1637–1864." Ph.D. diss., Boston University, 1982.

Handlin, David. *The American Home: Architecture and Society 1815–1915*. Boston: Little, Brown, 1979.

Hareven, Tamara, ed. *Anonymous Americans, Explorations in Nineteenth-Century Social History*. Englewood Cliffs, N.J.: Prentice-Hall, 1971.

Hayden, Dolores. *The Grand Domestic Revolution: A History of Feminist Designs for American Homes, Neighborhoods, and Cities*. Cambridge: MIT Press, 1981.

————. *Seven American Utopias: The Architecture of Communitarian Socialism, 1790–1975*. Cambridge: MIT Press, 1976.

Hayter, Earl. *The Troubled Farmer, 1850–1900*. De Kalb: Northern Illinois University Press, 1968.

Hedrick, Ulysses P. *History of Agriculture in the State of New York*. 1933. Reprint, New York: Hill & Wang, 1966.

————. *History of Horticulture in America to 1860*. New York: Oxford University Press, 1950.

Heininger, Mary L. S., et al. *A Century of Childhood, 1820–1920*. Rochester, N.Y.: Margaret Woodbury Strong Museum, 1984.

Herman, Bernard. *Architecture and Rural Life in Central Delaware, 1700–1900*. Knoxville: University of Tennessee Press, 1987.

Hewitt, Karen, and Louise Roomet, eds. *Educational Toys in America: 1800 to the Present*. Burlington, Vt.: Robert Hull Fleming Museum, 1979.

Heyl, John Vincent. *The Chautauqua Movement*. Boston: Chautauqua Press, 1886.

Higham, John. *Writing American History: Essays on Modern Scholarship*. Bloomington: Indiana University Press, 1970.

Hitchcock, Henry-Russell. *American Architectural Books*. Minneapolis: University of Minnesota Press, 1962.

Hofstadter, Richard. *The Age of Reform: From Bryan to F.D.R.* New York: Vintage, 1955.

Holland, Laurence, ed. *Who Designs America?* Garden City, N.Y.: Anchor Books, 1966.

Horowitz, Daniel Walker. *The Morality of Spending: Attitudes Toward the Consumer Society in America, 1875–1940*. Baltimore: Johns Hopkins University Press, 1985.

Hubka, Thomas. *Big House, Little House, Back House, Barn: The Connected Farm Buildings of New England*. Hanover and London: University Press of New England, 1984.

Jackson, John Brinkerhoff. *American Space: The Centennial Years, 1865–1876*. New York: Norton, 1972.

Jacobs, Stephen W. *Wayne County: The Aesthetic Heritage of a Rural Area*. Lyons, N.Y.: Wayne County Historical Center for Cultural Resources, 1979.

Jensen, Joan. *Loosening the Bonds: Mid-Atlantic Farm Women 1750–1850*. New Haven: Yale University Press, 1986.

————. *With These Hands: Women Working on the Land*. Old Westbury, N.Y.: The Feminist Press, 1981.

Johnson, Paul E. *A Shopkeeper's Millenium: Society and Revivals in Rochester, New York, 1815–1887*. New York: Hill & Wang, 1978.

Jones, Robert Leslie. *History of Agriculture in Ohio to 1880*. Kent, Oh.: Kent State University Press, 1983.

Juster, Norton. *So Sweet to Labor: Rural Women in America, 1865–1895*. New York: Viking, 1979.

Kasson, John. *Civilizing the Machine: Technology and Republican Values in America, 1776–1900*. New York: Penguin, 1976.

Kaufmann, Edgar, ed. *The Rise of an American Architecture*. New York: Praeger, 1970.

Kellar, Herbert Anthony, ed. *Solon Robinson: Pioneer and Agriculturist*. Indianapolis: Indiana Historical Bureau, 1936.

Kett, Joseph. *Rites of Passage: Adolescence in America, 1790 to the Present*. New York: Basic Books, 1977.

Kettell, Russell H. *Early American Rooms*. Portland, Me.: Southworth, Anthoensen Press, 1936.

Kimball, Fiske. *Domestic Architecture of the American Colonies and of the Early Republic*. 1922. Reprint, New York: Dover Publications, 1966.

Klingaman, David, and Richard Vedder, eds. *Essays in Nineteenth Century Economic History*. Athens: University of Ohio Press, 1975.

Koeper, Frederick. *Illinois Architecture from Territorial Times to the Present*. Chicago: University of Chicago Press, 1968.

Kostof, Spiro, ed. *The Architect: Chapters in the History of the Profession*. New York: Oxford University Press, 1977.

Kouwenhoven, John. *The Arts in Modern American Civilization*. 2nd ed. New York: Norton, 1967.

Kranzberg, Melvin, and Carroll Pursell, eds. *Technology in Western Civilization*. New York: Oxford University Press, 1967.

Kuhn, Anne Louise. *The Mother's Role in Childhood Education: New England Concepts, 1830–1860*. New Haven: Yale University Press, 1947.

Lampard, Eric. *The Rise of the Dairy Industry in Wisconsin*. Madison: State Historical Society of Wisconsin, 1963.

Lasch, Christopher. *Haven in a Heartless World: The Family Besieged*. New York: Basic Books, 1977.

Levy, Richard M. "The Professionalization of American Architects and Civil Engineers 1865–1917." Ph.D. diss., University of California-Berkeley, 1980.

Lounsbury, Carl. "From Craft to Industry: The Building Process in North Carolina in the Nineteenth Century." Ph.D. diss., George Washington University, 1983.

Lynes, Russell. *The Domesticated Americans*. New York: Harper & Row, 1963.

———. *The Tastemakers*. New York: Harper & Bros., 1954.

Maass, James. *The Gingerbread Age*. New York: Rinehart, 1957.

———. *The Victorian Home in America*. New York: Hawthorn Books, 1972.

Major, Howard. *The Domestic Architecture of the Early American Republic*. Philadelphia: Lippincott, 1926.

Marti, Donald. *To Improve the Soil and the Mind: Agricultural Societies, Journals, and Schools in the Northeastern United States, 1791–1865*. Ann Arbor, Mich.: University Microfilms International, 1979.

Martin, Charles. *Hollybush: Folk Building and Social Change in an Appalachian Community*. Knoxville: University of Tennessee Press, 1984.

Martin, Edgar W. *The Standard of Living in 1860*. Chicago: University of Chicago Press, 1942.

Marx, Leo. *The Machine in the Garden: Technology and the Pastoral Ideal in America*. New York: Oxford University Press, 1964.

Marzio, Peter. *The Democratic Art: Pictures for a Ninteeenth Century America*. Boston: David R. Godine, 1979.

Mayhew, Edgar, and Minor Myers. *A Documentary History of American Interiors*. New York: Scribner, 1980.

McKinley, Blaine. "Strangers in the Gates: Employer Reactions Toward Domestic Servants in America, 1825–1875." Ph.D. diss., Michigan State University, 1969.

McMahon, Sarah. "A Comfortable Subsistence: A History of Diet in New England, 1630–1850." Ph.D. diss., Brandeis University, 1982.

McNall, Neil Adams. *An Agricultural History of the Genesee Valley, 1790–1860*. Philadelphia: University of Pennsylvania Press, 1952.

Mead, Margaret, and Martha Wolfenstein, eds. *Childhood in Contemporary Culture*. Chicago: University of Chicago Press, 1955.

Meinig, Donald W., ed. *The Interpretation of Ordinary Landscapes*. New York: Oxford University Press, 1979.

Mergen, Bernard. *Play and Playthings: A Reference Guide*. Westport, Conn.: Greenwood, 1982.

Miller, Roberta Balstad. *City and Hinterland: A Case Study in Urban Growth and Development*. Westport, Conn.: Greenwood, 1979.

Morrison, Theodore. *Chautauqua: A Center for Education, Religion, and the Arts in America*. Chicago: University of Chicago Press, 1974.

Mott, Frank Luther. *History of American Magazines*. 5 vols. Cambridge: Harvard University Press, 1938–1968.

Mumford, Lewis. *Sticks and Stones: A Study of American Architecture and Civilization*. New York: Boni & Liverright, 1924.

Neely, Wayne Caldwell. *The Agricultural Fair*. New York: Columbia University Press, 1935.

Neil, J. Meredith, and Marshall Fishwick, eds. *Popular Architecture*. Bowling Green, Oh.: Bowling Green Popular Press, n.d.

Newcomb, Rexford. *Architecture of the Old Northwest Territory*. Chicago: University of Chicago Press, 1950.

Nissenbaum, Stephen. *Sex, Diet, and Debility in Jacksonian America: Sylvester Graham and Health Reform*. Westport, Conn.: Greenwood, 1980.

Noble, Allen. *Wood, Brick, and Stone: The North American Settlement Landscape*. Amherst: University of Massachusetts Press, 1984.

Ogilvie, William Edward. *Pioneer Agricultural Journalists*. Chicago: Arthur G. Leonard, 1927.

Osterud, Nancy Grey. "Strategies of Mutuality: Relations Among Women and Men in an Agricultural Community." Ph.D. diss., Brown University, 1984.

Pabst, Margaret. *Agricultural Trends in the Connecticut Valley, 1800–1900*. Smith College Studies in History, vol. 26. Northampton, Mass.: Department of History of Smith College, 1941.

Percival, Caroline. *Martha Van Rensselaer*. Ithaca: Cornell University Press, 1957.

Perrin, Richard. *Historic Wisconsin Buildings: A Survey of Pioneer Architecture, 1835–1870*. Milwaukee Public Museum Publications in History, number 4. Milwaukee: Milwaukee Public Museum, 1962.

Peterson, Charles, ed. *Building Early America: Contributions Toward the History of a Great Industry*. Radnor, Pa.: Chilton Book Co., 1976.

Peterson, Harold L. *Americans at Home: From the Colonists to the Late Victorians*. New York: Charles Scribner's Sons, 1971.

Pirtle, Thomas R. *History of the Dairy Industry*. 1926. Reprint, Chicago: Mojonnier Brothers, 1973.

Potter, David. *People of Plenty: Economic Abundance and the American Character*. Chicago: University of Chicago Press, 1954.

Prendergast, Norma. "A Sense of Home." Ph.D. diss., Cornell University, 1981.

Quimby, Ian, ed. *Material Culture and the Study of American Life*. New York: W. W. Norton, 1978.

Rapoport, Amos. *House Form and Culture*. Englewood Cliffs, N.J.: Prentice-Hall, 1969.

Rawls, Walton. *The Great Book of Currier & Ives' America*. New York: Abbeville Press, 1979.

Riley, Glenda. *Frontierswomen: The Iowa Experience*. Ames: Iowa State University Press, 1981.

Robinson, John Martin. *Georgian Model Farms*. New York: Oxford University Press, 1983.

Rodgers, Daniel T. *The Work Ethic in Industrializing America, 1850–1920*. Chicago: University of Chicago Press, 1978.

Rogers, Meyric. *American Interior Design: The Traditions and Development of Domestic Design From Colonial Times to the Present*. New York: Norton, 1947.

Rogin, Leo. *The Introduction of Farm Machinery in Its Relation to the Productivity of Labor in the Agriculture of the United States During the Nineteenth Century*. University of California Publications in Economics, vol. 9. Berkeley: University of California Press, 1931.

Roos, Frank J. *Bibliography of Early American Architecture*. Urbana: University of Illinois Press, 1968.

Rose, Flora. *A Page of Modern Education: Forty Years of Home Economics at Cornell University*. Ithaca: New York State College of Home Economics, 1940.

Rosenberg, Charles E. *No Other Gods, On Science and American Social Thought*. Baltimore: Johns Hopkins University Press, 1976.

Rossiter, Margaret. *The Emergence of Agricultural Science*. New Haven: Yale University Press, 1975.

————. *Women Scientists in America: Struggles and Strategies to 1940*. Baltimore: Johns Hopkins University Press, 1982.

Rothman, David. *The Discovery of the Asylum: Social Order and Disorder in the New Republic*. Boston: Little, Brown, 1971.

Russell, Howard S. *A Long, Deep Furrow: Three Centuries of Farming in New England*. Hanover, N.H.: University Press of New England, 1976.

Ryan, Mary. *Cradle of the Middle Class: The Family in Oneida County, New York, 1790–1865*. New York: Cambridge University Press, 1981.

Schafer, Joseph. *Social History of American Agriculture*. New York: Macmillan, 1936.

Schiffer, Margaret. *Chester County, Pennsylvania Inventories, 1684–1850*. Exton, Pa.: Schiffer Publishing, Ltd, 1974.

Schlereth, Thomas, ed. *Material Culture Studies in America*. Nashville, Tenn.: American Association for State and Local History, 1982.

Schlesinger, A. M. *Learning How to Behave: A Historical Study of American Etiquette Books*. New York: Macmillan, 1947.

Schmidt, Carl. *Early Architecture of the Genesee Valley*. Genesee, N.Y.: n.p., 1975.

————. *The Octagon Fad*. Scottsville, New York, 1958.

Schmidt, Carl, and Phillip Parr. *More About Octagons*. Scottsville, New York: n.d.

Schob, David E. *Hired Hands and Plowboys: Farm Labor in the Midwest, 1815–1860*. Urbana: University of Illinois Press, 1975.

Schorsch, Anita. *Images of Childhood: an Illustrated Social History.* New York: Mayflower Books, 1979.

Scully, Vincent. *The Shingle Style and the Stick Style: Architectural Theory and Design from Downing to the Origins of Wright.* rev. ed. New Haven: Yale University Press, 1971.

Seale, William. *The Tasteful Interlude: American Interiors Through the Camera's Eye, 1860–1917.* 2nd ed. Nashville, Tenn.: American Association for State and Local History, 1981.

Shannon, Fred A. *Farmer's Last Frontier: Agriculture, 1860–1897.* 1945. Reprint, White Plains, N.Y.: M. E. Sharpe, 1973.

Sklar, Kathryn K. *Catharine Beecher: A Study in American Domesticity.* New Haven: Yale University Press, 1973.

Smith, Ruby Green. *The People's Colleges.* Ithaca, N.Y.: Cornell University Press, 1949.

Smith-Rosenberg, Carroll. *Religion and the Rise of the American City.* Ithaca: Cornell University Press, 1971.

Solomon, Barbara Miller. *In the Company of Educated Women: A History of Women and Higher Education in America.* New Haven: Yale University Press, 1985.

Soltow, Lee. *Men and Wealth in the United States, 1850–1870.* New Haven: Yale University Press, 1975.

Stevenson, Katherine Cole, and H. Ward Jandl. *Houses By Mail: A Guide to Houses From Sears, Roebuck and Company.* Washington, D.C.: Preservation Press, 1986.

Stilgoe, John. *Common Landscape of America, 1580–1845.* New Haven: Yale University Press, 1982.

Stotz, Charles Morse. *The Architectural Heritage of Early Western Pennsylvania.* Pittsburgh: University of Pittsburgh Press, 1966.

Strasser, Susan. *Never Done: A History of American Housework.* New York: Pantheon, 1982.

Stratton, Joanna. *Pioneer Women: Voices From the Kansas Frontier.* New York: Simon and Schuster, 1981.

Tatum, George B. *Andrew Jackson Downing, Arbiter of American Taste, 1815–1852.* Ann Arbor, Mich.: University Microfilms, 1949.

Taylor, George Rogers. *The Transportation Revolution.* New York: Rinehart, 1951.

Tebbel, John William. *A History of Book Publishing in the United States.* 5 vols. New York: R. R. Bowker, 1972–1981.

Tomlan, Michael. "Popular and Professional American Architectural Literature in the Late Nineteenth Century." Ph.D. diss., Cornell University, 1983.

Torre, Susana, ed. *Women in American Architecture.* New York: Whitney Library of Design, 1977.

Tucker, Gilbert. *Historical Sketch of American Agricultural Periodicals.* Albany: privately printed, 1909.

Ucko, Peter, ed. *Man, Settlement, and Urbanism.* London: Duckworth, 1972.

Upton, Dell, and John Michael Vlach. *Common Places: Readings in American Vernacular Architecture.* Athens: University of Georgia Press, 1986.

Van Liew, Barbara. *Long Island Domestic Architecture of the Colonial and Federal Periods.* Setauket, N.Y.: Society for the Preservation of Long Island Antiquities, 1974.

Warner, Sam Bass. *Streetcar Suburbs: The Process of Growth in Boston, 1870–1900.* 2nd ed. Cambridge: Harvard University Press, 1978.

Waterman, Thomas. *The Dwellings of Colonial America.* Chapel Hill: University of North Carolina Press, 1950.

Webb, Walter Prescott. *The Great Plains.* Boston: Ginn and Co., 1931.

Wells, Camille, ed. *Perspectives in Vernacular Architecture.* Annapolis, Md.: Vernacular Architecture Forum, 1982.

Whiffen, Marcus, and Frederick Koeper. *American Architecture, 1607–1976.* Cambridge: MIT Press, 1981.

White, Morton, and Lucia White. *The Intellectual Versus the City.* Cambridge: Harvard University Press, 1962.

Whorton, James. *Crusaders For Fitness: The History of American Health Reformers, 1830–1920.* Princeton: Princeton University Press, 1982.

Wiebe, Robert. *The Search for Order 1877–1920.* New York: Hill and Wang, 1967.

Wilson, Harold Fisher. *The Hill Country of New England.* New York: Columbia University Press, 1936.

Wines, Richard. *Fertilizer in America: From Waste Recycling to Resource Exploitation.* Philadelphia: Temple University Press, 1985.

Wishy, Bernard. *The Child and the Republic: The Dawn of Modern American Child Nurture.* Philadelphia: University of Pennsylvania Press, 1968.

Woody, Thomas. *A History of Women's Education in the United States.* 2 vols. New York: The Science Press, 1929.

Wright, Gwendolyn. *Building the Dream: A Social History of American Housing.* New York: Pantheon, 1981.

———. *Moralism and the Model Home: Domestic Architecture and Cultural Conflict in Chicago, 1873–1913.* Chicago: University of Chicago Press, 1980.

Zelizer, Viviana. *Pricing the Priceless Child: The Changing Social Value of Children.* New York: Basic Books, 1985.

ARTICLES

Abbott, Richard. "The Agricultural Press Views the Yeoman 1819–1859." *Ag. History* 42 (January 1968): 35–44.

Adams, Donald R. "The Residential Construction Industry in the Early Nineteenth Century." *Journal of Economic History* 35 (December 1975): 794–806.

———. "The Standard of Living During American Industrialization." *Journal of Economic History* 42 (December 1982): 903–917.

Alexander, Edward. "Wisconsin, New York's Daughter State." *Wisconsin Magazine of History* 30 (September 1946): 11–30.

American Quarterly 35 (Bibliography 1983), special issue on material culture.

Ames, Kenneth. "Grand Rapids Furniture at the Time of the Centennial." *WP* 10 (1975): 24–29.

———. "Material Culture as Nonverbal Communication: An Historical Case Study." *Journal of American Culture* 3 (Winter 1980): 619–642.

Anderson, Russell. "New York Agriculture Meets the West, 1830–1850." *Wisconsin Magazine of History* 16 (December 1932): 163–199.

Anderson, William A. "Transmission of Farming as an Occupation." *Rural Sociology* 4 (December 1939): 433–448.

Ankarloo, Bengt. "Agriculture and Women's Work: Directions of Change in the West, 1700–1900." *Journal of Family History* 5 (Summer 1979): 111–120.

Ankli, Robert. "The Coming of the Reaper." In Gerald Nash, ed. *Issues in Economic History.* 3rd ed. Lexington, Mass.: D. C. Heath, 1980.

Appleby, Joyce. "The Changing Prospect of the Family Farm in the Early National Period." *Working Papers,* Regional Economic History Research Center 4 (1981): 1–16.

Atack, Jeremy, and Fred Bateman. "Egalitarianism, Inequality, and Age: The Rural North in 1860." *Journal of Economic History* 41 (March 1981): 85–94.

———. "The Egalitarian Ideal and the Distribution of Wealth in the Northern Agricultural Community." *Review of Economics and Statistics* 63 (February 1981): 124–129.

Baron, William, and Anne Bridges. "Making Hay in New England: Maine as a Case Study, 1800–1850." *Ag. History* 57 (April 1983): 165–181.

Bash, Wendell. "Changing Birth Rates in New York State, 1840–1870." Milbank Memorial Fund *Quarterly* 41 (April 1963): 161–183.

Bassett, T. D. Seymour. "A Case Study of Urban Impact on Rural Society: Vermont, 1840–1880." *Ag. History* 30 (January 1956): 28–35.

Bateman, Fred. "Improvement in American Dairy Farming, 1850–1910: A Quantitative Analysis." *Journal of Economic History* 28 (June 1968): 255–273.

Bateman, Fred, and Jeremy Atack. "The Profitability of Agriculture in 1860." *Research in Economic History* 4 (1979): 87–125.

Beales, Ross. "In Search of the Historical Child: Miniature Adulthood and Youth in Colonial New England." *AQ* 27 (October 1975): 379–398.

Bennett, Merrill K., and Rosamond Peirce. "Change in the American National Diet, 1879–1959." *Food Research Institute Studies* 2 (May 1961): 95–121.

Bidwell, Percy Wells. "The Agricultural Revolution in New England." *American Historical Review* 26 (July 1921): 683–703.

Bloch, Ruth. "American Feminine Ideals in Transition: The Rise of the Moral Mother, 1785–1815." *Feminist Studies* 4 (June 1978): 101–127.

Blocker, Jack S. "Market Integration, Urban Growth, and Economic Change in an Ohio County, 1850–1880." *Ohio History* 90 (Autumn 1981): 298–317.

Bloomberg, Susan, et al. "A Census Probe of Southern Michigan, 1850–1880." *Journal of Social History* 5 (Fall 1971): 26–45.

Bogue, Margaret B. "The Lake and the Fruit: The Making of Three Farm-Type Areas." *Ag. History* 59 (October 1985): 493–523.

Brady, Dorothy. "Relative Prices in the Nineteenth Century." *Journal of Economic History* 24 (June 1964): 164–203.

Bridges, William. "Family Patterns and Social Values in America, 1825–1875." *AQ* 17 (Spring 1965): 3–11.

Brobeck, Stephen. "Images of the Family: Portrait Paintings as Indices of American Family Structure, Culture, and Behavior, 1730–1860." *Journal of Psychohistory* 5 (Summer 1977): 67–80.

Brown, Richard D. "Emergence of Urban Society in Rural Massachusetts 1760–1820." *JAH* 61 (June 1974): 29–52.

———. "Spreading the Word: Rural Clergymen and the Communication Network of 18th-Century New England." *Proceedings,* Massachusetts Historical Society 94 (1982): 1–14.

Brown, Vernon J. "Country Life in the Eighties." *Michigan History* 17 (Spring 1933): 175–191.

Bruegman, Robert. "Central Heating and Forced Ventilation: Origins and Effects on Architectural Design." *JSAH* 37 (October 1978): 143–161.

Brumberg, Joan J. "Zenanas and Girlless Villages: The Ethnography of American Evangelical Women." *JAH* 69 (September 1982): 347–372.

Brunger, Eric. "Dairying and Urban Development in New York State 1850–1900." *Ag. History* 29 (October 1955): 169–174.

Bush, Corlann. "The Barn is His, The House is Mine: Agricultural Technology and Sex Roles." In George Daniels and Mark Rose, eds. *Energy and Transport.* Beverly Hills: Sage Publications, 1982.

Bushman, Richard L. "Family Security in the Transition from Farm to City, 1750–1850." *Working Papers,* Regional Economic History Research Center 4 (1981): 27–61.

———. "American High-Style and Vernacular Cultures." In Jack Greene and J. R. Pole, eds. *Colonial British America* (Baltimore: Johns Hopkins University Press, 1984).

Carman, Harry J. "Jesse Buel, Albany County Agriculturist." *New York History* 14 (July 1933): 241–250.

Clark, Christopher. "The Household Economy, Market Exchange, and the Rise of Capitalism in the Connecticut Valley 1800–1860." *Journal of Social History* 13 (Winter 1979): 169–191.

Clark, Clifford. "Domestic Architecture as an Index to Social History." *JIH* 7 (Summer 1976): 35–56.

Cohen, Yehudi. "Social Boundary Systems." *Current Anthropology* 10 (February 1969): 103–126.

Cole, Arthur H. "Agricultural Crazes, a Neglected Chapter in American Economic History." *American Economic Review* 16 (December 1926): 622–639.

———. "The Rise of the Price System and the Rites of Passage." *AQ* 14 (Winter 1962): 527–545.

———. "The Mystery of Fuel Wood Marketing." *Business History Review* 44 (Autumn 1970): 339–359.

Colman, Gould P. "Innovation and Diffusion in Agriculture." *Ag. History* 42 (July 1968): 173–187.

Condit, Carl W. "Architectural History in the United States: A Bibliographical Essay." *American Studies International* 16 (1977–78): 4–22.

Connally, Ernest A. "The Cape Cod House: An Introductory Study." *JSAH* 19 (May 1960): 47–56.

Cooke, Edward S. "Domestic Space in the Federal-Period Inventories of Salem Merchants." *Essex Institute Historical Collections* 116 (October 1980): 248–265.

Cott, Nancy. "Notes Toward an Interpretation of Antebellum Childrearing." *Psychohistory Review* 6 (Spring 1978): 4–21.

———. "Young Women in the Second Great Awakening in New England." *Feminist Studies* 3 (Fall 1975): 15–29.

Cowan, Ruth Schwartz. "The Industrial Revolution in the Home." *Technology and Culture* 17 (January 1976): 1–24.

Cox, Lawanda F. "The American Agricultural Wage Earner, 1865–1900." *Ag. History* 22 (April 1948): 95–114.

———. "Tenancy in the United States, 1865–1900." *Ag. History* 18 (July 1944): 97–105.

Cremin, Lawrence. "The Revolution in American Secondary Education, 1893–1918." *Teachers College Record* 56 (March 1955): 295–309.

Crosbie, Michael J. "From 'Cookbooks' to 'Menus': The Transformation of Architecture Books in Nineteenth-Century America." *Material Culture* 17 (1985): 1–23.

Cummings, Abbott Lowell. "Notes on Furnishing a Small New England Farmhouse." *Old-Time New England* 48 (Fall 1957): 65–84.

Danhof, Clarence. "The Farm Enterprise: The Northern United States, 1820–1860s." *Research in Economic History* 4 (1979): 127–191.

David, Paul. "The Mechanization of Reaping in the Antebellum Midwest." In Henry Rosovsky, ed., *Industrialization in Two Systems*. New York: Wiley, 1966.

Demaree, Albert L. "The Farm Journals, Their Editors, and Their Public, 1830–1860." *Ag. History* 15 (October 1941): 182–188.

Demos, John. "The American Family in Past Time." *American Scholar* 43 (Summer 1974): 422–447.

Demos, John, and Virginia Demos. "Adolescence in Historical Perspective." *Journal of Marriage and the Family* 31 (November 1969): 632–639.

Destler, Chester M. "The Gentleman Farmer and the New Agriculture: Jeremiah Wadsworth." *Ag. History* 46 (January 1972): 135–143.

Dodge, Stanley. "Bureau and the Princeton Community." *Annals*, American Association of Geographers 22 (September 1932): 159–209.

Doucet, Michael J., and John Weaver. "Material Culture and the North American House: The Era of the Common Man, 1870–1920." *JAH* 72 (December 1985): 560–588.

Douglas, Diane. "The Machine in the Parlor: A Dialectical Analysis of the Sewing Machine." *Journal of American Culture* 5 (Spring 1982): 20–30.

Durand, Loyal. "Historical and Economic Geography of Dairying in Northern New York." *Geographical Review* 57 (January 1967): 24–48.

———. "The Migration of Cheese Manufacture in the United States." *Annals*, Association of American Geographers, 42 (December 1952): 263–283.

Easterlin, Richard. "Population Change and Farm Settlement in the United States." *Journal of Economic History* 36 (March 1976): 45–75.

Edgerton, Samuel. "Heating Stoves in Eighteenth-Century Philadelphia." *APT Bulletin* 3 (1971): 14–104.

Ellis, David Maldwyn. "The Yankee Invasion of New York." *New York History* 32 (January 1951): 1–18.

Ellsworth, Clayton. "The Coming of Rural Consolidated Schools to the Ohio Valley 1892–1912." *Ag. History* 30 (July 1956): 119–128.

Erdman, H. E. "The Associated Dairies of New York as Precursors of American Agricultural Cooperatives." *Ag. History* 36 (April 1962): 82–91.

Esdaile, Katharine A. "The Small House and Its Amenities in the Architectural Handbooks of 1749–1827." *Transactions* of the Bibliographical Society 15 (1917–1919): 115–133.

Faragher, John Mack. "History from the Inside-Out: Writing the History of Women in Rural America." *AQ* 33 (Winter 1981): 537–557.

Farrell, Richard T. "Advice to Farmers: The Content of Agricultural Newspapers, 1860–1910." *Ag. History* 51 (January 1977): 209–217.

Feinstein, Karen W. "Kindergartens, Feminism, and the Professionalization of Motherhood." *International Journal of Women's Studies* 3 (January/February 1980): 28–39.

Fite, Gilbert. "The Development of Agricultural Fundamentalism in the Nineteenth Century." *Journal of Farm Economics* 44 (December 1962): 1203–1210.

Fleming, E. McClung. "Early American Decorative Arts as Social Documents." *Mississippi Valley Historical Review* 45 (September 1958): 276–285.

Fletcher, Stevenson W. "The Subsistence Farming Period in Pennsylvania Agriculture, 1640–1840." *Pennsylvania History* 14 (July 1947): 185–195.

Fox, Vivian. "Is Adolescence a Phenomenon of Modern Times?" *Journal of Psychohistory* 5 (Fall 1977): 271–292.

Fuller, Wayne. "The Rural Roots of the Progressive Leaders." *Ag. History* 42 (January 1968): 1–13.

Garnsey, Caroline J. "Ladies' Magazines to 1850: The Beginnings of an Industry." New York Public Library *Bulletin* 58 (February 1954): 74–89.

Garvin, James L. "Mail-Order Plans and American Victorian Architecture." *WP* 16 (Winter 1981): 309–334.

Gates, Paul W. "Agricultural Change in New York State, 1850–1890." *New York History* 50 (April 1969): 115–141.

Geary, Susan. "The Domestic Novel as a Commercial Commodity: The Making of a Best Seller in the 1850s." *Papers,* Bibliographical Society of America 70 (1976): 365–393.

Gilman, Roger. "The Romantic Interior." In George Boas, ed., *Romanticism in America.* Baltimore: Johns Hopkins University Press, 1940.

Glassie, Henry. "Eighteenth-Century Cultural Process in Delaware Valley Folk Building." *WP* 7 (1972): 19–59.

———. "Vernacular Architecture and Society." *Material Culture* 16 (Spring 1984): 5–25.

Glazer-Malbin, Nona. "Housework." (review essay) *Signs* 1 (Summer 1976): 905–922.

Graff, Harvey J. "Patterns of Dependency and Child Development in the Mid-Nineteenth Century City: A Sample from Boston, 1860." *History of Education Quarterly* 13 (Summer 1973): 129–143.

Green, Harvey. "Exploring Material Culture." *AQ* 32 (Summer 1980): 222–225.

Gross, Robert. "Culture and Cultivation: Agriculture and Society in Thoreau's Concord." *JAH* 69 (June 1982): 42–62.

———. "The Great Bean Field Hoax: Thoreau and the Agricultural Reformers." *Virginia Quarterly Review* 61 (Summer 1985): 483–497.

Halpin, Kay. "Sears, Roebuck's Best-Kept Secret." *Historic Preservation* 33 (September–October 1981): 25–29.

Hamlin, Talbot. "The Greek Revival in America and Some of its Critics." *Art Bulletin* 24 (September 1942): 244–259.

Handlin, David. "Efficiency and the American Home." *Architectural Association Quarterly* 5 (October/December 1973): 50–55.

Hargreaves, Mary. "Women in the Agricultural Settlement of the Northern Plains." *Ag. History* 50 (January 1976): 179–189.

Harris, Barbara. "Recent Work on the History of the Family: A Review Article." *Feminist Studies* 3 (Spring–Summer 1976): 159–172.

Harris, Michael. "Books for Sale on the Illinois Frontier." *American Book Collector* 21 (January 1971): 15–17.

———. "The General Store as an Outlet for Books." *Journal of Library History* 8 (July–October 1973): 124–132.

Hayden, Dolores, and Gwendolyn Wright. "Architecture and Planning." (review essay) *Signs* 1 (Summer 1976): 923–935.

Henretta, James. "Families and Farms: Mentalité in Pre-Industrial America." *WMQ* 3rd ser. 35 (January 1978): 3–33.

Hersey, George. "Godey's Choice." *JSAH* 18 (October 1959): 104–112.

Higgs, Robert. "Mortality in Rural America, 1870–1920." *Explorations in Economic History* 10 (Winter 1973): 177–195.

Hiner, N. Ray. "The Child in American Historiography: Accomplishments and Prospects." *Psychohistory Review* 7 (Summer 1978): 13–23.

————. "Adolescence in Eighteenth-century America." *History of Childhood Quarterly* 3 (Fall 1975): 253–281.

Hole, Donna C. "The Kitchen Dresser: Architectural Fittings in Eighteenth and Early Nineteenth Century Anglo-American Kitchens." *Petits Propos Culinaires* 9 (October 1981): 25–37.

Hutslar, Donald A. "The Ohio Farmstead: Farm Buildings as Cultural Artifacts." *Ohio History* 90 (Summer 1981): 221–237.

Inman, Pauline. "House Furnishings of a Vermont Family." *Antiques* 96 (August 1969): 228–234.

Interrante, Joseph. "You Can't Go to Town in a Bathtub: Automobile Movement and the Reorganization of American Rural Space, 1900–1930." *Radical History Review* 21 (Fall 1979): 151–168.

Jackson, John B. "The Westward-Moving House." *Landscape* 2 (Spring 1952): 10–18.

————. "Jefferson, Thoreau, and After." In Ervin Zube, ed., *Landscapes: Selected Writings of J. B. Jackson*. Amherst: University of Massachusetts Press, 1970.

Jeffrey, Kirk. "The Family as Utopian Retreat from the City: The Nineteenth Century Contribution." *Soundings* 55 (Spring 1972): 21–42.

Jensen, Joan M. "Churns and Butter Making in the Mid-Atlantic Farm Economy, 1750–1850." *Working Papers,* Regional Economic History Research Center 5 (1982): 60–100.

————. "Cloth, Butter, and Boarders: Women's Household Production for the Market." *Review of Radical Political Economics* 12 (Summer 1980): 14–24.

Johnstone, Paul. "In Praise of Husbandry." *Ag. History* 11 (April 1937): 80–96.

Jones, Robert Leslie. "The Beef Cattle Industry in Ohio Prior to the Civil War." *Ohio State Historical and Archaeological Quarterly* 64 (April 1955): 168–194.

————. "The Dairy Industry in Ohio Prior to the Civil War." *Ohio State Archaeological and Historical Quarterly* 56 (January 1947): 46–70.

————. "Introduction of Farm Machinery into Ohio Prior to 1865." *Ohio State Archaeological and Historical Quarterly* 58 (January 1949): 1–21.

Kaestle, Carl. "Social Change, Discipline, and the Common School in Early Nineteenth-Century America." *JIH* 9 (Summer 1978): 1–17.

Kaye, Frances. "The Ladies' Department of the Ohio Cultivator 1845–1855: A Feminist Forum." *Ag. History* 50 (April 1976): 414–424.

Keep, William. "Early American Cooking Stoves." *Old-Time New England* 22 (October 1931): 70–87.

Keppel, Ann M. "The Myth of Agrarianism in Rural Educational Reform, 1890–1914." *History of Education Quarterly* 2 (June 1962): 100–113.

Kerber, Linda. "Educating Women for the Republic, 1787–1805." In Stanley Elkins and Eric McKitrick, eds., *The Hofstadter Aegis: A Memorial*. New York: Alfred A. Knopf, 1974.

Kern, Stephen. "Explosive Intimacy: Psychodynamics of the Victorian Family." *History of Childhood Quarterly* 1 (Winter 1974): 437–463.

Kett, Joseph. "Adolescence and Youth in Nineteenth Century America." *JIH* 2 (Autumn 1971): 283–296.

Kihlstedt, Folke. "The Automobile and the Transformation of the American House." *Michigan Quarterly Review* 4 (Fall 1980–Winter 1981): 555–570.

Kniffen, Fred. "Folk Housing: Key to Diffusion." *Annals,* Association of American Geographers 55 (December 1965): 549–577.

Kniffen, Fred, and Henry Glassie. "Building in Wood in the Eastern United States: A Time-Place Perspective." *Geographical Review* 56 (January 1966): 40–66.

Krueger, Lillian. "Social Life in Wisconsin." (series) *Wisconsin Magazine of History* 22 (December 1938): 156–176; (March 1939): 312–329; (June 1939): 396–427.

Kwollek-Folland, Angel. "The Elegant Dugout: Domesticity and Moveable Culture in the United States, 1870–1900." *American Studies* 25 (Fall 1984): 21–37.

Lancaster, Clay. "Builders' Guides and Plan Books in American Architecture." *Magazine of Art* 41 (January 1948): 16–23.

Larkin, Jack. "Dimensions of Childhood." Unpublished paper, Old Sturbridge Village.

———. "The View from New England: Notes on Everyday Life in Rural America to 1850." *AQ* 34 (Bibliography 1982): 244–261.

Laslett, Barbara. "Family as a Public and Private Institution." *Journal of Marriage and the Family* 35 (August 1973): 480–495.

Lemmer, George. "Early Agricultural Editors and their Farm Philosophies." *Ag. History* 31 (October 1957): 3–23.

Lemon, James T. "Household Consumption in Eighteenth-Century America." *Ag. History* 41 (January 1967): 59–71.

Lerner, Gerda. "The Lady and the Mill Girl." *American Studies* 10 (Spring 1969): 1–15.

Lewandowski, Jan Leo. "The Plank Framed House in Northern Vermont." *Vermont History* 53 (Spring 1985): 104–121.

Lewis, Peirce F. "Common Houses, Cultural Spoor." *Landscape* 19 (January 1975): 1–22.

Littlejohn, J. "Temne Space." *Anthropological Quarterly* 36 (January 1963): 1–17.

Loehr, Rodney. "The Influence of England Upon American Agriculture, 1775–1825." *Ag. History* 11 (January 1937): 3–16.

———. "Self-Sufficiency on the Farm." *Ag. History* 26 (April 1952): 37–41.

MacFarlane, Janet. "Octagon Buildings in New York State." *New York History* 33 (April 1952): 216.

Madison, James. "Reformers and the Rural Church, 1900–1950," *JAH* 73 (December 1986): 645–668.

Malin, James. "The 'Vanity' Histories." *Kansas Historical Quarterly* 21 (Winter 1955): 598–643.

Marks, Bayly Ellen. "Rural Response to Urban Penetration: Baltimore and St. Mary's County, Maryland, 1790–1840." *Journal of Historical Geography* 8 (1982): 113–126.

Marsh, Margaret. "The Suburban House: The Social Implications of Environmental Choice." Paper, Organization of American Historians Annual Meeting, 1986.

Marti, Donald. "Agricultural Journalism and the Diffusion of Knowledge: The First Half-Century in America." *Ag. History* 54 (January 1980): 28–37.

———. "Early Agricultural Societies in New York: The Foundations of Improvement." *New York History* 48 (October 1967): 313–322.

———. "The Reverend Henry Colman's Agricultural Ministry." *Ag. History* 51 (July 1977): 524–540.

———. "Women's Work in the Grange: Mary Ann Mayo of Michigan, 1882–1903." *Ag. History* 56 (April 1982): 439–453.

Martin, Lawrence. "The Genesis of Godey's Lady's Book." *New England Quarterly* 1 (January 1928): 41–70.

Mayo, Edith. "Focus on Material Culture." *Journal of American Culture* 3 (Winter 1980): 595–599.

McClaugherty, Martha. "Household Art: Creating the Artistic Home, 1868–1893." *WP* 18 (Spring 1983): 1–26.

McGaw, Judith. "Women and the History of American Technology." *Signs* 7 (Summer 1982): 798–829.

McKelvey, Blake. "The Flower City: Center of Nurseries and Fruit Orchards." Rochester Historical Society *Publications* 18 (1940): 121–169.

McMullen, Haynes. "The Use of Books in the Ohio Valley Before 1850." *Journal of Library History* 1 (January 1966): 43–56.

McNall, Neil A. "King Wheat in the Genesee Valley." *New York History* 27 (October 1946): 426–441.

Mechling, Jay. "Advice to Historians on Advice to Mothers." *Journal of Social History* 9 (Fall 1975): 44–63.

Melder, Keith. "Ladies Bountiful." *New York History* 48 (July 1967): 231–254.

Mergen, Bernard. "Discovery of Children's Play." *AQ* 27 (October 1975): 399–421.

———. "Toys and American Culture: Objects as Hypotheses." *Journal of American Culture* 3 (Winter 1980): 743–747.

Merrill, Michael. "Cash is Good to Eat: Self-Sufficiency and Exchange in the Economy of the Rural United States." *Radical History Review* 4 (September 1976): 42–71.

Meyer, Douglas. "Folk Housing on the Illinois Frontier." *Pioneer America Society Transactions* 1 (January 1978): 30–42.

Mitchell, Robert J. "Tradition and Change in Rural New England." *Maine Historical Society Quarterly* 18 (Fall 1978): 87–107.

Modell, John. "Suburbanization and Change in the American Family." *JIH* 9 (Spring 1979): 621–646.

Modell, John, Frank Furstenberg, and Theodore Hershberg. "Social Change and Transitions to Adulthood in Historical Perspective." *Journal of Family History* 1 (Autumn 1976): 7–34.

Mutch, Robert. "Yeoman and Merchant in Pre-Industrial America." *Societas* 7 (Autumn 1977): 279–302.

Myers, Minor, Jr. "Who Bought Webster and Parkes's Encyclopedia?" *Antiques* 118 (May 1979): 1028–1032.

Naylor, Harriet J. "Rochester's Agricultural Press: A Mirror of Genesee Country Life." Rochester Historical Society *Publications* 18 (1940): 170–200.

Neil, J. Meredith. "What About Architecture?" *Journal of Popular Culture* 5 (Fall 1971): 280–288.

Noble, Allen G. "Variance in Floor Plans of Dutch Houses of the Colonial Period." *Pioneer America Society Transactions* 3 (1980): 46–56.

Norton, W. T. "Early Libraries in Illinois." *Journal of the Illinois State Historical Society* 6 (July 1913): 246–252.

Nylander, Jane. "Keeping Warm in Early Nineteenth-century New England." *Early American Life* 11 (October 1980): 46–49.

Oakes, Elinor F. "A Ticklish Business: Dairying in New England and Pennsylvania, 1750–1812." *Pennsylvania History* 47 (July 1980): 195–213.

Okada, Yasuo. "Squires' Diary: New York Agriculture in Transition, 1840–1860." *Keio Economic Studies* 7 (1970): 78–98.

———. "The Economic World of a Seneca County Farmer, 1830–1880." *New York History* 66 (January 1985): 5–29.

Olmstead, Alan T. "The Mechanization of Reaping and Mowing in American Agriculture, 1833–1870." *Journal of Economic History* 35 (June 1975): 327–352.

O'Neal, William B. "Pattern Books in American Architecture." In Mario di Valmarana, ed.,

Building By the Book. Palladian Studies in America I. Charlottesville: University of Virginia Press, 1984.

Peckham, Howard H. "Books and Reading on the Ohio Valley Frontier." *Mississippi Valley Historical Review* 44 (March 1958): 649–663.

Pederson, Jane. "The Country Visitors: Patterns of Hospitality in Rural Wisconsin, 1880–1925." *Ag. History* 58 (July 1984): 347–365.

Peterson, Fred. "Vernacular Building and Victorian Architecture: Midwestern American Farm Homes." *JIH* 12 (Winter 1982): 407–427.

Pillsbury, Richard. "Patterns in the Folk and Vernacular House Forms of the Pennsylvania Culture Region." *Pioneer America* 9 (July 1977): 12–31.

Prescott, Gerald. "Wisconsin Farm Leaders in the Gilded Age." *Ag. History* 44 (April 1970): 183–196.

Primack, Martin. "Farm Construction as a Use of Farm Labor in the United States, 1850–1910." *Journal of Economic History* 25 (March 1965): 114–125.

———. "Farm Capital Formation as a Use of Farm Labor in the United States, 1850–1910." *Journal of Economic History* 26 (September 1966): 348–359.

Pruitt, Bettye. "Self-Sufficiency and the Agricultural Economy of Eighteenth-Century Massachusetts." *WMQ* 3rd ser. 41 (July 1984): 333–364.

Quinan, Jack. "Asher Benjamin and American Architecture." *JSAH* 38 (October 1979): 244–270.

Rasmussen, Wayne. "The Civil War: A Catalyst of Agricultural Revolution." *Ag. History* 39 (October 1965): 187–194.

———. "The Impact of Technological Change on American Agriculture, 1862–1962." *Journal of Economic History* 22 (December 1962): 578–591.

Reinier, Jacqueline. "Concepts of Domesticity on the Southern Plains Agricultural Frontier, 1870–1920." In John Wunder, ed., *At Home on the Range.* Westport, Conn.: Greenwood, 1985.

Richardson, Herbert. "Farm Plans and Building Types in Harrison Township, New Jersey." *Pioneer America Society Transactions* 3 (1980): 88–121.

Rosenberg, Charles E. "Rationalization and Reality in the Shaping of American Agricultural Research, 1875–1914." *Social Studies of Science* 7 (1977): 401–422.

Rossiter, Margaret. "The Organization of the Agricultural Sciences." In A. Oleson and John Voss, eds., *The Organization of Knowledge in America.* Baltimore: Johns Hopkins University Press, 1979.

Rothenberg, Winifred. "The Market and Massachusetts Farmers, 1750–1850." *Journal of Economic History* 41 (June 1981): 283–313.

Rothman, Ellen. "Sex and Self-Control: Middle-Class Courtship in America, 1770–1870." *Journal of Social History* 15 (Spring 1982): 409–427.

St. George, Robert. "Set Thine House in Order: The Domestication of the Yeomanry in Seventeenth-Century New England." In *New England Begins.* Boston: Museum of Fine Arts, 1982.

Schlereth, Thomas. "The New England Presence in the Midwest Landscape." *Old Northwest* 9 (Summer 1983): 125–142.

Seaton, Beverly. "Idylls of Agriculture; or Nineteenth-century Success Stories of Farming and Gardening." *Ag. History* 55 (January 1981): 21–28.

Sewall, Richard H. "Michigan Farmers and the Civil War." *Michigan History* 44 (December 1960): 353–375.

Shammas, Carole. "The Domestic Environment in Early Modern England and America." *Journal of Social History* 14 (Fall 1980): 1–25.

Shepherd, Rebecca. "Restless Americans: The Geographical Mobility of Farm Laborers in the Old Midwest, 1850–1870." *Ohio History* 89 (Winter 1980): 25–46.

Sherman, Rexford. "Daniel Webster, Gentleman Farmer." *Ag. History* 53 (April 1979): 475–488.

Shettleworth, Earl G., and William Barry. "Walter Corey's Furniture Manufactory in Portland, Maine." *Antiques* 121 (May 1982): 1199–1206.

Shore, Miles F. "The Child and Historiography." *JIH* 6 (Winter 1976): 495–505.

Smith, David C. "Middle Range Farming in the Civil War Era: Life on a Farm in Seneca County, 1862–1866." *New York History* 48 (October 1967): 352–370.

Smith, Dorothy. "Household Space and Family Organization." *Pacific Sociological Review* 14 (January 1971): 53–79.

Smith, Kathleen. "Moore's Rural New Yorker: A Farm Program for the 1850s." *Ag. History* 45 (January 1971): 39–47.

Smith, Nancy A. "Pianoforte Manufacturing in Nineteenth-Century Boston." *Old-Time New England* 69 (Summer–Fall 1978): 37–48.

Smith-Rosenberg, Carroll. "The Female World of Love and Ritual." *Signs* 1 (Autumn 1975): 1–29.

Soltow, Lee, and Edward Stevens. "Economic Aspects of School Participation in the Mid-Nineteenth Century United States." *JIH* 8 (Autumn 1977): 221–243.

Sprague, Paul. "The Origin of Balloon Framing." *JSAH* 40 (December 1981): 312–319.

Stansell, Christine. "Women on the Great Plains." *Women's Studies* 4 (1976): 87–98.

Stearns, Bertha-Monica. "Early Western Magazines for Ladies." *Mississippi Valley Historical Review* 18 (December 1931): 319–331.

Stone, May N. "The Plumbing Paradox: American Attitudes Toward Late Nineteenth-Century Domestic Sanitary Arrangements." *WP* 14 (Autumn 1979): 284–309.

Sweeney, Kevin. "Mansion People: Kinship, Class, and Architecture in Western Massachusetts in the Mid-Eighteenth Century." *WP* 19 (Winter 1984): 231–255.

Swierenga, Robert. "The New Rural History: Defining the Parameters." *Great Plains Quarterly* 1 (Fall 1981): 211–223.

Taylor, George Rogers. "American Economic Growth Before 1840." *Journal of Economic History* 24 (December 1964): 427–431.

Taylor, Paul. "The American Hired Hand: His Rise and Decline." *Land Policy Review* 6 (Spring 1943): 3–17.

Thompson, E. P. "Time, Work-Discipline, and Industrial Capitalism." *Past and Present* 38 (1967): 56–79.

Thornton, Tamara. "The Moral Dimensions of Horticulture in Nineteenth-Century America." *New England Quarterly* 57 (March 1984): 3–25.

Throne, Mildred. "Book Farming." *Iowa Journal of History* 49 (April 1951): 117–143.

Tontz, Robert. "Memberships in General Farmers' Organizations in the United States 1874–1960." *Ag. History* 38 (July 1964): 143–148.

Trewartha, Glenn T. "Some Regional Characteristics of American Farmsteads." *Annals,* Association of American Geographers 38 (September 1948): 169–226.

Tryon, William S. "Book Distribution in Mid-Nineteenth Century America." *Papers,* Bibliographical Society of America 41 (July–September 1947): 210–230.

Ulrich, Laurel. "A Friendly Neighbor: Daily Work in Colonial Northern New England." *Feminist Studies* 6 (Summer 1980): 392–406.

Upton, Dell. "Ordinary Buildings: A Bibliographical Essay on American Vernacular Architecture." *American Studies International* 19 (Winter 1981): 57–76.

————. "Pattern-Books and Professionalism: Aspects of the Transformation of Domestic Architecture in America, 1800–1860." *WP* 19 (Summer/Autumn 1984): 108–150.

Van Wagenen, Jared. "Elkanah Watson: A Man of Affairs." *New York History* 13 (October 1932): 404–412.

Vanek, Joanne. "Work, Leisure, and Family Roles: Farm Households in the United States, 1920–1955." *Journal of Family History* 5 (Winter 1980): 422–431.

Vinovskis, Maris, and Richard Bernard. "Beyond Catharine Beecher." *Signs* 3 (Summer 1978): 857–870.

Waite, John G. "Stillwater, New York, House Specifications, 1843." *JSAH* 25 (March 1966): 59–60.

Walbert, Benjamin. "The Infancy of Central Heating in the United States, 1803–1845." *APT Bulletin* 3 (1971): 76–90.

Ward, J. W. "The Politics of Design." *Massachusetts Review* 6 (Autumn 1965): 661–689.

Weigley, Emma S. "It Might Have Been Euthenics: The Lake Placid Conference and the Home Economics Movement." *AQ* 26 (March 1974): 79–96.

Welker, Martin. "Farm Life in Central Ohio Sixty Years Ago." *Western Reserve Historical Society* 4 (1895): 23–87.

Welter, Barbara. "The Cult of True Womanhood." *AQ* 18 (Summer 1966): 151–174.

White, Frank G. "Stoves in Nineteenth Century New England." *Antiques* 110 (September 1979): 592–600.

Wilhelm, Hubert H. "New England in Southeastern Ohio." *Pioneer America Society Transactions* 2 (1979): 13–29.

Wines, Richard A. "The Nineteenth-Century Agricultural Transition in an Eastern Long Island Community." *Ag. History* 55 (January 1981): 50–83.

Withey, Lynne. "Household Structure in Urban and Rural Areas: The Case of Rhode Island, 1774–1800." *Journal of Family History* 3 (Spring 1978): 37–51.

Wohl, R. Richard. "The 'Country Boy' Myth and Its Place in American Urban Culture: The Nineteenth Century Contribution." *Perspectives in American History* 3 (1979): 77–156.

Wood, Charles B., III. "Survey and Bibliography of Writings on English and American Architectural Books." *WP* 2 (1965): 27–138.

Wright, Gwendolyn. "Sweet and Clean: The Domestic Landscape in the Progressive Era." *Landscape* 20 (October 1975): 38–44.

Yang, Donghyu. "Notes on the Wealth Distribution of Farm Households in the United States, 1860." *Explorations in Economic History* 21 (January 1984): 88–102.

Zelinsky, Wilbur. "Changes in the Geographic Patterns of Rural Population in the United States 1790–1960." *Geographical Review* 52 (1962): 492–524.

Sources of Biographical Data

Annett, Albert, and Alice Lehtinen. *History of Jaffrey, New Hampshire.* Jaffrey, N.H., 1934.

Atlas of Chenango County, New York. Philadelphia: Pomeroy and Whitman, 1875.

Atlas of Hartford (Ct) City and County. Hartford: Baker & Tilden, 1869.

Atlas of Monroe County, New York. New York: F. W. Beers, 1872.

Atlas of Seneca County (New York). Philadelphia: Pomeroy, Whitman, & Co., 1874.

Bagg, Moses M. *The Pioneers of Utica.* Utica, N.Y.: Curtis & Childs, 1877.

Baxter, Albert. *History of Grand Rapids Michigan*. New York: Munsell, 1891.

Bonner, R. I., ed. *Memoirs of Lenawee County* (Michigan). Madison, Wis.: Western Historical Association, 1909.

Boyd's Syracuse City Directory. 1866–70, 1874, 1879, 1880.

Bradsby, Henry, ed. *History of Bureau County Illinois*. Chicago: World Publishing Co., 1885.

Brown, Charles H. *William Cullen Bryant*. New York: Charles Scribner's Sons, 1971.

Bruce, Dwight, ed. *Onondaga's Centennial*. Boston: Boston History Company, 1897.

Bryant, William Cullen, II, and Thomas Voss, eds. *Letters of William Cullen Bryant*. 3 vols. New York: Fordham University Press, 1975.

Bryant Association Reunion of 1897.

Buffalo Architecture: A Guide. Cambridge: MIT Press, 1981.

Buffalo (New York) *Express*, May 3 & 4, 1890. Obituary, Lewis F. Allen.

"Campaign to Save Stately River Lea Succeeds." *Buffalo (New York) Evening News*, August 16, 1962.

Chapman, Gerard. "History in Houses: The William Cullen Bryant Homestead." *Antiques* 124 (October 1983): 782–788.

Chenango County (New York) Cemetery Records. 5:18.

Child, Hamilton. *Business Directory of Seneca County New York*. Syracuse, 1894.

————. *Monroe County (New York) Directory*. Syracuse, 1869–1870.

————. *Schenectady County (New York) Directory*. Syracuse, 1870–71.

————. *Wyoming County (New York) Directory*. Syracuse, 1870.

Clayton, W. W. *History of Onondaga County, New York*. Syracuse: D. Mason, 1878.

Collinsville, Illinois. City Directory, 1858.

Combination Atlas Map of Lenawee County Michigan. Chicago: Everts & Stewart, 1874.

Combination Atlas Map of Rock County (Wisconsin). Chicago: Everts, Baskin, and Stewart, 1873.

Commemorative Biographical Record of Hartford County Connecticut. Chicago: J. H. Beers, 1881.

Cutter, Daniel. *History of the Town of Jaffrey, New Hampshire*. Concord, N.H.: Republican Press Association, 1881.

Daily Journal (Syracuse) City Directory. 1866, 1867, 1869.

Dictionary of American Biography.

Disturnell, C. *Gazetteer of the State of New York*. Albany, 1843.

Douglas, Nancy, and Richard Hartung. *Rock County Historic Sites and Buildings*. Janesville, Wis.: Rock County Bicentennial Commission, 1976.

Durant, Samuel. *History of Oneida County (New York)*. Philadelphia: Ensign & Everts, 1878.

Eames, Charles M., comp. *Historic Morgan and Classic Jacksonville* (Illinois). Jacksonville, Ill.: Daily Journal, 1885.

Everhart, J. F. *History of Muskingum County (Ohio)*. Columbus: J. F. Everhart & Co., 1882.

Fairfield County (Ct.) Commemorative Biographical Record. Chicago: J. H. Beers, 1869.

Foster, Helen, and William Streeter. *Only One Cummington*. Cummington, Mass.: Cummington Historical Commission, 1974.

Fowkes, Henry, ed. *Historical Encyclopedia of Illinois and History of Christian County* (Illinois). Chicago: Munsell, 1908.

Goodspeed, Weston A., and C. Blanchard, eds. *Counties of Potter and Lake Indiana*. Chicago: F. A. Battey, 1882.

Goss, Dwight. *History of Grand Rapids (Michigan) and Its Industries*. Chicago: C. F. Cooper, 1906.

Grand Rapids (Michigan) City Directory. 1859–1860.

Grand Rapids (Michigan) *Eagle*. Obituary for J. F. Chubb, April 6, 1864.

Guernsey, Orrin, and Josiah Willard, eds. *History of Rock County and Transactions of the Rock County Agricultural Society.* Janesville, Wis.: W. M. Doty, 1856.

Harrington, George B. *Past and Present of Bureau County Illinois.* Chicago: Pioneer Publishing Co., 1906.

Hatfield, Julia. *The Bryant Homestead Book.* New York: G. P. Putnam & Son, 1870.

Hemenway, Abby Maria. *Vermont Historical Gazetteer.* Burlington, Vt., 1877.

History of Allegany County New York. New York: F. W. Beers, 1879.

History and Directory of Kent County Michigan. Grand Rapids: Dillenback and Leavitt, 1870.

History of Champaign County Ohio. Chicago: W. H. Beers, 1881.

History of Kent County Michigan. Chicago: Charles Chapman, 1881.

History of Lapeer County (Michigan). Chicago: H. R. Page, 1884.

History of Madison County Illinois. Edwardsville, Ill.: Brink & Co., 1882.

History of Monroe County, New York. Philadelphia: Everts, Ensign, & Everts, 1877.

History of Rock County Wisconsin. Chicago: Western Historical Company, 1879.

History of Wyoming County New York. New York: Beers, 1880.

Hitchcock, Charles, ed. *Atlas of the State of New Hampshire.* New York: Comstock & Cline, 1877.

Howard, R. H., and Henry E. Crocker, eds. *A History of New England.* Boston: Crocker & Co., 1881.

Howell, George R., and W. W. Munsell. *History of the County of Schenectady, New York.* New York: Munsell, 1886.

Huntington, Elijah B. *History of Stamford Connecticut.* Stamford: printed by the author, 1868.

Illinois State Business Directory. 1859–1860.

Illustrated Encyclopedia and Atlas Map of Madison County Illinois. St. Louis: Brink, McCormick, 1873.

Illustrated Historical Atlas of Indiana. Chicago: Baskin, Forster, & Co., 1876.

Judd, Oliver P. *History of the Town of Coventry.* Oxford, N.Y.: Oxford Review, 1912.

Lake, D. J. *Atlas of Washington County Ohio.* Philadelphia: Titus, Simmons, and Titus, 1875.

Leeson, Michael A. *History of Saginaw County Michigan.* Chicago: C. C. Chapman, 1881.

Leonard, Doris Parr. *Pioneer Tour of Bureau County.* Princeton, Il.: Bureau County Republican, 1954.

Lothrop, J. S. *Champaign County (Illinois) Directory,* 1870–71. Chicago: Rand, McNally, 1871.

Lydens, Z., ed. *The Story of Grand Rapids.* Grand Rapids, Mich.: Kregel Publishing, 1966.

Madison (Wisconsin) City Directory. 1858–1859.

Merrill, Mrs. G. D., ed. *Centennial Memorial History of Allegany County New York.* Alfred, N.Y., 1896.

Michigan Pioneer Collections. 10 (1886).

Monroe County Directory. 1869–1870. Syracuse, 1869.

New England Mercantile Union Business Directory. 1849.

Ohio State Business Directory. 1853–1854, 1855–1856.

"Old Homes at Princeton Form Interesting Link With Past." Peoria (Illinois) *Journal - Transcript,* October 18, 1942.

Ormsby's Syracuse City Directory. 1853–1854.

"Peers & Gauen—Building Materials." Edwardsville (Illinois) *Intelligencer,* Centennial Edition (1912): 61.

Portrait and Biographical Album of Rock County Wisconsin. Chicago: Acme, 1889.

Schenck, Lois. "The First Hundred Years." Bureau County (Illinois) *Republican,* August 6, 1936.

Schenectady Directory and City Register. 1841, 1860.

Smith, Henry P., ed. *History of the City of Buffalo and Erie County.* Syracuse: D. Mason & Co., 1884.

Smith, Henry P., and Rann, W. S., eds. *History of Rutland County Vermont.* Syracuse: D. Mason, 1886.

Smith, James Hadden. *History of Chenango and Madison Counties* (New York). Syracuse: D. Mason, 1880.

Sweet's New Atlas of Onondaga County New York. New York: Walker Brothers, 1874.

Syracuse (New York) City Directory. 1853, 1857.

Todd, Charles Burr. *History of Redding (Ct.).* New York: J. A. Gray, 1880.

United States Manuscript Census, Population and Agriculture Schedules, 1830 through 1900.

Wager, Daniel. *Oneida County* (New York). Boston: Boston History Co., 1896.

White, Truman C. *Our County and Its People.* (Erie County, N.Y.) Boston: Boston History Company, 1898.

PICTURE SOURCES AND CREDITS

Abbreviations

American Quarterly = **AQ**
Journal of Interdisciplinary History = **JIH**
William and Mary Quarterly = **WMQ**
Agricultural History = **Ag. History**
American Agriculturist = **AA**
Association for Preservation Technology Bulletin = **APT Bulletin**
Dictionary of American Biography = **DAB**
Genesee Farmer = **GF***
New England Farmer = **NEF**
Ohio Cultivator = **OC**
Prairie Farmer = **PF**
Country Gentleman = **CG**
Michigan Farmer = **MF**
Albany Cultivator = **AC**
Moore's Rural New Yorker = **Moore's**
Journal of the Society of Architectural Historians = **JSAH**
Winterthur Portfolio = **WP**
Journal of American History = **JAH**

*The original *Genesee Farmer* existed from 1831 to 1839. A *New Genesee Farmer* succeeded the original in 1840 under different management, but in the same city (Rochester) and almost immediately dropped the "New" from its title. I have chosen to use the same abbreviation for both journals.

Fig. 2–1.	Richard Rumery, Derby Line, Vermont
Fig. 2–2.	*AC* 6 (August 1839): 119. Cornell University Libraries
Fig. 2–3.	Personal collection of John F. Morgan. John F. Morgan, Pike, New York
Fig. 2–4, 2–5.	*Moore's* 11 (January 1860): 5. Pennsylvania State University, Libraries
Fig. 2–6.	The Author
Fig. 2–7, 2–8.	*Moore's* 11 (September 1860): 277. Pennsylvania State University Libraries
Fig. 2–9.	Personal collection of Duncan Bryant. Duncan Bryant, Princeton, Illinois
Fig. 2–10.	*PF* 5 (October 1845): 252–53. University of Illinois Library at Urbana-Champaign
Fig. 2–11.	Joel Nelson, Princeton, Illinois
Fig. 2–12.	Thomas Hubka, *Big House, Little House, Back House, Barn* (Hanover, N.H.: University Press of New England, 1984), 36. University Press of New England

Fig. 2–13, 2–14. *CG* 57 (June 16, 1892): 464. Pennsylvania State University Libraries

Fig. 2–15, 2–16. Personal collection of John Wing. Dohron Wilson, Mechanicsburg, Ohio

Fig. 2–17. *Moore's* 4 (April 23, 1853): 133. Cornell University Libraries

Fig. 2–18. *AA* 16 (January 1857): 33. Cornell University Libraries

Fig. 2–19. *AC* 3rd ser. 5 (August 1857): 249. Pennsylvania State University Libraries

Fig. 2–20. *AC* n.s. 5 (February 1847): 50. Cornell University Libraries

Fig. 2–21, 2–22. *GF* 19 (November 1858): 344. Pennsylvania State University Libraries

Fig. 2–23. *AC* n.s. 6 (February 1849): 57. Cornell University Libraries

Fig. 2–24, 2–25. *Moore's* 44 (March 7, 1885): 155. Pennsylvania State University Libraries

Fig. 2–26. *GF* 2 (November 3, 1832): 349. Pennsylvania State University Libraries

Fig. 2–27. *AA* 4 (January 1845): 22–23. Cornell University Libraries

Fig. 2–28. *AC* n.s. 3 (June 1846): 184–85. Cornell University Libraries

Fig. 2–29, 2–30. *AA* 7 (June 1848): 184. Cornell University Libraries

Fig. 2–31. Buffalo (NY) *Evening News*

Fig. 2–32. Lewis Falley Allen, *Rural Architecture* (New York: Orange Judd, 1860): 117. Pennsylvania State University Libraries

Fig. 3–1. *AA* 16 (March 1857): 60. Cornell University Libraries

Fig. 3–2. *AC* 6 (November 1849): 335. Pennsylvania State University Libraries

Fig. 3–3. *AC* 10 (July 1843): 69. Cornell University Libraries

Fig. 3–4, 3–5. *AC* n.s. 5 (August 1848): 248–49. Pennsylvania State University Libraries

Fig. 3–6, 3–7. *AA* 6 (July 1847): 184–85. Pennsylvania State University Libraries

Fig. 3–8. *AA* 6 (July 1847): 217. Cornell University Libraries

Fig. 3–9. *AC* n.s. 6 (January 1849): 25. Cornell University Libraries

Fig. 3–10. *PF* 13 (April 1853): 156–57. Princeton University Libraries

Fig. 3–11. Catharine Beecher, *Treatise on Domestic Economy* (Boston: Marsh, Capen, Lyon, & Webb, 1848), 267. Cornell University Libraries

Fig. 4–1. *Moore's* 47 (February 25, 1888): 123. Pennsylvania State University Libraries

Fig. 4–2. Ed Mineck Photographic Laboratory Services, Ed Mineck and Sue Holbink

Fig. 4–3, 4–4. *Moore's* 10 (March 5, 1859): 77. Pennsylvania State University Libraries

Fig. 4–5. *AC* 3rd ser. 6 (June 1858): 184. Pennsylvania State University Libraries

Fig. 4–6. *AC* 3rd ser. 4 (January 1856): 25. Pennsylvania State University Libraries

Fig. 4–7. *AC* 3rd ser. 9 (November 1861): 345. Pennsylvania State University Libraries

Fig. 4–8. *GF* 19 (June 1858): 185. Pennsylvania State University Libraries

Fig. 4–9. E. H. Leland, *Farm Homes* (New York: Orange Judd, 1881), 22. Cornell University Libraries

Fig. 4–10. *AA* 26 (February 1867): 65. Cornell University Libraries

Fig. 4–11. *AA* 35 (April 1876): 144. Cornell University Libraries

Fig. 4–12. *PF* 57 (April 1885): 251. Cornell University Libraries

Fig. 4–13. *Moore's* 20 (August 21, 1869): 533. Cornell University Libraries

Fig. 4–14, 4–15. *Moore's* 21 (March 19, 1870): 185. Cornell University Libraries

Fig. 4–16. *PF* n.s. 18 (August 18, 1866): 101. Cornell University Libraries

Fig. 4–17. E. H. Leland, *Farm Homes* (New York: Orange Judd, 1881), 16, 17. Cornell University Libraries

Fig. 4–18. James Stephens, Beverly, Ohio

Fig. 4–19. *Moore's* 26 (February 15, 1873): 105. Cornell University Libraries

Fig. 4–20.   D. J. Lake, *Atlas of Washington County Ohio* (Philadelphia: Titus, Simmons, and Titus, 1875): 42. Pennsylvania State University Libraries

Fig. 4–21.   *PF* 57 (June 13, 1885): 371. Cornell University Libraries

Fig. 4–22.   Lewis Falley Allen, *Rural Architecture* (New York: Orange Judd, 1860), 76. Pennsylvania State University Libraries

Fig. 4–23.   *Rural Affairs* 2 (1860): 262. Cornell University Libraries

Fig. 5–1.   A. J. Downing, *The Architecture of Country Houses* (1850. Reprint, New York: Dover Publications, 1969), 125. The Author

Fig. 5–2.   A. J. Bicknell, *Bicknell's Wooden and Brick Buildings* (New York: A. J. Bicknell, 1875), vol. 1, plate 70. Pennsylvania State University Libraries

Fig. 5–3.   Grand Rapids Public Library

Fig. 5–4.   *Illustrated Catalog of M.& H. Schrenkeisen* (New York: M.& H. Schrenkeisen, 1879), 83. Henry Francis du Pont Wintherthur Museum and Library, Collection of Printed Books

Fig. 5–5.   *Godey's* 24 (May 1842), f.p. Pennsylvania State University Libraries

Fig. 5–6, 5–7, 5–8, 5–9.   *Moore's* 47 (June 9, 1888): f.p. Cornell University Libraries

Fig. 5–10.   *AA* 40 (December 1881): f.p. Cornell University Libraries

Fig. 5–11.   Sereno Edwards Todd, *Todd's Country Homes and How to Save Money* (Hartford, Connecticut: Hartford Publishing Co., 1870), 105. Pennsylvania State University Libraries

Fig. 5–12.   Library of Congress

Fig. 5–13.   *Moore's* 20 (August 21, 1869): 533. Cornell University Libraries

Fig. 5–14, 5–15. *Moore's* 22 (August 20, 1870): 121. Cornell University Libraries

Fig. 5–16.   *PF* 12 (January 1852): 20. Cornell University Libraries

Fig. 5–17, 5–18. *Moore's* 41 (December 16, 1882): 849. Pennsylvania State University Libraries

Fig. 5–19.   *Moore's* 30 (December 5, 1874): 361. Cornell University Libraries

Fig. 5–20.   *Moore's* 7 (February 16, 1856): 53. Cornell University Libraries

Fig. 5–21.   *CG* 55 (January 5, 1888): 17. Cornell University Libraries

Fig. 5–22.   Leland, *Farm Homes,* 19. Cornell University Libraries

Fig. 6–1.   *AC* n.s. 5 (January 1848): 29. Cornell University Libraries

Fig. 6–2.   *PF* 7 (May 1847): 151–52. Cornell University Libraries

Fig. 6–3.   *GF* 11 (March 1850): 63. Pennsylvania State University Libraries

Fig. 6–4, 6–5.   *Moore's* 10 (January 1859): 5. Pennsylvania State University Libraries

Fig. 6–6.   *AC* n.s. 1 (March 1844): 120. Cornell University Libraries

Fig. 6–7.   *CG* 12 (July 15, 1858): 34. Pennsylvania State University Libraries

Fig. 6–8.   *CG* 37 (January 4, 1872): 9. Pennsylvania State University Libraries

Fig. 6–9.   *Moore's* 27 (April 19, 1873): 253. Cornell University Libraries

Fig. 6–10.   *Moore's* 22 (August 20, 1870): 121. Cornell University Libraries

Fig. 6–11.   *AA* 38 (April 1879): 147. Cornell University Libraries

Fig. 6–12.   *AA* 53 (January 1894): 24. Cornell University Libraries

Fig. 7–1.   *AA* 55 (February 23, 1895): 193. Cornell University Libraries

Fig. 7–2.   *Farm Journal* 38 (May 1914): 327. Pennsylvania State University Libraries

Fig. 7–3.   *Farm Journal* 38 (May 1914): 326. Pennsylvania State University Libraries

Fig. 7–4.   Martha Van Rensselaer et al., *A Manual of Homemaking* (New York: Macmillan, 1919), 14. Pennsylvania State University Libraries

Fig. 7–5.   Van Rensselaer, *Manual,* 15. Pennsylvania State University Libraries

Index